AF845772

DATA PROTECTION AND DIGITAL SOVEREIGNTY POST-BREXIT

One of the promises of Brexit was to allow the UK to regain its legislative sovereignty from the EU. However, after Brexit, UK data protection law must remain in line with EU standards in order not to lose the adequacy status that allows personal data to be transferred from the EU. This circumstance generates tensions between the EU, which is committed to preserving its digital sovereignty by ensuring an adequate protection of personal data even beyond its borders, and the UK's ambition to become a champion of the digital economy by adopting an innovative and pro-business legislation in the digital field.

The book analyses the latest legal and policy developments in this context, focusing on data protection but also exploring its intersection with other related regulatory areas, such as artificial intelligence and online safety. Renowned international experts contextualise current regulatory trends and policy proposals to understand whether a new UK model in the field of digital regulation is emerging and to what extent this will exacerbate existing tensions between the UK and the EU.

The book includes an accessible and detailed analysis of the major judicial decisions, laws, and current bills offering an invaluable guide to academics, practitioners and policymakers navigating the complex issues of cross-border data protection post-Brexit.

Data Protection and Digital Sovereignty Post-Brexit

Edited by
Edoardo Celeste
Róisín Á Costello
Edina Harbinja
and
Napoleon Xanthoulis

•HART•
OXFORD • LONDON • NEW YORK • NEW DELHI • SYDNEY

HART PUBLISHING

Bloomsbury Publishing Plc

Kemp House, Chawley Park, Cumnor Hill, Oxford, OX2 9PH, UK

1385 Broadway, New York, NY 10018, USA

29 Earlsfort Terrace, Dublin 2, Ireland

HART PUBLISHING, the Hart/Stag logo, BLOOMSBURY and the Diana logo are trademarks of Bloomsbury Publishing Plc

First published in Great Britain 2023

Copyright © The editors and contributors severally 2023

The editors and contributors have asserted their right under the Copyright, Designs and Patents Act 1988 to be identified as Authors of this work.

All rights reserved. No part of this publication may be reproduced or transmitted in any form or by any means, electronic or mechanical, including photocopying, recording, or any information storage or retrieval system, without prior permission in writing from the publishers.

While every care has been taken to ensure the accuracy of this work, no responsibility for loss or damage occasioned to any person acting or refraining from action as a result of any statement in it can be accepted by the authors, editors or publishers.

All UK Government legislation and other public sector information used in the work is Crown Copyright ©. All House of Lords and House of Commons information used in the work is Parliamentary Copyright ©. This information is reused under the terms of the Open Government Licence v3.0 (http://www.nationalarchives.gov.uk/doc/open-government-licence/version/3) except where otherwise stated.

All Eur-lex material used in the work is © European Union, http://eur-lex.europa.eu/, 1998–2023.

A catalogue record for this book is available from the British Library.

A catalogue record for this book is available from the Library of Congress.

Library of Congress Control Number: 2023936255

ISBN: HB: 978-1-50996-648-6
ePDF: 978-1-50996-650-9
ePub: 978-1-50996-649-3

Typeset by Compuscript Ltd, Shannon

To find out more about our authors and books visit www.hartpublishing.co.uk. Here you will find extracts, author information, details of forthcoming events and the option to sign up for our newsletters.

FOREWORD

FEDERICO FABBRINI

It is my pleasure to provide a foreword for this book on Data Protection and Digital Sovereignty Post-Brexit, which is the final deliverable of the Cross-Border Data Protection Network, a project led by Dublin City University (DCU) in partnership with the University of Southampton and Aston University, funded by the Irish Research Council (IRC) and the UK Economic and Social Research Council's (ESRC) newly established 'UK–Ireland' joint grant. This new funding scheme's purpose was to promote research between higher level academic institutions, and thus to build bridges between Ireland and the UK, at a time when Brexit was increasingly causing the emergence of new barriers between the governments and people of these shared islands.

The decision of the UK to leave the EU – a fateful step taken in a public referendum in June 2016, and eventually brought to bear in January 2020, with the entry into force of the Withdrawal Agreement (WA), later complemented by the EU–UK Trade and Cooperation Agreement (TCA) – has caused unprecedented consequences in society, the economy, politics and the legal system. In fact, under my leadership, DCU established in 2017 a Brexit Institute, which is Ireland's only and Europe's first centre specifically created to analyse Brexit from a research and policy perspective. The Brexit Institute houses a book series which now features four volumes examining the key steps of the Brexit process and its core implications.

The current book provides a welcome addition to the existing literature by zooming into a specific, but very important, aspect of the legal consequences of Brexit: namely, the protection of personal data and the transfer thereof, both in the private, commercial context and in that related to intelligence sharing and national security, which also has digital sovereignty implications. In this sectoral domain, as in others, Brexit has caused unprecedented legal headaches – which the TCA has temporarily resolved and a new Commission's adequacy decision has now sought to allay. Nevertheless, as this book points out, these legal issues are far from being settled, and new challenges – including questions connected to the emergence of artificial intelligence – are likely to be on the horizon.

From this point of view, the book fully fulfils the goal of the IRC–ESRC 'UK–Ireland' grant. To begin with, it brings together a dynamic group of scholars, proposing transnational solutions to face the newly emerging cleavages between the UK on the one hand and Ireland and the EU on the other. Moreover, it is to be commended that the book authors include observers from a diverse and international background. Finally, the book is coming out at an apt moment, and provides a timely assessment of the law three years after the WA. As such, it will certainly be of interest to scholars and practitioners with an expertise on privacy and data protection law across Europe and beyond.

ACKNOWLEDGEMENTS

This edited volume is the result of the 'Cross-Border Data Protection Network' (Cross-DPN) project, which aimed to create a multistakeholder network investigating the challenges of protecting data protection after Brexit and was jointly funded by the Irish Research Council and the UK Economic and Social Research Council. The network involved three partner organisations, Dublin City University, the University of Southampton (formerly the University of Portsmouth) and Aston University, and two associate partners, King's College London and the Institute of Advanced Legal Studies. Despite the challenges of the COVID-19 pandemic over two years (2020–22), the network organised four online and one hybrid event, bringing together leading academics, civil society leaders and public actors to engage with the challenges to data protection law caused by Brexit within the UK and on a cross-border basis between the UK, Ireland and, more broadly, the EU.

First of all, we would like to thank all the contributors to this edited volume for their commitment, professionalism and perseverance throughout this project. We are very grateful to our host institutions for supporting us and providing us with a stimulating and safe environment for our work during the pandemic. We are thankful also to the DCU Brexit Institute for co-hosting our final conference. Among the colleagues who have contributed to this project, we would like to sincerely thank Prof Federico Fabbrini for writing the foreword to this volume, and Charlee-Jane Kelly, James Byrne, Sorcha Montgomery, Havva Yesil and Cerys Lee for their assistance in the organisation of the online conferences, the dissemination of the network activities via social media and our website as well as their assistance during the editorial progress of this book. We are grateful to the team at Hart Publishing for enthusiastically supporting the publication of this edited volume and for their advice and editorial guidance. Lastly, we would like to extend our sincerest thanks to our partners, friends and family members for all their help and encouragement while preparing this volume during a period of unprecedented disruption to all of our lives.

Edoardo Celeste, Róisín Á Costello, Edina Harbinja and Napoleon Xanthoulis
Dublin–Birmingham–Southampton
January 2023

CONTENTS

PART III
PARALLEL CHALLENGES: REGULATING ARTIFICIAL INTELLIGENCE AND BEYOND

PART IV
DIGITAL SOVEREIGNTY TENSIONS AND CROSS-BORDER COOPERATION MECHANISMS

LIST OF CONTRIBUTORS

Christine Andreeva is a postdoctoral researcher at the Metropolitan University Prague, Czech Republic.

Edoardo Celeste is an Assistant Professor of Law, Technology and Innovation at the School of Law and Government of Dublin City University (DCU), Ireland, Programme Chair of the Erasmus Mundus Master in Law, Data and Artificial Intelligence (EMILDAI), and Deputy-Director of the DCU Law Research Centre.

Róisín Á Costello is an Assistant Professor in Law in the School of Law and Government of Dublin City University (DCU), Ireland.

Federico Fabbrini is a Full Professor of EU Law at the School of Law and Government of Dublin City University (DCU), Ireland, the Director of the DCU Law Research Centre and the Founding Director of Brexit Institute.

Edina Harbinja is a Reader in Law at Aston University, Birmingham.

Allison Holmes is a Lecturer in Law at the Law School of the University of Kent, UK.

Peter Hustinx is a non-executive director and member of the Management Board of the UK Information Commissioner's Office, former European Data Protection Supervisor (2004–14) and former President of the Dutch Data Protection Authority (1991–2004).

Karen McCullagh is a Lecturer in Media, Information Technology and Intellectual Property Law at the University of East Anglia, UK.

Lilian Mitrou is a Professor of Law at the Department of Information and Communication Systems Engineering of the University of the Aegean, Greece, a Visiting Professor at the Athens University of Economics and Business and the University of Piraeus, and the President of the Institute for Privacy Law, Data Protection and Technology (IPL), established by the European Public Law Organization.

Henry Pearce is a Senior Lecturer in Law at the University of Portsmouth and Deputy Editor of the *Computer Law & Security Review*.

Sotirios Santatzoglou is a Lecturer in Law at Keele University London, UK.

Maria Tzanou is an Associate Professor in Law at Keele University London, UK and Associate Editor of the *European Data Protection Law Review*.

Napoleon Xanthoulis is Senior Lecturer in Law at Southampton Law School.

TABLE OF CASES

TABLE OF LEGISLATION

1

Data Protection and Digital Sovereignty Post-Brexit: An Introduction

EDOARDO CELESTE, RÓISÍN Á COSTELLO,
EDINA HARBINJA AND NAPOLEON XANTHOULIS

I. The Legal Context: The UK as a Third Country

The UK's decision to withdraw from the EU generated manifold disruptive effects in economic, social and legal terms on both sides of the Irish Sea, as well as between these islands and mainland Europe.[1] Digital affairs have not been exempted from this disruption. With Brexit, the UK has left a group of states which is among the most advanced globally in protecting personal data, and which is currently at the forefront of legal innovation in regulating online content, services and disruptive digital technologies, including artificial intelligence-based tools.[2]

This volume, and the contributions within it, speak to the embeddedness and the prominence of digital affairs – and data protection in particular, not only in relations between the EU and third-party states, but also in the constitutional architecture and regulatory thinking of the Union and its Member States. This emphasis on data protection as both a constitutional value and a right that influences external relations makes data protection particularly important in a post-Brexit landscape. Perhaps nowhere is this more clearly illustrated than in the relations between the UK and Ireland, where data protection and the adequacy of the UK's data protection laws following Brexit have the potential not only to negatively impact intelligence sharing, trade and cross-border cooperation more generally, but also compliance with the Good Friday Agreement itself. The result is that ensuring the adequacy of the UK's data protection (and privacy)

[1] For a comprehensive overview of the topic see F Fabbrini (ed), *The Law & Politics of Brexit* (Oxford University Press, 2017); F Fabbrini (ed), *The Law & Politics of Brexit: Volume II: The Withdrawal Agreement*, 1st edn (Oxford University Press, 2020); F Fabbrini (ed), *The Law and Politics of Brexit. Volume III: The Framework of New EU-UK Relations*, 1st edn (Oxford University Press, 2021); F Fabbrini, *The Law and Politics of Brexit. The Protocol on Ireland/Northern Ireland*, 1st edn (Oxford University Press, 2022).

[2] See E Celeste, 'Data Protection' in Fabbrini, *The Law & Politics of Brexit: Volume III* (n 1).

laws post-Brexit is not only a legally complex and economically consequential matter – it is also one which is politically charged.

Following Brexit, the UK has become a 'third country' from a data protection perspective, meaning that personal data cannot be freely transferred from the EU to the UK absent a specific legal mechanism, in line with the requirements of the EU General Data Protection Regulation (GDPR). Indeed, the GDPR is directly applicable in all EU Member States and in the three countries composing the European Economic Area (EEA), ie Iceland, Norway and Liechtenstein. Data transfers occurring among these countries are not subject to any type of restriction, while transfers to third countries, including the UK, may occur if one of the conditions listed in chapter 5 GDPR is met.[3] The most comprehensive mechanism allowing data transfers from the EU to a third country consists in the adoption of a decision by the EU Commission declaring that the legal framework of the third country offers an 'adequate' level of data protection. According to Article 45 GDPR and in line with the case law developed by the Court of Justice of the EU (CJEU), the assessment of the Commission should not be limited to the foreign country's legislation on data protection but should look at the legal framework in general, including areas that might have an impact on the protection of personal data, such the possibility of law enforcement authorities to access personal data transferred from the EU.[4]

In June 2021, the EU Commission adopted two decisions – one covering data transfers under the GDPR and one transfers under the Law Enforcement Directive – declaring that the UK data protection regime offers an adequate level of protection, thus allowing for the transfer of personal data from the EU to the UK.[5] This set of decisions prevented the possibility of a sudden stop to data transfers to the UK. Indeed, the exit of the UK from the EU – and thus its acquisition of the third country status – occurred on 31 January 2020. Until the end of December 2020, data transfers between the two jurisdictions were allowed as if Brexit had not occurred in light of a legal arrangement during what was called the 'transition period'. The Trade and Cooperation Agreement (TCA) signed on 30 December 2020 introduced a further grace period of six months – ending in June 2021 – during which the UK could still be considered as an EU Member

[3] See C Kuner, 'Extraterritoriality and Regulation of International Data Transfers in EU Data Protection Law' (2015) 5 *International Data Privacy Law* 235.

[4] See M Tzanou, 'European Union Regulation of Transatlantic Data Transfers and Online Surveillance' [2017] *Human Rights Law Review* https://academic.oup.com/hrlr/Article/3061949/European; M Tzanou, '*Schrems I* and *Schrems II*: Assessing the Case for the Extraterritoriality of EU Fundamental Rights' in F Fabbrini, E Celeste and J Quinn (eds), *Data Protection beyond Borders: Transatlantic Perspectives on Extraterritoriality and Sovereignty* (Hart Publishing, 2021).

[5] EU Commission, Commission Implementing Decision (EU) 2021/1772 of 28 June 2021 pursuant to Regulation (EU) 2016/679 of the European Parliament and of the Council on the adequate protection of personal data by the United Kingdom; EU Commission, Commission Implementing Decision (EU) 2021/1773 of 28 June 2021 pursuant to Directive (EU) 2016/680 of the European Parliament and of the Council on the adequate protection of personal data by the United Kingdom.

State from a data protection perspective and the EU Commission could have time to assess UK law with the perspective of adopting an adequacy decision.[6]

II. Towards a New UK Data Protection Model?

Despite the UK's long-standing membership of the EU and the de facto alignment of UK data protection law with the GDPR at the time of Brexit, the EU Commission's decision to adopt an adequacy determination vis-à-vis the UK was vocally contested. Objectors pointed in particular to the architecture of UK national security law, which has been repeatedly judged by both national and European courts as failing to align with fundamental rights standards, as an issue of concern.[7] This circumstance alone would suffice to argue that there is a serious risk in terms of the sustainability of the newly adopted adequacy decision – a risk which now exceeds mere academic speculation following the recent case law of the Court of Justice of the EU that invalidated, for the second time, the EU Commission's adequacy decision adopted in relation to the USA.[8]

One might think, in these circumstances, that the precarious equilibrium created by the adequacy decision would cause the UK to desist from introducing new regulations in the digital field that could threaten its adequacy status vis-à-vis the EU, especially in light of the strategic and economic importance of data exchanges with EU Member States. Yet, in September 2021 the UK government published a consultation document that included the blueprint of a new model for data regulation, not accidentally entitled 'Data: A New Direction'. In this, the UK government proposed its vision to emancipate UK law from the bureaucratic aspects of EU law, give new economic elan to the UK digital economy and lay the basis to make the UK a global champion in the tech sector.[9] The answers to the consultation later informed a new piece of legislation presented on 18 July 2022: the Data Protection and Digital Information Bill.[10]

[6] For a more detailed reconstruction of the provisions of the TCA related to data protection, see Celeste, 'Data Protection' (n 2).

[7] See ibid; E Celeste, 'The Court of Justice and the Ban on Bulk Data Retention: Expansive Potential and Future Scenarios' (2019) 15 *European Constitutional Law Review* 134. See also Santatzoglou and Tzanou, 'An (In)adequate Data Protection Regime after Brexit? Bulk Surveillance Powers, National Security and the Future of EU–UK Data Transfers', ch 5 in the current volume.

[8] See *Facebook Ireland and Schrems* [2020] CJEU C-311/18, ECLI:EU:C:2020:559; Tzanou, '*Schrems I* and *Schrems II*' (n 4).

[9] UK Department of Digital, Culture, Media and Sport, 'Data: A New Direction' (2021) https://assets.publishing.service.gov.uk/government/uploads/system/uploads/attachment_data/file/1022315/Data_Reform_Consultation_Document__Accessible_.pdf; UK government, 'Data: A New Direction – Government Response to Consultation' www.gov.uk/government/consultations/data-a-new-direction/outcome/data-a-new-direction-government-response-to-consultation.

[10] UK Parliament, 'Data Protection and Digital Information Bill' https://bills.parliament.uk/bills/3322.

On the one hand, the departure from the EU offers to the UK the possibility to reacquire its legislative sovereignty in the digital field, as much advocated in the Brexit rhetoric. On the other hand, adopting a new regulatory model governing data protection – and digital technologies more broadly – poses new challenges both internally and from a cross-border cooperation perspective. Firstly, departing from the EU data protection model concretely means challenging a framework to which the UK contributed so much as a Member State over the past three decades. Concepts, principles and processes that are embedded in the UK data protection sector now risk being unilaterally changed for political purposes or in the name of revitalising the UK economy after Brexit. Will this restyling of UK data protection law succeed in its objective of making the UK more economically attractive as well as removing barriers to innovation?

Secondly, the consequences of this choice are not limited to the UK context, but exacerbate existing tensions between various countries' willingness to protect their digital sovereignty. The EU aims to continue to be a global standard setter in the data protection field. Protecting the EU digital sovereignty also means preserving the EU ideal of fundamental rights-compliant development of technology.[11] The UK, by departing from the EU, seeks to compete on the international plane against, on the one hand, superpowers in the tech sector, such as the USA and China, and, on the other hand, large markets like the EU. Yet, the UK is still linked to the EU from a data protection perspective by the adequacy decisions allowing data transfers between the two jurisdictions. This umbilical cord keeps the UK within the EU orbit, as severing it would mean losing access to a huge amount of EU personal data. The adequacy status prevents the UK from departing radically from EU data protection law for the fear of losing this special position.[12] At the same time, this means not being fully sovereign in the digital sector, always having to assess whether a reform would eventually lead to the loss of the adequacy status.

This edited volume aims to investigate the challenges and implications of the latest UK law and policy strategies in the data protection field – and in 'neighbouring' regulatory areas that have an impact on data protection, such as artificial intelligence (AI) or online safety regulation. The book analyses the UK's data protection status after Brexit and reflects on the consequences of the emergence of a new data protection model in the UK. It also seeks to offer the reader an analysis that incorporates digital sovereignty concerns, examining emerging tensions both at national level and on an EU cross-border basis as they have been raised (or exacerbated) by Brexit. Beyond data protection and cross-border data transfers, the volume also considers broader questions of digital regulation, including digital sovereignty and the 'Brussels effect', and the importation of regulatory and

[11] See E Celeste, 'Digital Sovereignty in the EU: Challenges and Future Perspectives' in Fabbrini et al (n 5).

[12] See Celeste, 'Data Protection' (n 2). See also Santatzoglou and Tzanou, ch 5 in this volume.

rights standards beyond the borders of the EU. In doing so, the authors analyse the data protection law reform proposals and other technology law reforms in the UK (namely online safety, AI regulation and human rights law reform), which, combined, may affect the UK data protection adequacy and the broader UK–EU political and economic relationship. Many authors thus exemplify and assess the legal, political and economic effects of regulatory convergence and divergence between the UK and EU. In all, the volume argues for a more robust and coordinated international cooperation on data protection and digital regulation more broadly, including the collaboration between various relevant digital and data protection regulators in the UK and the EU.

III. Building on the Cross-Border Data Protection Network Project

This edited collection is the result of the 'Cross-Border Data Protection Network' project, which was jointly funded by the Irish Research Council and the UK Economic and Social Research Council and aimed to create a multistakeholder network investigating the challenges of vindicating data protection rights after Brexit. Over two years (2020–22), the network organised five events, bringing together prominent academics, civil society leaders and public actors to engage with the challenges to data protection law caused by Brexit within the UK and on a cross-border basis between the UK, Ireland and, more broadly, the EU. The network involved three partner organisations, Dublin City University, the University of Southampton (formerly the University of Portsmouth) and Aston University, and two associate partners, King's College London and the Institute of Advanced Legal Studies.

The volume includes a selection of the scholarship generated by the network's members during this two-year process, collecting reflections on data protection law in a post-Brexit UK, the impacts on British legislative sovereignty of EU data protection law, the influence of Brexit on national privacy laws within the UK, and the broader socio-political and economic results of the changing data protection and technology regulation landscape between the UK and Ireland and the UK and EU.

IV. Structure of the Book

The book is divided into four parts. Part 1 critically assesses the potential directions of a new, post-Brexit UK regulatory strategy in the digital field, starting with an analysis of the Data Protection and Digital Information Bill. One of the core points examined by the contributors in this first part is whether and to what extent it will be possible for the UK to find an innovative way of regulating data without significantly departing from the existing EU regulatory model, thus jeopardising its adequacy status. In chapter two, entitled 'Post-Brexit UK Data Protection: Staying the Course or Charting a New Direction?', Karen McCullagh analyses how the planned Data Protection and Digital Information Bill would align with the requirements of the EU adequacy status. While the Bill aims to update and simplify the UK data protection framework in order to enable economic growth, McCullagh argues that multiple amendments proposed in the Bill mean that the 'UK GDPR' would look quite different to the EU version, thus increasing the risk that the EU might question the adequacy of the UK regime for the purposes of data transfers.

In chapter three, entitled 'Brexit and Data Protection Law: A Missed Opportunity for Innovative Reform?', Henry Pearce considers how a departure from the EU might offer the UK an opportunity to think differently about data protection and argues that personal data may not be the most suitable conceptual hub on which to base the regulation of contemporary data-handling activities. In light of this – Pearce argues – Brexit could be seen as an opportunity to locate a potential alternative approach to data protection law based on the notion of information harms. This approach – he argues – would result in a more granular way of regulating data processing activities, as part of which the application of legal rules would be dependent on the contextual peculiarities of specific data uses. This would, in turn, allow for the law to move beyond the categories of personal data and anonymous data established in EU law and adopt a more responsive approach to data protection.

Part 2 of the book continues this analysis, focusing on the law enforcement and national security sectors. The contributions to this section map how data exchange regimes in the law enforcement context have changed post-Brexit and examine the extent to which current UK law regulating the use of data by law enforcement and national security agencies can still be considered to offer an adequate level of data protection. Paradoxically, when the UK was part of the EU, UK national security law largely fell outside the scope of EU law and consequently outside the scrutiny of the CJEU. However, as the contributors to this part note, the UK, having acquired the status of a 'third country' from a data protection perspective, now confronts a situation in which the UK regime's regulation of access to and use of data by law enforcement and national security authorities is one of the core elements to be assessed when determining whether the UK offers an adequate level of data protection, in line with the requirements of the GDPR. The contributors highlight how, in light of the peculiarities of the UK national security and law enforcement regimes, the equilibrium of the recently adopted UK adequacy decision is precarious, drawing in particular on recent case law from the Court of Justice of the EU and the European Court of Human Rights.

In chapter four, 'Counter-terrorism, Information-Sharing and Law Enforcement Cooperation Post-Brexit', Christine Andreeva explains that the EU counter-terrorism apparatus was being redesigned in light of security threats and political pressures within the Union when the UK began the process of exiting the EU. This circumstance made both negotiating parties even more aware of the mutual benefit of an EU–UK partnership in this field, and led to very specific arrangements being negotiated between the parties. In particular, Andreeva examines the TCA in the area of law enforcement cooperation and information exchange, and, by comparing it to the previous EU instruments in this domain, reflects on the long-term consequences of Brexit on cross-border counter-terrorism cooperation between the EU and the UK. Andreeva stresses that this new arrangement is 'unprecedented with regard to a non-EU and non-Schengen third country'. As the TCA could never match the extent of law enforcement and judicial cooperation of the UK at the time of its EU membership, the new arrangements are considered a step backwards when it comes to information-sharing.

Chapter five, written by Sotirios Santatzoglou and Maria Tzanou, complements this analysis by focusing on UK internal national security laws. Their contribution, 'An (In)adequate Data Protection Regime after Brexit? Bulk Surveillance Powers, National Security and the Future of EU–UK Data Transfers', opens with a historical analysis of the UK criminal policy that led to the consolidation of UK mass surveillance practices, highlighting in particular the influence of political strategies – from both sides of the political spectrum – in enhancing crime control through surveillance in the UK. The second part of the chapter stresses how, paradoxically, after Brexit, national security matters have become the rationale for an increased EU review of the UK legal framework in the context of transborder data transfers. Regrettably – Santatzoglou and Tzanou argue – after the UK's departure from the EU, the UK will no longer have an explicit fundamental right to data protection and the Charter of Fundamental Rights of the EU will apply extraterritorially in the field of law enforcement and national security, but not in relation to all types of data processing. However, in light of its historico-political analysis, the chapter concludes that bulk surveillance powers will not be removed and this thus represents one of the main vulnerabilities of the UK adequacy status.

Moving to the more quotidian deployment of surveillance in the name of national security, in chapter six, '"Serious and Systemic"? Live Facial Recognition Technology in the UK and Its Impact on Adequacy', Allison M Holmes examines how domestic regulation of facial recognition technology – and, in particular, live facial recognition (LFR) in the UK – could impact any adequacy decision. Ultimately, Holmes concludes that the arrangements governing LFR in the UK represent a clear divergence from EU standards governing the use of personal data and the vindication of fundamental rights.

Part 3 of the book turns to address the diverse manners in which data protection is affected through disparate pieces of legislation within the UK legal order. This part of the book is concerned, in particular, with two major areas of reform in which both the EU and the UK are actively, and heavily, engaged – namely, AI and online safety. The contributions to this part explain how data protection law informs regulatory strategies in these two interlinked areas and analyse the extent to which new policies in the field of AI and online safety are simultaneously shaping the evolution of data protection law. As the contributors examine, both the EU and the UK have declared their intention to become leaders in the field of AI and have prioritised online safety as an area of particular concern. This requires both a complex co-regulation strategy between regulators and private companies and a clear delimitation of the admissible use of AI technology in particular. The result, the contributions argue, is a regulatory race between the EU and the UK, motivated by a mix of economic interests and fundamental rights protection justifications.

In chapter seven, entitled 'Regulation versus Innovation? A Comparative Analysis of EU and UK Policy Responses to Artificial Intelligence', Lilian Mitrou examines the current attempts to regulate artificial intelligence in the UK and the EU from a comparative perspective. The chapter contextualises this analysis within the cross-border data protection-related concerns and challenges generated by Brexit and the recent proposals of the UK government to depart from the EU standards and establish a new data model. Mitrou's examination is based on the Proposal for an AI Act submitted by the European Commission on 21 April 2021 and the strategy and policy papers on AI published up to August 2022 by the UK government. Mitrou analyses the need for regulating AI and discusses the advantages and challenges of transitioning from the ethical guidelines on AI to regulation. She highlights the difficulty in defining what AI is in a sufficiently flexible and future-proof manner, and compares the main regulatory priorities of the EU and the UK, examining the at first sight dichotomic couple of fundamental rights protection versus innovation. Her chapter concludes by reflecting upon the timing of the current regulatory proposals and on the role of AI regulation as a tool for setting global standards and protecting digital sovereignty.

Chapter eight, by Edina Harbinja, expands the horizon of research by considering the relationship between data protection regimes and other sectors of technology regulation. Her chapter, entitled 'Regulatory Divergence: The Effects of UK Technology Law Reforms on Data Protection and International Data Transfers', examines examples of ongoing law reforms in technology law in the UK, discussing their effects on data protection and commercial data transfers. In particular, the chapter assesses implications of the regulation of online safety and AI in the UK, questioning their effect on the UK data protection regime and its adequacy status. The chapter challenges these reforms on the basis of their mutual divergence and inconsistency. It concludes that these proposals should be considered holistically. Otherwise, a piecemeal reform could lead to unintended and adverse consequences, not only on the enforceability of these proposals, but also on the UK's data protection adequacy and, notably, data protection and privacy rights of individuals in the UK.

Part 4 contextualises the developments analysed in the first three parts of the book by adopting digital sovereignty as an interpretative lens. The contributions in this part explain how, on the one hand, EU data protection law aims to ensure an adequate level of protection both within the territory of the Union and in circumstances when data is transferred to a third country such as the UK. This implies that the UK, even after Brexit, will be subject to a significant Brussels effect in the digital field lest it risk losing its adequacy status. Equally, the UK has justified Brexit, both prior to and following the referendum, by referring to the need for increased legislative sovereignty, as demonstrated by its recent reform proposals in the digital sector. The question remains, however, whether the choice to depart from the EU data protection model is motivated merely by short-term economic interests (what contributors call digital 'sovereignism') but will, de facto, betray the UK's long-standing support for digital rights, as actively demonstrated in the 47 years that it was an EU Member State. The book will conclude with an analysis of the cross-border cooperation mechanisms that will help prevent future regulatory friction between the EU and the UK, and which may offer the basis for joint development of regulatory solutions in the digital field.

In chapter nine, 'The Brussels Effect: Regulatory Standard-Setting and Constitutional Conflicts in Post-Brexit Privacy Law', Róisín Á Costello critically examines how EU values are exported through regulatory standards as part of the so-called 'Brussels effect'. The chapter argues that importing regulatory standards may now result in an unintended importation of rights standards, and, crucially, it may also mean that such a dual importation must take place to satisfy the requirements of the GDPR following the *Schrems II* case. As such, the UK, if it seeks to adopt a new data protection model that still meets the EU adequacy ruling, is required to critically examine the congruence of its own national constitutional tradition with European privacy values. Costello concludes by arguing that this raises particular challenges for the UK, given its progressive attempts following Brexit to shed or minimise the influence of EU law and the jurisprudence of the European Court of Human Rights.

Chapter ten, by Edoardo Celeste, builds on this analysis and specifically explores the implications of recent UK reform of data protection from a digital sovereignty perspective. His contribution, 'Brexit and the Risks of Digital Sovereignism', recontextualises recent UK regulatory and policy moves as part of ongoing clashes concerning digital sovereignty between the EU and the UK. The chapter analyses the risks and limits of the digital sovereignty claims, questioning whether they are degenerating into a form of 'digital sovereignism', backed by economic protectionism instances and guided by economic interests. Celeste concludes on the core question of whether announced UK data policies merely denote a marketing strategy or rather provide evidence for a more serious constitutional value crisis. To avoid an economic war and 'a digital sovereignty arm-wrestle', Celeste argues that the solution is to foster international cooperation on data protection and digital regulation more broadly, to understand its core objectives and how they can be achieved while supporting the plurality of values and technical innovation.

Chapter eleven, entitled 'Towards a Successful Cross-Border Regulatory Cooperation', by Peter Hustinx, a former EU data protection supervisor, concludes the volume by analysing the potential mechanisms to ensure effective regulatory cooperation on both sides of the English Channel. His contribution looks at the scope for institutional cooperation in the post-Brexit context by the authorities responsible for the supervision and enforcement of data protection laws in the UK and the EU. In doing so, it first sets out how the UK Information Commissioner's Office has invested in developing a global framework for regulatory cooperation in the context of the Global Privacy Assembly and the results of these efforts so far. It then discusses a few alternative frameworks and their current practice, notably in the Council of Europe, the Organisation for Economic Cooperation and Development and the European Union context. Against this background, the chapter examines how such regulatory cooperation between the UK and EU Member States – at a regional scale or in bilateral settings – is currently or could in the future be organised, illustrating some critical conditions for success. Hustinx concludes by arguing that UK adequacy will continue to play a vital role, not only as a precondition for a successful cross-border regulatory cooperation, but also in a much larger context.

PART I

Towards a New UK Data Protection Model?

2

Post-Brexit UK Data Protection: Maintaining Alignment with or Diverging from the GDPR?

KAREN McCULLAGH

I. Introduction

When the UK was preparing to leave the EU and become a third country for EU data protection purposes, it opted to maintain alignment with EU data protection laws, including the General Data Protection Regulation (GDPR), and considered a variety of mechanisms to effectuate seamless EU–UK personal data transfers before applying for a GDPR adequacy assessment by the European Commission (the Commission).[1] Then, after the adoption of the adequacy decision by the Commission on 28 June 2021, the UK government announced an intention to consult on proposed changes to UK data protection law with a view to modernising the law to foster and encourage innovation by removing barriers and reducing burdens on organisations, to allow the UK to 'operate as the world's data hub' while maintaining high data protection standards so as not to jeopardise the EU–UK adequacy decision.[2] Mindful of these developments, this chapter has two goals, the first of which is to explain why the UK was initially reluctant to apply for an adequacy decision, before outlining how the Commission assesses adequacy. The second is to outline proposed changes to UK data protection law and consider whether the UK is seeking merely to make appropriate use of the white space in the GDPR and the degree of divergence permitted from the EU standard or to substantially diverge from the GDPR.

[1] European Commission, Implementing Decision of 28 June 2021 pursuant to Regulation (EU) 2016/679 of the European Parliament and of the Council on the adequate protection of personal data by the United Kingdom, C(2021) 4800 final, https://ec.europa.eu/info/sites/default/files/decision_on_the_adequate_protection_of_personal_data_by_the_united_kingdom_-_general_data_protection_regulation_en.pdf.

[2] DCMS, 'Data: A New Direction' (10 September 2021) https://assets.publishing.service.gov.uk/government/uploads/system/uploads/attachment_data/file/1022315/Data_Reform_Consultation_Document__Accessible_.pdf.

The chapter demonstrates that the UK government has, over time, resiled from many of the more radical reform proposals it initially consulted on. It concludes that if implemented in their current form, many of the proposed changes are minor and only a few of the proposed changes would result in significant divergence from the GDPR and would cause the EU to question whether to attach conditions to the renewal of the adequacy decision or refuse to renew it in due course.

II. Rationale for Seeking to Obtain and Retain an Adequacy Decision

During post-Brexit referendum negotiations, the UK government acknowledged that personal data transfers between the EU and the UK were vital to the UK economy: EU personal data-enabled services exports to the UK were worth approximately £42bn (€47bn) in 2018 and exports from the UK to the EU were worth £85bn (€96bn), and this motivated the UK to ensure the continued free flow of personal data between the two.[3] It also acknowledged that the GDPR would continue to have extraterritorial application to data controllers offering goods or services to individuals or monitoring the behaviour of individuals in EEA countries, thereby necessitating ongoing compliance with the GDPR,[4] but that as a third country for data protection purposes it would not benefit from de jure recognition of its data protection laws as providing an adequate standard of protection to facilitate EEA–UK personal data transfers, and it therefore reviewed the appropriateness of a variety of mechanisms for effectuating such transfers for meeting the UK's needs. In this regard, it considered whether data flows would be best facilitated by requiring data controllers and processors to rely on model clauses or other legal mechanisms to effectuate transfers such as consent or seeking either a sectoral or whole-country adequacy decision from the Commission.[5]

Although it concluded that an adequacy decision would be the 'least burdensome' option and would offer 'stability and certainty for businesses', particularly small and medium-sized businesses that could not easily absorb the legal costs associated with drafting and obtaining approval for model clauses or other legal mechanisms to effectuate transfers,[6] it was reluctant to apply for one because that would require the UK to accept the jurisdictional element of an adequacy assessment. That is, the UK would have to submit to an evaluation of its laws and practices by the Commission; to accept that whilst there would be dialogue

[3] DCMS, 'Explanatory Framework for Adequacy Discussions, Section A: Cover Note' 1, https://assets.publishing.service.gov.uk/government/uploads/system/uploads/attachment_data/file/872228/A_-_Cover_Note.pdf.

[4] GDPR, Art 3, 679.

[5] House of Lords, European Union Committee, 'Brexit: The EU Data Protection Package' (18 July 2017) HL Paper 7, ch 3, paras 112–15.

[6] ibid.

between the EU and the UK regarding its legal framework and practices pertaining to data protection, the decision whether to make a finding (or not) of adequacy would be made by the Commission on a unilateral basis; to accept that EU law would continue to have extraterritorial impact in the UK in respect of personal data transferred to it from EEA countries; and further, to accept that if an adequacy decision were adopted, it could, as a 'living document', be revoked or not renewed by the Commission on a unilateral basis if it formed the view that the UK no longer provides an adequate level of protection. It was anathema to some government ministers who had promoted Brexit as an opportunity for the UK to 'free' itself from the EU law and EU institutions, which they viewed as imposing burdensome and unnecessary red tape that hindered business competitiveness.[7]

Accordingly, the UK government initially pursued a strategy of exceptionalism, calling for the EU and UK to agree to 'mutually recognise' each other's data protection frameworks, with UK data protection law 'deemed' adequate, that is, without the Commission conducting a GDPR adequacy assessment.[8] The UK further proposed to deal with disputes through the inclusion of horizontal data protection clauses in any bilateral agreement concluded between the EU and the UK; the underlying motivation was to prevent a *Schrems* scenario, that is, the EU having the power to unilaterally revoke an adequacy decision, thereby immediately halting EU–UK data transfers should the UK be found to be substantially in breach of the GDPR.[9]

The UK was likely emboldened to pursue this course of action because the Commission has drafted horizontal clauses on cross-border data flows and personal data protection for inclusion in trade agreements with the aim of reducing barriers to trade, such as forced data localisation in a state's territory.[10] However,

[7] For further discussion of the UK's pre- and post-Brexit data protection laws and rationale for continued compliance with the GDPR, see K McCullagh, 'Post-Brexit Data Protection in the UK – Leaving the EU but not EU Data Protection Law Behind' in G González Fuster, R Van Brakel and P de Hert (eds), *Research Handbook on Privacy and Data Protection Law: Values, Norms and Global Politics* (Edward Elgar Publishing, 2022) 35–58.

[8] HM Government, 'The Exchange and Protection of Personal Data – a Future Partnership Paper' (24 August 2017) https://assets.publishing.service.gov.uk/government/uploads/system/uploads/attachment_data/file/639853/The_exchange_and_protection_of_personal_data.pdf.

[9] Case C-362/14 *Maximillian Schrems v Data Protection Commissioner* (*Schrems I*) ECLI:EU:C:2015:650. For case commentary, see L Azoulai and M Van Der Sluis, 'Institutionalizing Personal Data Protection in Times of Global Institutional Distrust: *Schrems*' (2016) 53 *CML Rev* 1343.

[10] TFEU, Art 216(1) allows authority for the conclusion of an international agreement to be 'provided for in a legally binding Union act', which would allow EU legislation to set out criteria for data protection agreements with third countries. In 2018, the European Commission endorsed horizontal provisions for inclusion in trade agreements that allow the EU to tackle protectionist practices in third countries in relation to digital trade while ensuring that trade agreements cannot be used to challenge the high level of protection guaranteed by the EU Charter of Fundamental Rights and the EU legislation on the protection of personal data. See European Commission, 'EU Horizontal Provisions on Cross-Border Data Flows and Protection of Personal Data and Privacy in the Digital Trade Title of EU Trade Agreements' https://trade.ec.europa.eu/doclib/docs/2018/may/tradoc_156884.pdf. For further discussion on the inclusion of horizontal clauses in EU trade agreements, see S Yakovleva and K Irion, 'Pitching Trade against Privacy: Reconciling EU Governance of Personal Data Flows with External Trade' (2020) 10 *International Data Privacy Law* 201.

the UK only partially succeeded in realising this goal because the Commission currently envisages using horizontal clauses in situations only when an adequacy decision cannot be realistically adopted; instead, it advocates that trade negotiations and applications for an adequacy assessment follow separate but parallel tracks[11] 'to keep trade deals uncontroversial'.[12] Therefore, whilst the EU–UK Trade and Cooperation Agreement (TCA) does contain data protection clauses and does not, at the UK's insistence, refer to data protection as a fundamental right, it is important to note that the insertion of data protection provisions and the wording thereof was agreed upon only after the UK had conceded that it would need to apply for an adequacy assessment such that the horizontal data protection provisions would have limited transitional effect, that is, pending the conclusion of the adequacy assessment.[13] Moreover, whilst the EU did agree to 'mutual adequacy recognition', it was in conjunction with the UK's acceptance that this did not eliminate the need for the Commission to assess the adequacy of the UK's data protection framework.[14]

The Commission insisted on conducting an assessment of adequacy because, as Lynskey has observed, whilst mutual respect for fundamental rights and data protection standards is assumed within EU Member States, such trust does not automatically exist in relation to third countries; rather, it must be built through formal legal relationships, and an adequacy assessment provides that mechanism.[15] The UK's change in status from trusted Member State to third country explains why the UK was de facto 'adequate' on the eve of the end of the transition period, whereas the following day it was not. The UK applying for and obtaining an adequacy decision would reinstate that trust, because rather than negotiating the standard of protection that the UK would agree to provide, the Commission was instead empowered to unilaterally determine whether the UK provided an adequate level of protection. Relatedly, to ensure that the UK would address any deficiencies in its law and practices, and not immediately seek to diverge from the GDPR after adoption of an adequacy decision, the Commission inserted both monitoring provisions and a sunset clause in the adequacy decision. To this end, the EU–UK adequacy decision adopted on 28 June 2021 is subject to continuous monitoring (the Commission may suspend, repeal or amend the decision at any time if it forms the view that developments render the UK's legal

[11] Commission, 'European Commission Letter on Cross-Border Data Flows and EU Trade Agreements' (1 March 2018) https://data.consilium.europa.eu/doc/document/ST-6687-2018-INIT/en/.

[12] JH Vela, J Plucinska and H von der Burchard, 'EU Trade, the Martin Selmayr Way' *Politico* (21 February 2018).

[13] Trade and Cooperation Agreement between the European Union and the European Atomic Energy Community, of the one part, and the UK of Great Britain and Northern Ireland, of the other part [2020] OJ L444/14, Art FINPROV.10A.

[14] For further information on mutual adequacy recognition, see McCullagh (n 7).

[15] O Lynskey 'Extraterritorial Impact in Data Protection Law through an EU Law Lens' in F Fabbrini, E Celeste and J Quinn (eds), *Data Protection beyond Borders: Transatlantic Perspectives on Extraterritoriality and Sovereignty* (Hart Publishing, 2021) 191–210.

framework inadequate)[16] and includes a sunset clause which stipulates that it will expire on 27 June 2025 if the Commission has not made a renewed finding of adequacy by then.[17]

III. A Post-Brexit Opportunity for GDPR Divergence?

Soon after the adoption of the adequacy decision, the UK government published its National Data Strategy, in which it announced an intention to reform its data protection laws by identifying post-Brexit opportunities for 'unlocking the value of data' and securing 'a pro-growth and trusted data regime', while preserving strong data subject rights and seeking to retain its adequacy status under the GDPR.[18]

To this end, the Data Protection and Digital Information Bill (DPDI Bill) was laid before Parliament on 18 July 2022,[19] after the government had published its response[20] to the 'Data: A New Direction' (DaND) consultation.[21] The DPDI Bill was positioned as part of a series of legislative proposals intended to seize the benefits of Brexit by creating an 'ambitious, pro-growth and innovation-friendly data protection regime'. A central theme in the consultation and the DPDI Bill was reducing perceived burdens on organisations by updating and simplifying the UK's data protection framework and removing the red tape and administrative burden on businesses.

The DPDI Bill's passage through the UK's legislative process was unexpectedly paused in September 2022 to 'allow ministers to consider the legislation further' following changes to the UK's governmental leadership (Liz Truss replaced Boris Johnson as Prime Minister and leader of the Conservative Party). That same month, the government announced the Retained EU Law (Reform and Revocation) Bill (Reform and Revocation Bill). This Bill proposes to amend the European Union (Withdrawal) Act 2018, which was the basis for the retention of the GDPR (as the UK GDPR), in UK law post-Brexit. It proposes to revoke any EU-derived subordinate legislation and any retained direct EU legislation unless specifically listed under retained law. It was unclear whether this would include revocation of the UK GDPR as part of a 'bonfire of regulations'.

[16] GDPR, Art 45(4); European Commission, Implementing Decision (n 1) recital 281.

[17] GDPR, Art 45(3); European Commission, Implementing Decision (n 1) Art 4, recitals 289–90.

[18] DCMS policy paper, 'National Data Strategy' (9 September 2020).

[19] Data Protection and Digital Information Bill (DPDI Bill) 143, 2022–23, 18 July 2022, https://publications.parliament.uk/pa/bills/cbill/58-03/0143/220143.pdf.

[20] DCMS, Data: A New Direction – Government Response to Consultation' (23 June 2022) www.gov.uk/government/consultations/data-a-new-direction/outcome/data-a-new-direction-government-response-to-consultation#:~:text=The%20government%20launched%20its%20consultation,the%20UK's%20National%20Data%20Strategy.

[21] DCMS, 'Data: A New Direction' (n 2).

Thereafter, in October 2022, the Secretary of State for Culture, Media and Sport (DCMS), Michelle Donelan, gave a speech in which she announced that 'We inherited GDPR from the EU, and its bureaucratic nature is still limiting the potential of our businesses … We will be replacing GDPR with our own business-and consumer-friendly British data protection system'.[22] Her speech initially caused a stir in the business, legal and technology communities, not least because no warning had been given and it created uncertainty and confusion regarding the status of the DPDI Bill. It left unanswered the question whether the DPDI Bill would be abandoned or would be revised to change some provisions in the UK GDPR, and relatedly whether this would be the endpoint of reforms or merely a stopgap measure whilst a new bespoke data protection regime is created.

The Secretary of State's citation of findings of a survey of businesses conducted by her department in which half of the respondents reported 'excessive caution' amongst staff when handling people's data[23] and of a working paper by researchers at Oxford University suggesting they found the GDPR 'caps businesses profits by 8%' in support of her claim that a reduction in red tape could unlock economic gains[24] gave some credence to reports that the UK GDPR could be repealed.

If the UK GDPR were repealed and UK data protection laws completely rewritten, a nuanced approach to its redrafting would be needed, for if the protections currently found in the UK GDPR were watered down, the EU–UK adequacy decision would be jeopardised. It could also bring about a two-tier data rights system – with the UK being on the lower tier, falling behind the EU level of protection. It could also increase the compliance burden and associated costs of businesses operating in both the EEA and the UK as they would be required to comply with the GDPR for EEA–UK personal data transfers and any new law introduced by the UK.

Unsurprisingly, concern was expressed that there was a lack of evidence of the need for radical reform. For example, one commentator observed that the Secretary of State may have selectively reported the Oxford University research in support of political goals, since the researchers had caveated their research as a 'work in progress' and urged caution when interpreting findings – noting, for example, that negative effects on business performance which the paper links to the GDPR 'may partly reflect temporary adjustment costs, meaning that its effects might taper-off in the future'.[25] A data protection solicitor similarly commented that:

> It would seem to me that the premise that the GDPR limits the potential of businesses is unfounded. The GDPR provides a moral and ethical approach to data protection to

[22] M Donelan, '2022 Speech to Conservative Party Conference', www.ukpol.co.uk/michelle-donelan-2022-speech-to-conservative-party-conference/.

[23] ibid.

[24] ibid.

[25] N Lomas, 'UK Pauses Data Reform Bill to Rethink How to Replace GDPR' (Tech Crunch, 4 October 2022) https://techcrunch.com/2022/10/03/uk-data-reform-bill-replace-gdpr/; C Chen, CB Frey and

> standardise the responsibilities of those who process personal data. The UK GDPR and Data Protection Act 2018 build on these standards.[26]

And another law firm reported that 'the general consensus from many of our clients with [p]an-European operations is that any substantial divergence from the EU could potentially increase the costs of compliance'.[27]

On a positive note, the deputy director for domestic data protection policy at DCMS subsequently confirmed that 'The adequacy agreement with the EU, which allows seamless EEA–UK personal data flows, will be "at the heart" of the finalised bill'.[28] However, he also advised that the return of the DPDI Bill to Parliament would be further delayed to facilitate additional consultation, stating that ministers

> need space to work with all groups to check we go as far as we can to enable growth and innovation while protecting high standards and maintaining our parallel policy objective of looking after EU adequacy and doing so as quickly as possible.[29]

This announcement allayed fears that the government was planning to diverge to a significant degree from the GDPR or use powers in the Reform and Revocation Bill to repeal the UK GDPR in due course.

Thereafter, on 8 March 2023 the Secretary of State for Science, Innovation and Technology (DSIT, formerly DCMS), introduced the Data Protection and Digital Information (No 2) Bill (DPDI Bill No 2) to Parliament,[30] taking the place of the DPDI Bill, which will now not proceed further in Parliament. The accompanying press release states that it will 'introduce a simple, clear and business-friendly framework that will not be difficult or costly to implement – taking the best elements of GDPR and providing businesses with more flexibility about how they comply with the new data laws'.[31] It further notes that the Bill will 'ensure … [the] new regime maintains data adequacy with the EU', a point which has been questioned since it was originally announced that the UK would reform its data protection laws.[32]

G Presidente, 'Privacy Regulation and Firm Performance: Estimating the GDPR Effect Globally', The Oxford Martin Working Paper Series on Technological and Economic Change, Working Paper No 2022-1, 25.

[26] Bindmans, 'The Future of UK Tech Law – Data Privacy Laws in the UK' (*Bindmans Blog*, 4 October 2022) www.bindmans.com/knowledge-hub/blogs/the-future-of-uk-tech-law/.

[27] Ashurst, 'Is This Goodbye to the UK GDPR?' (*Ashurst Blog*, 7 October 2022) www.ashurst.com/en/news-and-insights/legal-updates/is-this-goodbye-to-the-uk-gdpr/; Ashurst, 'Themes and Discussions from Ashurst Data Protection Roundtable' (*Ashurst Blog*, 7 October 2022) www.ashurst.com/en/news-and-insights/legal-updates/themes-and-discussions-from-ashurst-data-protection-roundtable/.

[28] O Rowland, 'Update on Data Policy' Westminster eForum Policy Conference (31 October 2022).

[29] ibid.

[30] Data Protection and Digital Information (No 2) Bill (DPDI Bill No 2) 265, 2022–23, 8 March 2023, https://publications.parliament.uk/pa/bills/cbill/58-03/0265/220265v2.pdf.

[31] DSIT, 'Press Release: British Businesses to Save Billions Under New UK Version of GDPR' (8 March 2023) www.gov.uk/government/news/british-businesses-to-save-billions-under-new-uk-version-of-gdpr.

[32] ibid.

While the DPDI Bill No 2 proposes to amend both the UK GDPR and the Privacy and Electronic Communications (EC Directive) Regulations 2003, the analysis in this chapter focuses solely on a selection of proposals relating to the UK GDPR. It explores whether the proposals would, if implemented, lead to significant divergence from the GDPR or would merely clarify definitions, reduce administrative burdens, and make appropriate use of white space in the GDPR to facilitate innovation.

It is imperative that the proposals in the DPDI Bill No 2 strike the correct balance between improving on the UK GDPR yet not diverging too far from the GDPR to satisfy the 'essentially equivalent' standard. If the latter occurs, then the EU may revoke the existing EU–UK adequacy agreement or refuse to renew it in due course with serious financial and legal consequences for the UK economy. Indeed, if the adequacy decision were to be revoked or not renewed, UK businesses could lose more than £1bn in reduced trading revenue and £420m in compliance costs over five years,[33] something the government is keen to avoid. Accordingly, at this juncture, it is appropriate to explain how UK adequacy was and will be assessed.

IV. Assessing Adequacy: 'Essential Equivalence'

When assessing adequacy, the Commission was and will be (when the UK seeks renewal of the existing adequacy decision) tasked with determining whether the UK provides an 'essentially equivalent' level of protection to that guaranteed in the EU. As confirmed in *Schrems*, UK law does not need to mirror the GDPR point by point[34] so long as it contains the core requirements set out in Article 45 GDPR and further elaborated on in Court of Justice of the EU (CJEU) case law and the European Data Protection Board (EDPB)'s Recommendations on Essential Guarantees for Surveillance Measures[35] and its 'adequacy referential'.[36] In effect, the Commission conducts an in-depth assessment of (i) de jure substantive protection of personal data in UK data protection law, (ii) de facto procedural protection and remedies and (iii) access to EU personal data by a third country's law enforcement authorities, each of which are discussed below.

[33] DCMS, 'Data: A New Direction: Analysis of Expected Impact' para 71, https://assets.publishing.service.gov.uk/government/uploads/system/uploads/attachment_data/file/1016471/Data_Reform_Impact_Analysis_Paper.pdf.

[34] *Schrems I* (n 9) para 81.

[35] EDPB Recommendations 02/2020 on the European Essential Guarantees for Surveillance Measures, adopted on 10 November 2020, https://edpb.europa.eu/our-work-tools/our-documents/preporki/recommendations-022020-european-essential-guarantees_en.

[36] Article 29 Working Party, 'Adequacy Referential' adopted on 28 November 2017, as last revised and adopted on 6 February 2018, WP254 rev.01 (endorsed by the EDPB, the Article 29WP successor body) https://edpb.europa.eu/our-work-tools/general-guidance/endorsed-wp29-guidelines.

A. De Jure Substantive Protection of Personal Data in UK Data Protection Law

The de jure substantive protection of personal data in UK law is assessed by reference to the criteria set out in Article 45(2) of the GDPR. This involves reviewing the UK's legislative framework and making a normative judgement about the UK's political structures and values, including respect for the rule of law, human rights and fundamental freedoms. It also necessitates an assessment of UK data protection law and derogations therein, and the UK's international commitments in respect of the European Convention on Human Rights (ECHR) and the Council of Europe.

When the UK applied for an adequacy assessment, the Commission reviewed several aspects of the UK's legislative framework to make a normative judgement about its political structures and values, including respect for the rule of law, human rights and fundamental freedoms, by reference to the fundamental right to a private and family life (Article 7) and to protection of personal data (Article 8) enshrined in the Charter of Fundamental Rights of the European Union 2000 (the Charter). The UK government had refused to retain the Charter in UK law on the basis that it 'only applies to Member States when acting within the scope of EU law, so its relevance is removed by our withdrawal from the EU'. It had similarly refused, in the name of restoring legislative sovereignty, to accept a proposed amendment that would have retained wording from Article 8 of the Charter in the Data Protection Bill (now the Data Protection Act 2018 (DPA)) during the legislative enactment process.[37] The Commission was nevertheless satisfied that, by virtue of a combination of common law, Article 8 of the ECHR (as incorporated into UK law by the Human Rights Act 1998 (HRA)) and the data protection rights in both the UK GDPR[38] and the DPA, the UK provides an essentially equivalent level of protection to the EU.[39] However, both the EDPB and the European Parliament (EP) emphasised the importance of UK adherence to the ECHR, implying that if the UK were to withdraw from the ECHR in the future

[37] HM Government, *Legislating for the United Kingdom's Withdrawal from the European Union* (Cm 9446, 16 May 2017) [2.23]; HM Government, *Charter of Fundamental Rights of the EU Right by Right Analysis* (5 December 2017) https://assets.publishing.service.gov.uk/government/uploads/system/uploads/attachment_data/file/664891/05122017_Charter_Analysis_FINAL_VERSION.pdf; European Union (Withdrawal) Bill, HC Deb 21 November 2017, vol 631 col 902; Joint Committee on Human Rights, *Legislative Scrutiny: The EU (Withdrawal) Bill: A Right by Right Analysis, Appendix: Commentary on the Right by Right Analysis* (2017–19, HL 70, HC 774).

[38] The Data Protection, Privacy and Electronic Communications (EU Exit) (Amendments etc) (EU Exit) Regulations 2019, SI 491/2019 came into effect at the end of the transition period on 31 December 2020. It retained the GDPR in UK law. All references to EU institutions were removed and replaced with appropriate UK bodies, and it was renamed as the UK GDPR.

[39] DCMS, 'Explanatory Framework for Adequacy Discussions, Section B: Wider Context'; DCMS, 'Explanatory Framework for Adequacy Discussions, Section C: The UK's Legislative Framework'.

it would trigger a review of the decision.[40] Significantly, in response to a petition asking the UK government to withdraw the UK from the ECHR and the jurisdiction of the European Court of Human Rights, the UK government confirmed that 'It is not currently government policy to seek withdrawal from ECHR',[41] so this aspect of the EU–UK adequacy decision should not prove problematic when it is reviewed in due course.

The Commission also considered the UK's international commitments in the form of 'legally binding conventions or instruments', as well as its 'participation in multilateral or regional systems'. In this regard, the UK's accession to both Convention 108 (the Convention for the Protection of Individuals with regard to Automatic Processing of Personal Data) and the additional (modernising) protocol[42] was looked upon favourably, particularly as the intelligence services data protection obligations in the DPA are based on Convention 108. Likewise, the membership of the Information Commissioner's Office (ICO) to a number of international initiatives, including the Global Privacy Assembly[43] and the Global Privacy Enforcement Network,[44] through which it and other supervisory authorities from member countries share best practices for addressing cross-border challenges and the practical aspects of privacy law enforcement cooperation, develop shared enforcement priorities and support joint enforcement initiatives and awareness campaigns, was accepted as evidence of the UK's strong and continuing commitment to data protection.[45]

UK data protection laws and derogations therein were also examined because Article 45(2)(a) provides that the third country shall have 'relevant legislation'. As the GDPR was implemented during the pre-withdrawal period and was retained in UK law upon exit (albeit renamed as the UK GDPR), the Commission was for

[40] EDPB Opinion 14/2021 regarding the European Commission Draft Implementing Decision pursuant to Regulation (EU) 2016/679 on the adequate protection of personal data in the United Kingdom, para 49; see also the European Parliament's concern over the UK's recognition of Gibraltar as adequate without conducting an assessment equivalent to the GDPR adequacy assessment; European Parliament Resolution of 21 May 2021 on the adequate protection of personal data by the United Kingdom (2021/2594(RSP)) General Observation 2; European Commission, Implementing Decision (n 1) recital 277.

[41] UK Government and Parliament, Response to Petition to Withdraw the UK from the European Convention on Human Rights, 28 February 2023, https://petition.parliament.uk/petitions/618456.

[42] Modernised Convention for the Protection of Individuals with Regard to the Processing of Personal Data, CM/Inf (2018)15-fina; Convention for the protection of individuals with regard to automatic processing of personal data: ETS No108, 28 January 1981 (entered into force 1 October 1985).

[43] Formerly known as the International Conference of Data Protection and Privacy Commissioners. It is a global forum for more than 130 data protection and privacy authorities from across the globe which seeks to connect and support efforts at domestic and regional level, and in other international forums, to enable authorities better to protect and promote privacy and data protection.

[44] Global Privacy Enforcement Network, www.privacyenforcement.net. In June 2007, the Organisation for Economic Cooperation and Development (OECD) governments adopted a Recommendation on Cross-border Cooperation in the Enforcement of Laws Protecting Privacy and established an informal network of Privacy Enforcement Authorities Discuss to develop and share best practices regarding the practical aspects of privacy law enforcement cooperation; cross-border challenges; enforcement and awareness campaigns.

[45] DCMS, 'Explanatory Framework for Adequacy Discussions, Section A: Cover Note' (n 3) 3.

the most part easily satisfied that UK law contained essentially equivalent concepts and definitions regarding, for example, personal data, processing principles, rights and safeguards, and material and geographic scope, with only a few immaterial differences in the UK law.

Yet it was not all plain sailing. A provision in the DPA exempted public bodies from certain aspects of the fundamental data protection rights and principles, such as the right of access and the right of a data subject to know with whom their data has been shared when processing personal data for purposes related to immigration control, was closely scrutinised.[46]

Whilst the Commission noted in its draft adequacy decision that the immigration exemption was broadly formulated, it was nonetheless satisfied that an adequate level of protection was provided in UK law because the exemption would 'be applied on a case-by-case basis, only to the extent necessary to achieve a legitimate aim and in a proportionate manner'.[47] However, both the EDPB and the EP voiced concerns, with the EDPB calling on the Commission 'to provide further information on the necessity and proportionality of the immigration exemption, in particular having regard to the broad scope of application *ratione personae*',[48] and to further explore whether additional safeguards exist in the UK legal framework or could be envisaged, for example 'through legally binding instruments that would complement the immigration exemption enhancing its foreseeability by and the safeguards for data subjects, also allowing for a better and prompt assessment and monitoring of the necessity and proportionality requirements'.[49] The EP similarly called upon the Commission to either seek the removal of the immigration exemption from the DPA or for it to reformed to 'provide sufficient safeguards for data subjects'.[50] The Commission did not act in response to these concerns. Rather, shortly before the adequacy decision was adopted, the Court of Appeal in England & Wales ruled in *The Open Rights Group & Anor, R (On the Application Of) v The Secretary of State for the Home Department & Anor* that the exemption did not include the necessary limitations and safeguards to protect the fundamental rights and freedoms of individuals.[51] This ruling prompted the Commission to exclude transfers for the purposes of UK immigration control from the scope of the adopted adequacy decision, but it agreed to reassess the exemption once UK legislators had addressed the issues raised in the judgment, which is appropriate given that an adequacy decision is a 'living' document that can and should be revised in light of changing circumstances.[52]

[46] DPA, Sch 2, part 1, para 4.
[47] Draft adequacy decision, para 65.
[48] EDPB Recommendations 02/2020 (n 35) para 13.
[49] ibid.
[50] European Parliament Resolution (n 40) para 11.
[51] [2021] EWCA Civ 800.
[52] European Commission press release 'Data Protection: Commission Adopts Adequacy Decisions for the UK (28 June 2021) https://ec.europa.eu/commission/presscorner/detail/en/ip_21_3183. UNTIL the incompatible immigration exemption is remedied, personal data transfers for immigration control purposes may only be made using the transfer mechanisms in Arts 46–49 of the GDPR.

As for proposed changes, four are worthy of discussion to illustrate that if implemented in their current form, they represent minor changes that would provide additional flexibility for organisations and by addressing unnecessary administrative burdens and are therefore unlikely to jeopardise the EU–UK adequacy decision or its renewal in due course.

Firstly, the UK is proposing to redefine the parameters of what constitutes personal data by revising its test of identifiability to allow more data to be considered anonymous and outside the scope of the UK GDPR.

Currently, personal data is defined as 'any information relating to an identified or identifiable natural person'. An 'identifiable individual' is one who can be identified directly or indirectly. To determine whether an individual is indirectly identifiable, account should be taken of all the means 'reasonably likely' to be used either by the controller or by another person. Data which has been anonymised to the extent that it does not meet the standard of 'personal data' does not fall within the scope of the UK GDPR.[53]

The DPDI Bill proposed, and the DPDI Bill No 2 continues to propose, that information will relate to identifiable living individuals only where they are 'identifiable by the controller or processor by "reasonable means" at the time of the processing' or 'where the controller or processor knows, or ought reasonably to know, that another person will, or is *likely to, obtain the information as a result of the processing*, and the living individual will be, *or is likely to be, identifiable that person by reasonable means at the time of the processing*'.[54]

This would limit the assessment of identifiability to the controller or processor and persons who are likely to receive the information, rather than anyone in the world (who might have the means to identify the data subject but are unlikely ever to access the data). It also proposes that identifiability be assessed at the time of processing – for example, where an organisation receives personal data without identifiers, but with a right to gain access to the identifiers on the occurrence of defined events in the future, such data would not be considered personal data until such events occur. This aspect of the proposed definition merely reflects the wording of recital 26 of the GDPR, which states that 'To determine whether a natural person is identifiable, account should be taken of all the means reasonably likely to be used' to identify the natural person, and that in ascertaining reasonable likelihood, 'account should be taken of all objective factors, such as the costs of and the amount of time required for identification, taking into consideration the available technology at the time of the processing and technological developments'. It confirms that account should not be taken of means that are technically feasible but are unlikely to be used. This reflects the approach of Advocate General Campos Sánchez-Bordona in *Breyer v Bundesrepublik Deutschland*, in which he opined that if the contrary perspective were adopted, it would never be possible

[53] UK GDPR, Art 4.
[54] DPDI Bill (n 19) cl 1(2); DPDI Bill No 2 (n 30), cl 1(2).

to rule out with absolute certainty 'that there is no third party in possession of additional data which may be combined with that information and are, therefore, capable of revealing a person's identity'.[55] As the UK was in the past the subject of infraction proceedings[56] for an overly narrow interpretation of personal data, it will no doubt attract intense scrutiny when adequacy is reviewed. However, given that it mirrors the position adopted in *Breyer* and is a mere gloss on the definition in the GDPR that adds clarity, this change is unlikely to prove problematic when the UK adequacy decision is reviewed.

Secondly, the DPDI Bill proposed (and the DPDI Bill No 2 continues to propose) to introduce a new lawful basis for processing, namely processing that is necessary for the purpose of 'recognised legitimate interests'. Under the current law data controllers are required to identify a lawful ground before processing personal data. These grounds include processing that is necessary for the legitimate interest of a data controller.[57] However, this can only be relied on to the extent that the organisation's interests are not outweighed by the interests of the individual (the 'balancing test'). In the DaND consultation, the UK government contended that applying the balancing test is too complex and forces organisations to inappropriately rely on another lawful ground: consent. This prompted the government to remove the balancing test (though not the necessity test) for a limited list of legitimate interests specified in the DPDI Bill. The proposed list (in a new annex to the UK GDPR) is automatically deemed to have a legitimate interest lawful basis without requiring an assessment balancing such interest with the rights and interests of the relevant data subject(s). At present, the lists of purposes include processing for reasons of 'public interest'. as well as public security, emergency response, crime prevention and detection, democratic engagement and safeguarding children/vulnerable adults.

The DPDI Bill No 2 proposes to add to the non-exhaustive list of activities that may be regarded as in a data controller's legitimate interest to process. It proposes to do so by moving illustrative activities currently listed in recitals to the operative part of the UK GDPR.[58] The listed activities are: direct marketing, intraorganisational transmission of data and network and information systems security. Data

[55] See Opinion of AG Campos Sánchez-Bordona in Case C-582/14 *Patrick Breyer v Bundesrepublik Deutschland* [2016] ECLI:EU:C:2016:339, para 65.

[56] C Pounder, 'European Commission Explains Why UK's Data Protection Act Is Deficient', http://amberhawk.typepad.com/amberhawk/2011/02/european-commission-explains-why-uks-dataprotection-act-is-deficient.html; C Pounder, 'Copy of Correspondence between Dr Chris Pounder and EU Commission & Ombudsman', http://amberhawk.typepad.com/files/dp_infraction_reasons.pdf; C Pounder, 'European Commission Raises Infraction Threat to UK on Failing to Implement Directive 95/46/EC Properly via the Data Protection Act', http://amberhawk.typepad.com/amberhawk/2014/10/european-commission-raises-infraction-threat-touk-on-failing-to-implement-directive-9546ec-properly.html; the infraction proceedings were halted when Directive 95/46/ec was repealed and replaced by the GDPR.

[57] UK GDPR, Art 6(1)(f).

[58] Recitals 47, 48 and 49 of the UK GDPR become a new Art 6(9).

controllers will still be required to ensure their interests are not outweighed by the data subject's rights and interests. And, as commentary in the Explanatory Notes to the Bill confirms that any legitimate commercial activity can be a legitimate interest, provided the processing is necessary and the balancing test is carried out, this change is unlikely to prove problematic when the EU–UK adequacy decision is reviewed. However, the DPDI Bill No 2 further stipulates that the Secretary of State for Science, Innovation and Technology (DSIT) may in the future amend this list so that more processing may be conducted on a legitimate interest basis without necessitating a balancing test. The Secretary of State will therefore need to ensure that any additional categories comply with forthcoming EDPB guidance on legitimate interests once it is issued to retain the current UK adequacy decision and ensure its renewal in due course.

Thirdly, the DPDI Bill proposed and the DPDI Bill No 2 includes a proposal that was not included in the DaND consultation. The proposal is to remove Article 27 of the UK GDPR, which would mean that overseas controllers and processors without an office or other establishment in the UK but who offer goods or services in the UK or monitor the behaviour of UK data subjects would no longer be required to appoint a UK representative as their local point of contact. The government's rationale is that 'in order to identify an organisation's representative, one must first identify the relevant controller or processor anyway, resulting in duplication and an unnecessary burden on organisations'.[59] Whilst this is viewed as an example of the government seeking to remove unnecessary red tape and barriers to trade, some legal experts have commented that 'the evidence presented on the impact of the change is far less convincing'[60] because 'it is increasingly being adopted around the world',[61] noting that the requirement to appoint a representative is also a feature of data protection of other countries beyond the EEA, including China, Thailand, Turkey, Serbia, Switzerland and Thailand. In effect, the UK could remove the Article 27 requirement without jeopardising the EU–UK adequacy decision only to find that it needs to include a similar provision to secure data transfers with another country.

Fourthly, a proposal in the DaND consultation for the UK to use a different test than that in the GDPR when assessing the adequacy of third countries could, if implemented, have given the Commission serious pause for thought when reassessing UK adequacy. It proposed that UK adequacy assessments would involve a risk- and outcome-based approach that considered 'actual risks' to data subjects' data protection rights in the applicant third country, rather than 'academic or immaterial' risks. The underpinning rationale was that practices undermining

[59] DPDI Bill Explanatory Notes, https://publications.parliament.uk/pa/bills/cbill/58-03/0143/en/220143en.pdf, para 185.

[60] A Mätzler and C Mason, 'The Value of a UK Representative: A Response to the Data Protection and Digital Information Bill', Privacy Law & Business UK Report (November 2022).

[61] ibid.

data subject rights may exist in some specific sectors but not in others such that transfers to the sectors in which the risk to the data subject is low or immaterial should not be impeded. However, it was not clear how the 'likelihood and severity of risks to data protection rights' would be assessed. The ICO was therefore not alone in calling for clarification of 'how a risk-based approach would work in practice'.[62] Ultimately, this proposal was not included in the DPDI Bill.

Instead, the DPDI Bill No 2 includes what appears at first glance to be a new 'data protection test' involving a determination of whether the standard of protection provided for data subjects in a third country is 'not materially lower' than the standard of data protection provided in the UK. The test would be applied by both the Secretary of State (when making adequacy decisions) and data controllers (when deciding whether it is safe to use other transfer mechanisms).[63] The test mirrors the criteria of Article 45 GDPR inasmuch as it specifies that the following factors should be considered: respect for the rule of law and for human rights, and any relevant international obligations; the existence of a data protection regulator and the extent of their enforcement powers; arrangements for redress by individuals, whether through the courts or otherwise; and the constitution, traditions and culture of the country in question. The explanatory notes to the Bill clarify that the test would not require a 'point-by-point comparison' between the other country's regime and the UK's. Rather, the assessment would be 'based on outcomes i.e., the overall standard of protection for a data subject'.[64]

While there is some scope for flexible interpretation of what constitutes a 'material' lowering of the standard of protection, the change looks at first glance like mere semantics, ie replacing the words 'essentially equivalent' with 'not materially lower', a view confirmed by a Department for Digital, Culture, Media and Sport (DCMS) representative (the government department sponsoring the Bill) when speaking at a National Data Strategy Forum in mid-July 2022, who emphasised that there had been discussions with the Commission and EU Member States to check that these proposed changes would not jeopardise the adequacy decision, which suggests that the changes are cosmetic and would be unproblematic when UK adequacy were reviewed in due course. However, if the wording changes significantly during the passage of the Bill or its interpretation subsequently results in a significant lowering of the UK standard such that a third country (eg the USA) is found adequate by the UK when it has not been found adequate by the EU, this element of the DPDI Bill No 2 would warrant intense scrutiny by the Commission and could jeopardise the renewal of the EU–UK adequacy decision in due course.

[62] ICO, 'Response to DCMS Consultation "Data: A New Direction"' (6 October 2021) https://ico.org.uk/media/about-the-ico/consultation-responses/4018588/dcms-consultation-response-20211006.pdf; Open Rights Group, 'Response to Data: A New Direction' (19 November 2021) www.openrightsgroup.org/publications/open-rights-group-response-to-data-a-new-direction/.

[63] DPDI Bill (n 19) Sch 5; DPDI Bill No 2 (n 30) Sch 5.

[64] DPDI Bill Explanatory Notes (n 59) para 704.

B. De Facto Procedural Protection and Remedies

The Commission is also required, when assessing adequacy, to make a de facto determination that data protection does not just exist on paper but is effectively operationalised in the third country. In this regard, Article 45(2)(a) GDPR requires the UK to have 'effective and enforceable data subject rights and effective administrative and judicial redress for the data subjects whose personal data are being transferred',[65] and also to have 'an effective independent supervisory authority with adequate enforcement powers for assisting and advising data subjects in exercising their rights, and for cooperation with EU supervisory authorities'.[66] In effect, the Commission seeks confirmation that the oversight and enforcement powers exercised by the UK national supervisory authority (the ICO) and the courts do not just exist on paper but are real and operational, so that data subjects have effective rights, means of recourse and remedies available to them.

When assessing adequacy, the Commission commented favourably on the relatively large number of staff at the ICO, together with the sources of its funding, and on the high number of complaints received and investigations opened by the ICO since the GDPR came into effect. It also recorded that UK domestic courts have oversight of data protection matters, and that there are mechanisms for EU data subjects to obtain redress either from the ICO or from the courts. However, the EP noted that it was not clear that the ICO was using its enforcement and fining powers effectively. Specifically, it noted that the ICO had a poor track record of enforcement action under predecessor legislation[67] and had not used its enforcement powers under the GDPR while the UK was a Member State of the EU, leading the EP to question whether this is a structural weakness of the ICO.[68] Consequently, both the EDPB opinion and the EP resolution called for monitoring by the Commission of the ICO's exercise of its enforcement powers.[69] Specifically, the EDPB noted that it was satisfied that the ICO has adequate enforcement powers 'on paper', but asked for continuous monitoring to ensure that those powers are in fact exercised effectively.[70]

Although proposals in the DPDI Bill No 2 to replace the Information Commissioner with an Information Commission, a collegiate body with members appointed by the Secretary of State, are not likely to cause immediate concern,

[65] GDPR, Art 45(2)(a).

[66] GDPR, Art 45(2)(b).

[67] C Pounder, 'Adequacy of the UK's Data Protection Regime; now the UK Has Left the EU, the Battle Lines Are Drawn' (3 February 2020) https://amberhawk.typepad.com/amberhawk/2020/02/adequacy-of-the-uks-data-protection-regime-now-the-uk-has-left-the-eu-the-battle-lines-are-drawn.html; European Commission press release, 'Data Protection: Commission Requests UK to Strengthen Powers of National Data Protection Authority, as Required by EU Law' (24 June 2010); Ministry of Justice, 'Letter to Dr Chris Pounder' (5 May 2011) https://amberhawk.typepad.com/files/uk-deficiency-details_may-2011-1.pdf.

[68] European Parliament Resolution (n 40) General Observation 6.

[69] European Parliament Resolution (n 40) Enforcement of the GDPR, 6.

[70] EDPB Opinion 14/2021 (n 40) paras 111 and 113.

the Commission will undoubtedly review whether the appointments are undermining the independence of the Information Commissioner when reviewing adequacy.

In addition, the proposals to impose new duties on the Information Commission, including 'promoting innovation and competition',[71] and for it to have regard to the government's strategic priorities (which will be set out by the Secretary of State in an official 'statement of priorities' laid before Parliament) when exercising its regulatory functions,[72] and a power for the Secretary of State to approve statutory Codes of Practice are likely to warrant close scrutiny by the Commission. As the European Data Protection Supervisor has observed, 'any changes that make it less independent or require it to push through a political agenda will naturally force the Commission to raise concerns, ask questions, and seek assurances'.[73] If the UK government uses these provisions, either immediately or over time, to limit the independence and regulatory freedom of the ICO, they are likely to prove a bar to achieving a finding of adequacy when the UK adequacy decision is reviewed.

C. Access to EU Personal Data by the Third Country's Authorities

The element of the UK adequacy assessment that was expected to be most unpredictable and controversial was the powers in the Investigatory Powers Act 2016 (IPA 2016) that permit UK security and intelligence services such as MI5, MI6 and GCHQ to both access personal data and share it with other countries for law enforcement and national security purposes.

As the CJEU expressly held in *Schrems II* that the national security exemption in the EU Treaties only applies to national security-related activities of the EU Member States and does not apply to national security-related activities of third countries',[74] the UK could not rely on this exemption to shield its surveillance law from scrutiny by the Commission. Moreover, as a third country, it should have been assessed by reference to the EU Charter and related CJEU jurisprudence and the essential security guarantees developed by the EDPB, and not by reference to the ECHR and related jurisprudence (by which the bulk interception by security intelligence agencies in Member States are assessed). The main difference between CJEU jurisprudence and that of the European Court of Human Rights (ECtHR) is that in *Digital Rights Ireland* the CJEU held that 'generalised, indiscriminate'

[71] DPDI Bill (n 19) cl 27; s 120B; DPDI Bill No 2 (n 30) cl 27.

[72] DPDI Bill (n 19) cl 28; DPDI Bill No 2 (n 30) cl 28.

[73] N Hodge, 'EDPS: UK GDPR Reforms Could Create Friction with EU' (*Compliance Week*, 13 July 2022) /www.complianceweek.com/data-privacy/edps-uk-gdpr-reforms-could-create-friction-with-eu/31851.article.

[74] Case C-311/18 *Data Protection Commissioner v Facebook Ireland Ltd* (*Schrems II*) ECLI:EU:C:2020:559, para 81.

collection of personal data is incompatible with the Charter (while making a very limited exception in relation to bulk collection to deal with a most serious, real threat to the very foundations and functioning of the state, which must still be strictly limited in time and place),[75] whereas the ECtHR held in *Big Brother Watch* that the decision to operate a bulk interception regime falls within the wide margin of appreciation granted to countries and instead requires very strong oversight and supervisory procedures, and that all the relevant parameters should be expressly stated in the relevant law.[76]

It is highly doubtful that the processing of personal data by UK security and intelligence agencies, especially bulk communication data, complies with the EU Charter of Fundamental Rights. Specifically, the indiscriminate bulk collection of communications metadata ('related communications data') from transatlantic undersea cables is contrary to principles established by the CJEU (*Tele2/Watson*,[77] *Digital Rights Ireland*,[78] *Schrems II*,[79] *Privacy International*,[80] and *La Quadrature du Net*),[81] as reflected in the EDPB's 'European Essential Guarantees for Surveillance Measures'.[82]

Yet, the Commission selectively highlighted compliance with the ECHR and EU Charter and glossed over problematic aspects to find the UK adequate.[83] For instance, it cited paragraphs in the *Big Brother* ECtHR judgment that found predecessor UK surveillance law compliant with the ECHR[84] as evidence that the UK provides an adequate level of protection. Notably, it did not mention that the *Big Brother* case held that some aspects of the UK's predecessor legislation were in violation of the ECHR, merely noting, in a footnote, that 'It is important to bear in mind that this judgment concerned the previous legal framework (RIPA 2000) that did not contain some of the safeguards (including prior authorisation by an independent Judicial Commissioner) introduced by the IPA 2016'.[85] Significantly,

[75] Joined Cases C-293/12 and C-594/12 *Digital Rights Ireland Ltd v Minister for Communications, Marine and Natural Resources and Others and Kärntner Landesregierung and Others*, ECLI:EU:C:2014:238, paras 48 and 52.

[76] *Big Brother Watch And Others v The United Kingdom* App nos 58170/13, 62322/14 and 24960/15 (Grand Chamber judgment) paras 338–40.

[77] Joined Cases C-203/15 and C-698/15 *Tele2 Sverige AB and Watson and Others* ECLI:EU:C:2016:970, para 120.

[78] *Digital Rights Ireland* (n 75).

[79] *Schrems II* (n 74).

[80] Case C-623/17 *Privacy International v Secretary of State for Foreign and Commonwealth Affairs and Others* ECLI:EU:C:2020:790.

[81] Joined Cases C-511/18, C-512/18 and C-520/18 *La Quadrature du Net and Others v Premier ministre and Others* ECLI:EU:C:2020:791.

[82] EDPB Recommendations 02/2020 (n 35).

[83] Korff contends, inter alia, that the draft decision completely failed to assess (or even note) the UK's intelligence agencies' actual surveillance practices: D Korff, 'The Inadequacy of the EU Commission Draft GDPR Adequacy Decision on the UK, Executive Summary' (3 March 2021); www.ianbrown.tech/wp-content/uploads/2021/03/KORFF-The-Inadequacy-of-the-EU-Commn-Draft-GDPR-Adequacy-Decision-on-the-UK-210303final.pdf.

[84] European Commission, Implementing Decision (n 1) fnn 269, 294, 365, 385, 441 and 505 and para 269.

[85] ibid fn 37.

the Commission did not expressly assess whether these safeguards in the IPA 2016 met the ECHR standards. Likewise, although the Commission considered *Tele2/Watson*, a case in which the CJEU ruled that the UK's predecessor legislation[86] breached EU law because it allowed for general and indiscriminate retention of citizens' data by law enforcement authorities and further determined that access to and use of mandatorily retained communications data should, with the exception of cases of validly established urgency, 'be subject to a prior review carried out either by a court or by an independent administrative body',[87] it did not explore in detail whether these deficiencies are addressed in the IPA 2016.

The Commission's conclusion that any interference with the fundamental rights of individuals 'will be limited to what is strictly necessary to achieve the legitimate objective in question, and that effective legal protection against such interference exists',[88] was therefore criticised by both the EDPB and the EP. Nevertheless, the Commission did not require the UK to amend the surveillance powers in IPA 2016 prior to adoption of the adequacy decision.

The adequacy assessment also required a review of procedures and practices for the onward data transfers of personal data from an applicant third country to other third countries for intelligence purposes since such transfers could undermine the GDPR and fundamental rights protections. The UK's membership of the Five Eyes alliance countries[89] and past sharing of personal data of individuals in EEA countries with each other and the UK's continued sharing of data with the USA via the US–UK Communications and Intelligence Agreement should have been a cause for concern for the Commission when assessing adequacy.[90] In an explanatory framework document, the UK government cited positive comments in a report from the UN Special Rapporteur for the Right to Privacy regarding how the UK has 'equipped itself with a legal framework and significant resources designed to protect privacy without compromising security' as confirmation that the UK has world-leading measures in place.[91] But in that same report, the Special Rapporteur was critical of international intelligence-sharing arrangements on the basis that they are 'not transparent to the public' and safeguards to avoid facilitating non-compliant surveillance by allies are not clearly set out in the IPA 2016,[92] and further commented that:

> Intelligence sharing must not result in a backdoor to obtain or facilitate for others the obtaining of intelligence free from domestic safeguards, nor a loophole for foreign

[86] The Data Retention and Investigatory Powers Act 2014.

[87] *Tele2/Sverige* (n 77) reaffirming *Digital Rights Ireland* (n 75).

[88] Draft adequacy decision, recital 268.

[89] The Five Eyes alliance comprises the UK, the USA, Canada, Australia and New Zealand.

[90] European Parliament, 'Report on the US NSA surveillance programme, surveillance bodies in various Member States and their impact on EU citizens' fundamental rights and on transatlantic cooperation in Justice and Home Affairs' (2013/2188(INI)).

[91] DCMS, 'Explanatory Framework for Adequacy Discussions, Section H: National Security Data Protection and Investigatory Powers Framework', 1.

[92] OHCHR, 'End of Mission Statement of the Special Rapporteur on the Right to Privacy at the Conclusion Of his Mission to the United Kingdom of Great Britain and Northern Ireland, London,

> Governments with lower standards on the protection of privacy (or other human rights) to obtain intelligence from UK intelligence that could give rise to human rights violations.[93]

Consequently, he endorsed calls for greater public scrutiny of such arrangements and for the establishment of strong safeguards and an oversight system to ensure that intelligence sharing is subjected to the same standards of privacy protection – and the Commission should have paid keen attention to this aspect of the IPA 2016 when assessing adequacy. These concerns were echoed by the EDPB, which called for further examination of safeguards in respect of overseas disclosures and in the EP resolution, which observed 'in relation to the US, UK citizens are subject to some informal safeguards between GCHQ and the NSA … these safeguards would not protect EU citizens or residents whose data may be subject to onward transfers and sharing with the NSA.'[94] Even so, the Commission did not make these amendments prior to adoption of the adequacy decision.

Although a review of powers in the IPA 2016 was outside the scope of the DaND consultation and DPDI Bill No 2, the provisions in the IPA 2016 could nevertheless prove problematic when the UK applies for a renewal of the adequacy decision because the Commission has a track record of seeking incremental changes to bring a third country's surveillance laws and practices into closer alignment with EU law when it seeks renewal of its adequacy decision.[95]

V. Conclusions: Alignment with or Divergence from the GDPR?

In conclusion, the legal and trade benefits of securing an adequacy decision to facilitate seamless EEA–UK personal data transfers persuaded the UK government to overcome its initial reluctance to apply for one when the UK left the EU and became a third country for data protection purposes, and it is now keen to retain it for those same reasons.

Whilst some of the political rhetoric accompanying the consultation and legislative proposals emphasised divergence from the GDPR and EU institutions as a supposed 'Brexit Dividend', the government appears to have resiled from the more radical divergence proposals in response to consultation feedback and input from the ICO. Many of the proposals seek to clarify definitions, make appropriate use of white space in the UK GDPR to facilitate innovation and

29 June 2018' www.ohchr.org/en/statements/2018/06/end-mission-statement-special-rapporteur-right-privacy-conclusion-his-mission?LangID=E&NewsID=23296.

[93] ibid.

[94] European Parliament Resolution (n 40) Mass Surveillance, 16.

[95] The Commission used annual reviews of the (now revoked) EU–US Privacy Shield Decision to require the USA to make changes to its laws and practices.

reduce administrative burdens. For example, the DaND consultation proposed to utilise a risk-based approach when assessing third country adequacy, but this proposal was not included in the DPDI Bill, nor is it included in the DPDI Bill No 2. Instead, it proposes to use a 'not materially lower' test akin to the 'essentially equivalent' test in the GDPR when assessing third country adequacy. Several other proposed changes in the DPDI Bill No 2 (eg the proposed narrower definition of personal data) represent an evolution rather than revolution in UK data protection law and are therefore likely to be favourably received during any review of the adequacy decision by the Commission.

Nevertheless, a few proposed changes, eg in the potential reduction of ICO independence and the Secretary of State having the power to add to the list of recognised legitimate interests, will, if implemented unchanged, attract scrutiny by the Commission, who will seek confirmation that they do not constitute significant divergence from the GDPR. To avert this, the UK should seek to maintain a close working relationship with the Commission and heed any guidance issued by it on how to revise provisions in the UK GDPR in a manner that maintains alignment with the GDPR; otherwise, the EU–UK adequacy decision or some aspects of it might not be renewed in due course.

The UK's continued alignment with the GDPR is appropriate as significant divergence from it would not be a prudent course of action when the global trend is towards higher rather than lower data protection standards and many of the UK's trading partners are using the GDPR as their operational benchmark on a global basis. Diverging from the EU standard of data protection would not give the UK a competitive advantage since many organisations are subject to both the UK and the EU regime. Instead, it could jeopardise the renewal of the EU–UK adequacy decision in due course and place additional burdens on businesses with multinational operations since it would require them to operate multiple standards to trade in the UK, the EU and beyond.

3

Brexit and Data Protection Law: A Missed Opportunity for Innovative Reform?

HENRY PEARCE

I. Introduction

Since leaving the EU on 31 January 2020, the UK has had the legislative freedom to diverge from EU data protection rules. This new-found freedom represents an opportunity for data protection law in the UK to evolve. On 18 July 2022, the UK government introduced its Data Protection and Digital Information Bill in the House of Commons. The Bill was purported to refresh and revamp the UK's data protection framework. In reality, however, the Bill is unambitious and envisages an outdated model of data protection constructed around the notion of personal data – a vague and complex concept. This chapter argues that persisting with a personal data-based approach to data protection law is short-sighted and tentatively proposes an alternative approach.

The chapter comprises four core sections following this brief introduction. Section II provides a brief overview of data protection law in the UK and some Brexit-related implications. Section III considers the concept of personal data and explains its central role in current and prospective data protection frameworks. Through an analysis of the constituent elements of its current and prospective definitions, the fourth section argues that personal data is not a suitable concept around which to base the regulation of contemporary data-handling activities. The fifth section sketches a potential alternative approach to data protection law based on the notion of information harms. The chapter concludes with a summary of its core arguments.

II. Brexit and Data Protection Law in the UK

On 31 January 2020, the UK left the EU, meaning it was no longer directly bound by EU law and the doctrine of supremacy.[1] Observers were quick to comment on the possible data protection-related implications of this major constitutional shift. Early scholarship of the issue focused on transfers of personal data between the UK and the EU, and particularly on challenges associated with the UK being granted an adequacy decision by the European Commission (EC).[2] Following a period of uncertainty, on 19 February 2021, two draft decisions were published by the EC for transfers of personal data from the EU to the UK (one under the General Data Protection Regulation (EU GDPR) and one under the Law Enforcement Directive).[3] The draft decisions were adopted by the EC on 28 June 2021, thereby allowing unimpeded transborder personal data flows to continue between the EU and the UK.[4]

The adoption of the adequacy decisions reflected the EC's findings that, despite Brexit, the UK's domestic data protection system (ie the UK General Data Protection Regulation (UK GDPR) and the Data Protection Act 2018 (DPA)) continues to be based on the same rules that were applicable when the UK was an EU Member State (ie the EU GDPR). The adequacy relationship between the EU and the UK, however, will likely be precarious and unstable. As noted elsewhere, the UK's data retention regime and national surveillance mechanisms make the UK's adequacy decisions ominously susceptible to challenge by the Court of Justice of the EU (CJEU).[5] The likelihood of this prospect will only increase if the UK, no longer bound by the doctrine of supremacy, uses its newfound legislative freedom to introduce changes that cause the UK's data protection framework to diverge from the EU GDPR.[6]

[1] The doctrine of supremacy of EU law, as established in Case 6/64 *Costa v ENEL*, holds that EU law takes precedence over conflicting national laws of EU Member States.

[2] See, eg C Kuner et al, 'The Global Data Protection Implications of "Brexit"' (2016) 6(3) *International Data Privacy Law* 167; A Murray, 'Data Transfers between the EU and UK post Brexit?' (2017) 7(3) *International Data Privacy Law* 149; L Moerel and R Tigner, 'Data Protection Implications of Brexit' [2016] *European Data Protection Law Review* 381; O Butler, 'The Implications of a "No-Deal" Brexit for Data Protection in the United Kingdom' (2019) 3(1) *Journal of Data Protection & Privacy* 8; P de Hert and V Papakonstantinou, 'The Rich UK Contribution to the Field of EU Data Protection: Let's Not Go for "Third Country" Status after Brexit' (2017) 33(3) *Computer Law & Security Review* 254; A Vanberg and M Maunick, 'Data Protection in the UK post-Brexit: The Only Certainty Is Uncertainty' [2018] *International Review of Law, Computers & Technology* 190; K McCullagh, 'Brexit: Potential Trade and Data Implications for Digital and "Fintech" Industries' (2017) 7(1) *International Data Privacy Law* 3.

[3] European Commission, 'Data Protection: European Commission Launches Process on Personal Data Flows to UK' (19 February 2021) https://ec.europa.eu/commission/presscorner/detail/en/ip_21_661.

[4] European Commission, 'Data Protection: Commission Adopts Adequacy Decisions for the UK' (28 June 2021) https://ec.europa.eu/commission/presscorner/detail/en/ip_21_3183.

[5] E Celeste, 'Cross-Border Data Protection after Brexit' (2021) DCU Brexit Institute Working Paper 4.

[6] See, eg O Butler, 'The End of the Transition Period: Implications for Data Protection after Brexit' (2020) 4(1) *Journal of Data Protection & Privacy* 22. See also McCullagh (n 2).

Though deviation from EU data protection rules could place the UK's adequacy decisions in jeopardy, the potential for divergence has seemingly never been far away. For instance, in a 2016 speech, Baroness Neville-Rolfe, then the Minister for Data Protection, opined that any significant post-Brexit variation of data protection policy was unlikely, but nonetheless suggested that 'the detailed future may be different'.[7] The prospect of legislative divergence again arose on 10 September 2021, when the Department for Digital, Culture, Media and Sport (DCMS) launched a public consultation on its reform paper 'Data: A New Direction'.[8] The paper outlined numerous proposed changes to the UK's data protection framework that were intended to reduce barriers to innovation, reduce compliance burdens on businesses, boost trade and improve public services.[9] Responses to the consultation were mixed, with critics suggesting that the proposed reforms would weaken many established data protection rules and, in so doing, jeopardise the EU/UK adequacy relationship.[10] On 18 July, the Data Protection and Digital Information Bill (the Data Protection Bill), which, if enacted, will pass into law some of the proposed reforms set out in the DCMS's reform paper and amend several substantive provisions of the UK GDPR and DPA, was introduced in the House of Commons.[11]

Concerns regarding possible losses of adequacy notwithstanding, the legislative freedom brought about by Brexit represents an opportunity for UK lawmakers to think creatively about the future of data protection law, and to develop new approaches to data protection that move beyond the increasingly criticised traditional European-inspired model on which the EU GDPR and UK GDPR are based.[12] However, despite the proposed reforms set out in the Data Protection Bill purporting to be bold and innovative, they are in reality disappointingly unambitious and envisage a model of data protection that is outdated and likely unsustainable. The reason for this is that, irrespective of its proposed changes, the Data Protection Bill still envisages a model of data protection based on the troublesome concept of personal data.

[7] HM Government, 'The EU Data Protection Package: the UK Government's Perspective', speech by Baroness Neville-Rolfe DBE CMG, Minister for Data Protection, at the Privacy Laws & Business Annual Conference on Data Protection (4 July 2016) www.gov.uk/government/speeches/the-eu-data-protection-package-the-uk-governments-perspective.

[8] DCMS, 'Data: A New Direction' (10 September 2021) https://assets.publishing.service.gov.uk/government/uploads/system/uploads/attachment_data/file/1022315/Data_Reform_Consultation_Document__Accessible_.pdf.

[9] ibid.

[10] See, eg W Damen et al, 'Data Protection in post-Brexit Britain: A Response to the Government of the United Kingdom's Public Consultation on Reforms to the Data Protection Regime ("Data: A New Direction")' (Leadership, Enterprise & Diversity Laboratory, University of Birmingham, 2021).

[11] Data Protection and Digital Information Bill, https://publications.parliament.uk/pa/bills/cbill/58-03/0143/220143.pdf.

[12] See, eg B-J Koops, 'The Trouble with European Data Protection Law' (2014) 4(4) *International Data Privacy Law* 250.

III. Personal Data

The substantive rules of the UK GDPR apply to the processing (ie almost any imaginable use)[13] of 'personal data'. In other words, once data qualifies as 'personal', the UK GDPR's extensive complement of obligations and protections is triggered and will apply in their entirety.[14] Whether compliance with the UK GDPR is required, therefore, hinges on whether personal data are being processed. Consequently, this model of data protection can be described as 'personal data-based'. The model of data protection envisaged by the Data Protection Bill would also operate on this basis. Accordingly, a clear understanding of the notion of personal data is, and will continue to be, vital for the smooth operation of the law. This section sets out the concept of personal data and explains the factors data controllers must consider when determining whether data are personal.

Article 4(1) of the UK GDPR defines personal data as: 'any information relating to an identified or identifiable natural person ("data subject")'. There are, therefore, two collective conditions for data to be personal. First, the data must relate to a person. Second, the person to whom the data relate must either be identified or be identifiable from the data. Ordinarily, the first condition will often be embraced by the second (because data that enable a person's identification will normally relate to that person). Recital 26 of the UK GDPR then specifies that anonymous data are not personal: 'The principles of data protection should … not apply to anonymous information, namely information that does not relate to an identified or identifiable natural person.'

The UK GDPR's criterion for identifiability is also set out in Recital 26:

> To determine whether a natural person is identifiable, account should be taken of all the means reasonably likely used to be used … either by the controller or by another person to identify the natural person directly or indirectly. To ascertain whether means are reasonably likely to be used to identify the natural person, account should be taken of all objective factors, such as the costs and the amount of time required for identification, taking into consideration the available technology at the time of the processing and technological developments.

Article 4(1) and Recital 26, therefore, establish that the concept of personal data is capable of embracing a wide range of information types. The terms 'relate to', 'directly' and 'indirectly' prima facie allow for a broad spectrum of interpretation. The requirement that data controllers must take account of 'the means reasonably likely to be used' to identify necessarily implies that whether information

[13] See UK GDPR, Art 4(2).

[14] Of note are the requirements that data controllers must only process personal data in accordance with the six data protection principles, and that data controllers must observe and uphold a range of rights provided to data subjects regarding their personal data.

constitutes personal data will depend on context, and may require data controllers to consider factors external to the data themselves when determining whether they are personal.[15]

The Data Protection Bill adopts the same personal data-based approach as the UK GDPR and DPA, but seeks to amend the definition of personal data by adding a subjective element from the perspective of the controller, processor or recipient(s) as to whether information is either personal data or anonymous. Under the Bill, information will only be personal data if it:

- 'relates to' an individual who is 'identifiable ... by the controller or processor by reasonable means at the time of the processing'; or
- the controller or processor 'knows, or ought reasonably to know, that another person will, or is likely to, obtain the information as a result of the processing, and the individual will be, or is likely to be, identifiable ... by that person by reasonable means at the time of the processing'.[16]

By limiting personal data to information that relates to an individual 'at the time' it is processed, either by a controller, processor or other individual who is likely to obtain the information, the Data Protection Bill's definition is clearly narrower than the definition contained in the UK GDPR. Nevertheless, despite its more limited scope, the definition of personal data contained in the Data Protection Bill is at its core substantively the same as that contained in the UK GDPR. Personal 'data' remains 'information' that 'relates to' 'identifiable' persons. For these reasons, previous case law relating to the interpretation of these terms under the UK GDPR and DPA is likely to continue to be relevant to the interpretation of the provisions of the Data Protection Bill should it be passed into law.

There are numerous reasons why continued reliance on the personal data-based model of data protection, as envisaged by the Data Protection Bill, might be considered desirable.[17] If, however, we are to examine a range of semantic and practical challenges inherent in the personal data concept, as defined both currently and prospectively, it becomes apparent that the continued reliance on this approach has the potential to undermine data protection law's practical viability.

[15] On the potentially expansive nature of the notion of indirect identification, and how data controllers may have to consider a range of contextual factors (eg uses of prima facie non-personal data) when determining whether data are 'personal', see the recent CJEU decision in C-184/20 ECLI:EU:C:2022:601.

[16] See Data Protection and Digital Information Bill, Part 1.

[17] One might argue, for example, that personal data represent an extension of one's personhood and thus from a fundamental rights perspective it is absolutely right that the law should seek to provide individuals to whom such data relate with the most extensive form of legal protection as possible in relation to their use. On the notion of personal data as an extension of personhood, see H Pearce. 'Personality, Property and Other Provocations: Exploring the Conceptual Muddle of Data Protection Rights under EU Law' (2018) 4(2) *European Data Protection Law Review* 190.

IV. The Problem with Personal Data

As set out above, the concept of personal data acts as a threshold to the applicability of substantive data protection rules. The ability of data controllers to delineate between personal and non-personal data, therefore, is paramount to determining whether compliance with substantive data protection rules is necessary.[18] However, this a task increasingly beset by complexity. The reason for this is twofold. First, the current and prospective legislative definitions of personal data are inherently semantically vague, inasmuch as they do not allow us to categorically identify the things to which they apply and do not apply.[19] This has impeded the development of a stable understanding of what the personal data concept encompasses. Second, these interpretative difficulties have been, and will continue to be, exacerbated by developments in digital technologies. Through an analysis of the constituent elements of personal data's definition, this section argues that personal data is a concept around which it is unsuitable to base an entire area of law.

A. 'Relating to'

The first troublesome element of the personal data definition is the requirement that information must 'relate to' an identified or identifiable natural person. The matter of when information will relate to an individual has proved contentious, and despite UK and EU courts seeking to address this question over the last 20 or so years, a clear elucidation of this notion has not emerged.

Approximately two decades ago, in *Durant*, the Court of Appeal infamously adopted a strict interpretation of the words 'relate to', thereby establishing a very narrow approach to the personal data concept.[20] It was held that information would only 'relate to' a person if it was either biographical in a significant sense or affected a person's privacy. This approach diverged considerably from subsequent CJEU jurisprudence that unequivocally stressed that the personal data concept should not be subject to either qualifying criterion.[21] The *Durant* decision was seemingly overturned in *Edem*, where it was held that data could be personal without any significant biographical nexus to an individual.

[18] Significant liability may be incurred if data are incorrectly classified. Data controllers who process personal data, perhaps in the mistaken belief said data are anonymous, in a way that infringes the substantive provisions of the UK GDPR shall be subjected to administrative fines of up to £8.7 million or, in the case of undertakings, up to 2% of the total worldwide annual turnover, whichever is higher. See Art 83(4) UK GDPR.

[19] Some observers, for example, have referred to the terminology used by the UK GDPR to define personal data as 'slippery language'. See V Janeček, 'Ownership of Personal Data in the Internet of Things' (2018) 34 *Computer Law & Security Review* 1039.

[20] *Durant v Financial Services Authority* [2003] EWCA Civ 1746.

[21] See, eg Case T-194/04 *Bavarian Lager v Commission* [2007] ECR II-4523.

Here, the Court of Appeal held that information would relate to a person when it was 'obviously about' them.[22] More recently, in *TLU*, the Court of Appeal appeared to imply that the biographical nexus and 'obviously about' tests should both be used to determine whether data are personal, but did not explain either how the two tests should interact or what their relationship was, leaving a residual uncertainty.[23] As noted elsewhere, uncertainty regarding the 'relate to' criterion has historically resulted in major practical difficulties for data controllers.[24]

The approach of the CJEU to the interpretation of the 'relate to' criterion has been more decisive than that of UK courts but is problematic for other reasons. In *YS*, the CJEU held that information 'about' an individual will 'relate to' them, but that analyses of that information will not themselves 'relate to' the individual.[25] In *Nowak*, a substantially more expansive approach was adopted, and it was held that information will relate to an individual if it is used (or is likely to be used) to evaluate them, treat them in a certain way, influence their behaviour or impact on their rights and interests.[26] Information, therefore, can relate to an individual by way of the purpose and impact of its uses, as well as its content (ie information will relate to an individual if its uses have an impact on said individual, even if it is not about them). In its guidance on the interpretation of the UK GDPR, the Information Commissioner's Office (ICO), the UK's data protection regulator, has since endorsed this interpretation.[27]

If adopted in the future, however, this approach will likely significantly aggravate the above-mentioned difficulties in elucidating a clear meaning of the 'relate to' criterion to such an extent that it may render the personal data-based model of data protection unworkable. This is mainly due to the way in which its adoption will necessarily result in the scope of the personal data concept becoming virtually unlimited. This, in turn, will lead to illogical applications of the law involving data protection rules being applied to information types which have no obvious relationship to the individuals to whom they nominally relate, and will render compliance with data protection rules either extremely burdensome or close to impossible. For example, when considering whether to employ a job applicant, an employer will likely not only review the applicant's application, but will also consider other information, such as budgetary constraints and organisational gaps. This information is not obviously about the applicant but, under the CJEU's expansive approach, could still be the applicant's personal data as it

[22] *Edem v IC & Financial Services Authority* [2014] EWCA Civ 92.

[23] *Secretary of State for the Home Department v TLU* [2018] All ER (D) 85 (Jun).

[24] C Millard and W Kuan Hon, 'Defining "Personal Data" in E-Social Science' (2012) 15(1) *Information, Communication & Society* 66.

[25] Case C-141/12 *YS and Others* ECLI:EU:C:2014:2081.

[26] Case C-434/16 *Nowak* ECLI:EU:C:2017:994.

[27] ICO, 'Guide to the General Data Protection Regulation' (1 January 2021) https://ico.org.uk/media/for-organisations/guide-to-data-protection/guide-to-the-general-data-protection-regulation-gdpr-1-1.pdf.

would be used for the purposes of determining whether to hire the applicant; a decision that would impact on the applicant's rights and interests. Observers have described such a possibility as 'absurd',[28] but it is an entirely feasible, if not probable, extension of the approach set out by the CJEU in *Nowak*. The widening of the personal data concept to potentially include information of this sort (eg corporate data) could significantly increase compliance obligations for data controllers, who, in addition to having to wrestle with the above-mentioned uncertainty regarding when information relate to an individual, would have to consider a possibly unlimited range of information types and uses when making such determinations.

The perils of this situation are compounded by the way in which key aspects of our lives are increasingly transformed into digital data. The emergence of ubiquitous computing, high levels of social media usage and increased utilisation of sensor-embedded physical environments (frequently referred to as 'the internet of things') mean that digital data about people's behaviours are ceaselessly generated on their own behalf and by others.[29] The ways in which this phenomenon presents various challenges in the data protection field have been widely discussed in the literature.[30] However, not only does datafication give rise to numerous data protection-related challenges in their own right, it simultaneously threatens the sustainability of the personal data-based approach to data protection itself.

As mentioned above, under the *Nowak* standard, information will relate to a person when it is used, or is likely to be used, for the purpose of evaluating or influencing the behaviour of a person. However, in an increasingly 'datafied' world, where aspects of everyday life are collected via participation in nominally 'smart' environments and converted into machine-readable data, essentially all and any information can be described as such. Purtova, for example, has highlighted how, although data collected from smart environments (eg data pertaining to rainfall, wind direction and foot traffic) will not habitually be 'about' people, they will frequently be collected for the purposes of assessing and influencing peoples' behaviour (such data may be used, for example, to adjust the speed at which escalators run, promote physical activity, change the warmth and intensity

[28] B Wong, 'Delimiting the Concept of Personal Data after the GDPR' (2019) 39 *Legal Studies* 527.

[29] See D Lupton and B Williamson, 'The Datafied Child: The Dataveillance of Children and Implications for Their Rights' (2017) 19(5) *New Media & Society* 780; L Dencik and S Stevens, 'Regimes of Justification in the Datafied Workplace: The Case of Hiring' [2021] *New Media & Society*; U Mejias and N Couldry, 'Datafication' (2019) 8(4) *Internet Policy Review*; V Mayer-Schönberger and K Cukier, *Big Data: A Revolution That Will Transform How We Live, Work and Think* (J Murray, 2013).

[30] See, eg R Weber, 'Internet of Things – New Security and Privacy Challenges' (2010) 26(1) *Computer Law & Security Review* 23; R Weber, 'Internet of Things: Privacy Issues Revisited' (2015) 31(5) *Computer Law & Security Review* 618; M Rhoen, 'Rear View Mirror, Crystal Ball: Predictions for the Future of Data Protection Law Based on the History of Environmental Protection Law' (2017) 33 *Computer Law & Security Review* 603.

of street lighting or predict and de-escalate deviant behaviours).[31] With this being the case, this information will frequently 'relate to' individuals by way of its intended purpose and impact. Pursuant to this, given the high dimensionality of contemporary datasets (ie the way in which they consist of numerous data points about each individual, thereby making each individual's record unique), it is likely that individuals will frequently be identifiable from the data collected.[32]

The upshot of this is as follows. As significant amounts of information gathered from smart environments will likely relate to identifiable persons by way of their purpose and impact, this information will be personal data. If this is the case, then the processing of personal data will literally be everywhere, all around us. Under the personal data-based model to data protection, therefore, data protection law will apply to nearly every aspect of our everyday interactions and behaviours. Ergo, data protection law will effectively become the 'law of everything'. Were this to happen, compliance with the law would become impossible, thereby depriving it of its value and legitimacy.[33]

B. 'Identified or Identifiable'

The second troublesome element of the personal data definition is the notion of an 'identified or identifiable' person. Identifiability in this context amounts to the ability of a data controller or another person to distinguish one person from others by linking them to information of some kind.[34] As set out above, if this cannot be done, the information will be legally anonymous. The notion of identifiability and how it should be interpreted has, however, again proven challenging for data controllers and the courts, and again these difficulties have been exacerbated by technological developments, particularly those in the field of anonymisation.

Anonymisation is a word used to refer to an action applied to data that aims to eliminate the possibility of an individual being identified from those data.[35] This is not a new phenomenon. Efforts to scientifically guarantee the anonymity of data can be traced back at least as far as the 1970s.[36] Despite often being used as a broad collective term, 'anonymisation' spans a wide range of techniques, each with their own functions. Some, for example, involve the removal of directly

[31] N Purtova, 'The Law of Everything. Broad Concept of Personal Data and Future of EU Data Protection Law' (2018) 10(1) *Law, Innovation and Technology* 40.
[32] ibid.
[33] ibid.
[34] ICO (n 27).
[35] S Saxby, A Knight and H Pearce, 'Piercing the Anonymity Veil: Re-identification Risk and the UK Transparency Agenda' in S Kierkegaard (ed), *Information Ethics and Security: Future of International World Time* (IATL, 2014).
[36] See, eg T Dalenius, 'Towards a Methodology for Statistical Disclosure Control' (1977) 15 *Statistical Review* 429.

identifiable characteristics from datasets, whereas others aggregate datasets to provide summary-level statistics that do not include individual-level data.[37]

As set out above, existing and prospective data protection rules do not apply to the processing of anonymous data. Ergo, converting 'personal data' to 'anonymous data' via the use of anonymisation techniques will remove those data from the scope of the law. Anonymisation, therefore, is often advocated as a way of processing data free from data protection obligations.[38] However, despite historically being championed as a way through which data controllers can absolve themselves of data protection obligations, over the last 20 or so years technical critics of anonymisation have demonstrated that conventional techniques are incapable of providing a 100 per cent guarantee of anonymity. In an increasing number of situations, nominally 'anonymised' data will be at risk of being 'de-anonymised' and re-rendered personal.[39] This is significant for data protection law. As established above, the wording of the UK GDPR and the Data Protection Bill is premised on the idea that personal data can be categorically distinguished from anonymous data. Given the limits of anonymisation techniques, however, this position has become divorced from reality, as the line between personal and anonymous data has become blurred, thereby making determinations regarding whether data are personal or anonymous extremely difficult to perform. In turn, this raises difficult normative questions as to the suitability of persisting with a model of data protection law based on a personal/anonymous dichotomy.[40]

Various observers have contended, however, that although perfect anonymisation is unachievable, anonymisation remains an important tool for protecting individuals' data protection interests. Several have argued that though the law should not look to anonymisation for absolute guarantees of anonymity, identifiability exists on a continuum and thus identification from data will depend on probability and context.[41] Others have noted that, as set out above, Article 4(1) and

[37] A detailed consideration of different anonymisation techniques is beyond the scope of this chapter. For an overview of a number of prominent techniques, see Article 29 Data Protection Working Party (2014) Opinion 05/2014 on Anonymisation Techniques.

[38] Z Alexin, 'Does Fair Anonymization Exist?' (2014) 28(1) *International Review of Law, Computers & Technology* 2.

[39] See particularly L Sweeney, 'Simple Demographics Often Identify People Uniquely' (Carnegie Mellon University, 2000) Data Privacy Working Paper; A Narayanan and V Shmatikov, 'Robust De-anonymization of Large Datasets (How to Break Anonymity of the Netflix Prize Dataset)' (University of Texas at Austin, 2006) 403–18; Y de Montjoye et al, 'Unique in the Crowd: The Privacy Bounds of Human Mobility' (2013) 3 *Scientific Reports* no 1376; L Rocher, J Hendrickx and Y de Montjoye, 'Estimating the Success of Re-identifications in Incomplete Datasets Using Generative Models' (2019) 10 *Nature Communications* no 3069. See also P Ohm, 'Broken Promises of Privacy: Responding to the Surprising Failure of Anonymization' (2009) 57 *UCLA Law Review* 1701; F Aldhouse, 'Anonymisation of Personal Data: A Missed Opportunity for the European Commission' (2014) 30(4) *Computer Law & Security Review* 403.

[40] These questions were first brought to the attention of the legal world by Paul Ohm in 2010: Ohm (n 39).

[41] See A Cavoukian and K El Emam, 'Dispelling the Myths Surrounding De-identification: Anonymization Remains a Strong Tool for Protecting Privacy' (Information and Privacy Commissioner,

Recital 26 of the UK GDPR establish that a 100 per cent guarantee of non-identifiability is not required for data to be legally anonymous (ie because identifiability from data must be assessed by way of reference to the means 'reasonably likely' to be used to identify an individual or individuals), and so anonymisation's failings need not be fatal for the law. Pursuant to this, it has been suggested that the law allows for a risk-based approach to personal data, according to which data will only be personal if, having taken account of all the means that might 'reasonably likely' be used to identify an individual, there is a significant risk of identification occurring.[42] Pursuant to this, if the risk of identification following the application of anonymisation techniques is insignificant, this will amount to the achievement of what has been described as 'functional anonymisation'.[43] This scalar interpretation of the notion of identifiability appears to be broadly consistent with both UK and EU case law, which, to some extent at least, have seemingly tentatively endorsed the possibility of an approach to data categorisation in this vein.[44]

Crucially, however, both the CJEU and the UK courts have failed to provide a definitive answer to the question: 'when, and at which point, will data become legally anonymous?'. This is problematic. Even if the courts were to fully endorse a risk-based approach to data categorisation that recognised the notion of identifiability as scalar/existing on a spectrum (as a means of addressing the problems caused by anonymisation's limitations), the application of data protection rules under both current and prospective data protection frameworks would themselves remain binary (ie they would apply either completely or not at all, due to data protection rules being triggered in their entirety as soon as personal data are processed, but not at all in the event non-personal data are processed). Because of this, a risk-based approach would still require data controllers to map out the

Ontario, 2011); E Rubinstein and W Hartzog, 'Anonymization and Risk' [2015] *Washington Law Review*; P Schwartz and D Solove, 'Reconciling Personal Information in the United States and European Union' (2014) 102 *California Law Review* 877; S Stalla-Bourdillon and A Knight, 'Anonymous Data v Personal Data – A False Debate: An EU Perspective on Anonymization, Pseudonymization and Personal Data' (2017) 43(2) *Wisconsin Law Journal* 284; S Esayas, 'The Role of Anonymisation and Pseudonymisation under EU Data Privacy Rules: Beyond the "All or Nothing" Approach' (2015) 6(2) *European Journal of Law and Technology*.

[42] See Stalla-Bourdillon and Knight (n 41); R Hu et al, 'Bridging Policy, Regulation, and Practice? A Techno-legal Analysis of Three Types of Data in the GDPR' in R Leenes et al (eds), *Data Protection and Privacy: The Age of Intelligent Machines* (Hart Publishing, 2017); M Mourby et al, 'Are "Pseudonymised" Data Always Personal Data? Implications of the GDPR for Administrative Data Research in the UK' (2018) 34(2) *Computer Law & Security Review* 222; M Finck and F Pallas, 'They Who Must Not Be Identified – Distinguishing Personal from Non-personal Data under the GDPR' (2020) 10(1) *International Data Privacy Law*.

[43] M Elliot et al, 'Functional Anonymisation: Personal Data and the Data Environment' (2018) 34(2) *Computer Law & Security Review* 204.

[44] See, eg *Information Commissioner v Miller* [2018] UKUT 229; *Information Commissioner v Magherafelt District Council* [2012] UKUT 263 AAC; *Queen Mary University of London v (1) The Information Commissioner and (2) Alem Mathees* EA/2015/0269; Case C-582/14 *Breyer* ECLI:EU:C:2016:930. For an overview of UK case law in this area, see F Aldhouse, 'Anonymisation of Personal Data: A Missed Opportunity for the European Commission' (2014) 30(4) *Computer Law & Security Review* 403.

precise rate at which personal data and anonymous data accrete from completely non-identifiable to completely identifiable, and for them to be able to map the point at which identification legally occurs. Significant liability would hang on the exact nature of this mapping, and yet there is a dearth of judicial guidance on how exactly this could or should be accomplished, or how one mapping should be judged superior or inferior to another.

In the absence of conclusive judicial guidance, other observers and institutions have issued their own advice on how 'identifiability' from data should be assessed. Both the ICO and the UK Anonymisation Network (UKAN), for instance, have published guidance which stresses that questions regarding identifiability from data cannot be confined to an analysis of the data in question in isolation, but must also encompass a consideration of the 'environment' and ongoing 'situation' of those data.[45] A full assessment of possible identifiability from data, in fact, will require a continuous evaluation of any other existing data, including data held by other parties (as well as data that may come into existence in the future), which could be linked to the data resulting in identification, as well as the existence of any 'motivated intruders' (and their capabilities) who would seek to de-anonymise the data.[46] As noted above, so long as this is done, it should be possible for data controllers to 'functionally anonymise' data in their possession.[47]

In a very best-case scenario, however, this will often be a task fraught with difficulty. Modelling the 'environment' of data will often be a complicated, resource-intensive exercise, particularly for data controllers working with high-dimensionality datasets, as extensive research and expert guidance will likely be required in order to fully comprehend the different components of said environment (eg other data in the environment, the infrastructure, other agents/parties).[48] With this being the case, and considerable expenditure and expert consultation potentially being required for compliance with legal rules, questions arise as to whether it is appropriate for the law to continue to operate on this basis.

C. 'Information' and 'Data'

The final troublesome elements of the definition of personal data considered here are the notions of 'information' and 'data' themselves. As set out above, under both the UK GDPR and the Data Protection Bill, personal 'data' is 'information'

[45] ICO, 'Anonymisation: Managing Data Protection Risk Code of Practice' (2012); M Elliot et al, *The Anonymisation Decision-Making Framework* (UKAN, 2016).

[46] ibid.

[47] Elliot et al (n 45).

[48] Stalla-Bourdillon and Knight (n 41).

relating to an identified or unidentified person. Recital 26 of the UK GDPR also specifically refers to 'personal information' as well as 'personal data'. Despite their apparent fundamental importance, the meanings of both 'information' and 'data' have seemingly been taken for granted by the courts, who have generally treated the two terms as interchangeable and have made little effort to elucidate the differences between them or articulate their meaning.

Whilst the courts have been reticent in their attempts to distinguish and define information and data, however, observers in other fields have extensively argued how information and data are conceptually distinct and that it is important for them to be recognised as such. There is now a sizeable body of philosophical literature, for instance, which supports a definition of information as 'data plus meaning'. In other words, data is raw material that is used to generate information, and information is data that has been processed into a form that is meaningful.[49] The fact that the courts and the UK GDPR itself do not recognise this nuance is potentially problematic. Disconnections between law and philosophical hermeneutics of this sort often result in the development of poor understandings of the law, the unsatisfactory application of legal rules, and the emergence of constitutive disconnections between the law and wider culture.[50]

On a related note, observers have highlighted how, despite judicial ambivalence as to their intricacy, information and data are notoriously complex concepts that are capable of coming in many forms and of having many meanings. Floridi provides an instructive example of this nuance:

> Something may count as information in more than one sense, depending on the context. For example, a person's iris may be an instance of information as reality (the pattern of the membrane in the eye), which provides information for reality (eg as a biometric means to open a door by verifying the identity of a person), or about reality (eg the identity of the person).[51]

Not only is information a complex notion, however: the notion of data on which it is based is similarly multifaceted. In regular everyday use, 'data' is a term commonly understood as referring to items typically found in databases, or those which information management systems are designed to convey to users in the form of information (eg statistics, numbers, names, addresses, weights). Data of this sort

[49] See, eg L Floridi, 'Is Semantic Information Meaningful Data?' (2005) 20(2) *Philosophy and Phenomenological Research* 351. See also G Silver and M Silver, *Systems Analysis and Design* (Addison Wesley, 1989); G Davis and M Olson, *Management Information Systems: Conceptual Foundations, Structure, and Development* (McGraw-Hill, 1985).

[50] See F Mootz, 'Law and Philosophy, Philosophy and Law' (1994] 26 *Toledo Law Review* 146; G Leyh, 'Legal Education and the Public Life' in G Leyh (ed), *Legal Hermeneutics: History, Theory and Practice* (University of California Press, 1992) 269.

[51] L Floridi, *Information: A Very Short Introduction* (Oxford University Press, 2010) 74.

has been defined by observers as 'primary data'.[52] However, the full meaning of the term 'data' extends beyond primary data alone, and there are several other notable forms in which data can exist of which people, including data controllers, are often unaware. These include:

- *Metadata* – data which provide indications about the nature of primary data. For example, the contents of an email are primary data, whereas the time and date the email was sent are metadata.[53]
- *Operational data* – data regarding the use of other (usually primary) data within a data system. For example, a car may have a yellow light on the dashboard that, when flashing, indicates that the car's systems are malfunctioning. The flashing of the yellow light may indicate that the car's low battery indicator (a red flashing light) is not working properly, thereby undermining the hypothesis that the battery is flat.[54]
- *Derivative data* – data that are extracted from other (usually primary) data that reveal patterns, clues or inferential evidence about things other than those directly addressed by the data themselves. For example, from an analysis of a person's credit card bill, it will frequently be possible to derive the card-holder's whereabouts at a given time.[55]

A possible implication of the often under-appreciated breadth of the terms 'data' and 'information' in a general sense, therefore, is that the terms 'personal data' and 'personal information' will apply to a wider range of material than might initially be assumed by many data controllers based on their reading of the UK GDPR and the Data Protection Bill. Article 4(1) of the UK GDPR, for example, lists a number of identifiers as examples of things that might constitute personal data, all of which can be described as primary data as per the understanding set out above (eg names, identification numbers, location data). No reference is made to examples of other types of data (eg operational or derivative data) that, depending on context, could also fall within the scope of the personal data concept. This could plausibly lead to some data controllers incorrectly interpreting Article 4(1) as implying that personal data's scope is narrower than it is.[56]

[52] ibid 28.

[53] See J Pomerantz, *Metadata* (MIT Press, 2015).

[54] Floridi (n 51) 29.

[55] ibid.

[56] For example, within some organisations data protection rules and requirements are frequently viewed by staff as a vague and confusing process. Decisions over matters of data protection are frequently taken on a 'will this do?' basis, and are often dictated by internal rules of offices, or what senior members of staff without any data protection knowledge (possibly erroneously) believe is the law. See E Harbinja et al, 'BILETA Response to UK Government Consultation: Data a New Direction' (BILETA, 2021). On perceptions and possibly misunderstandings of data protection rules more generally, see D Hallinan, M Friedewald and P McCarthy, 'Citizens' Perceptions of Data Protection and Privacy in Europe' (2012) 28(3) *Computer Law & Security Review* 263.

These possible difficulties regarding the scope and breadth of the personal data concept have again been exacerbated by technological developments, particularly advances in data mining technology.[57] Developments in the data mining field mean that physical objects and materials are now increasingly 'mined' for the purpose of revealing important information. For example, biological material (eg organs, skin cells) is frequently analysed for the sake of revealing new information and insights into clinical conditions and the development of new medical treatments.[58] The use of physical objects in this way, however, when considered against the background of the law's failure to disambiguate information and data, may ultimately undermine the feasibility of maintaining a logical boundary between data and information and the physical material that constitutes their medium.[59] As noted by Bygrave, as physical objects are increasingly mined for information, it will become increasingly difficult to justify any meaningful distinction between the former and the latter. The upshot of this is the possible applicability of the terms 'personal data' and 'personal information' extending to physical materials per se, as opposed to data or information derived from said materials (eg blood cells themselves, as opposed to data or information derived from blood cells).[60] UK and European Court of Human Rights jurisprudence has suggested there is nothing present in the statutory definition of personal data that prima facie disallows such an interpretation.[61] A necessary consequence of this would be data controllers, when attempting to determine whether they are processing personal data, having to consider the possibility of physical objects constituting personal data per se, rather than confining their analyses to information as traditionally understood, adding a further layer of complexity to a task that, as set out above, will often already be extremely complicated.

[57] Broadly speaking, data mining can be described as the process of finding anomalies, patterns and correlations within large datasets to predict outcomes. See D Larose and C Larose, *Discovering Knowledge in Data: An Introduction to Data Mining* (J Wiley & Sons, 2014) 2.

[58] See B Prainsack, 'The Powers of Participatory Medicine' (2014) 12(4) *PLoS Biology*; R Li et al, 'Electronic Health Records and Polygenic Risk Scores for Predicting Disease Risk' (2020) 21 *Nature Reviews Genetics* 493; N Artzi et al, 'Prediction of Gestational Diabetes Based on Nationwide Electronic Health Records' (2020) 26 *Nature Medicine* 71; G Taskler et al, 'Opportunities, Pitfalls, and Alternatives in Adapting Electronic Health Records for Health Services Research' (2021) 41(2) *Medical Decision Making* 133; L Beesley et al, 'The Emerging Landscape of Health Research Based on Biobanks Linked to Electronic Health Records: Existing Resources, Statistical Challenges, and Potential Opportunities' (2020] 39(6) *Statistics in Medicine* 773; A Callahan, NH Shah and JH Chen, 'Research and Reporting Considerations for Observational Studies Using Electronic Health Record Data' (2020] 172 *Annals of Internal Medicine* 79.

[59] L Bygrave, *Data Privacy Law: An International Perspective* (Oxford University Press, 2014) 126.

[60] L Bygrave, 'The Body as Data? Biobank Regulation via the "Back Door" of Data Protection Law' (2010) 2(1) *Law, Innovation and Technology* 1.

[61] See *LS, R (on application of) v South Yorkshire Police (Consolidated Appeals)* 2004 UKHL39; *S and Marper v UK* (2009) 48 EHHR 50 [68].

V. A Non-personal Approach to Data Protection Law?

The personal data-based model of data protection explicitly distinguishes personal data from all other data types, and establishes that the processing of the former will trigger legal rules and protections, whilst processing of the latter will not. There are major problems with this duality that have been, and will continue to be, exacerbated by technological advancement.

First, the concept of personal data is semantically vague to the point that determining to what it does and does not apply is increasingly a task laden with considerable difficulty, particularly in the context of contemporary data-handling practices. Though UK and EU courts have sought to address these difficulties and provide clarification, the approaches they have adopted have not been entirely adequate. In reality, successfully negotiating the challenge of determining whether data are personal will frequently require data controllers to engage with reams of technical guidance and seek expert consultation, and even then to some extent they will only be able to guess at what is required for legal compliance. This puts the personal data-based approach to data protection law in its entirety at odds with widely accepted legal maxims which hold that in order to be 'good' the content of legal rules must be clear to whom they apply.[62]

Second, even if these difficulties could be overcome, given the amount of information in the world that is either about or relates to individuals in terms of purpose or impact, it is a term that could conceivably come to encompass all and any information types and uses. These semantic and practical challenges inherent in the personal data concept risk the law becoming unworkable and therefore devoid of meaning. Because of these factors alone, there are now compelling reasons as to why we should at the very least think about moving away from the traditional personal data-based approach to data protection.

One possible way of circumventing the above-mentioned challenges inherent in the personal data-based approach to data protection that has been hitherto relatively unexplored is to move to an information harms-based approach to data protection, underpinned by the notion of risk. In other words, rather than the law concerning itself with whether data are personal and using this as the central trigger for the application of data protection rules, the rules could be triggered according to the level of potential harm inherent in data processing activities. Under such an approach, the extent to which data protection rules and obligations would apply to data controllers would operate on a sliding scale, depending on the nature of the processing operations for which they were responsible, as well

[62] See particularly L Fuller, *The Morality of Law* (Yale University Press, 1969). See also A Le Sueur, M Sunkin and J Murkens, *Public Law* (Oxford University Press, 2013) 78–112; R Brownsword and M Goodwin, *Law and the Technologies of the Twentieth Century* (Cambridge University Press, 2012).

as their possible impact on any affected individuals, irrespective of whether any data involved were nominally personal. What follows below is a sketch of what a harm-based approach to data protection could look like in practice.

A. Towards a Harm-Based Approach to Data Protection

The starting point for discussions of how a harm-based approach to data protection law might operate is the notion of harm itself. If legal rules were to apply according to the level of overall harm inherent in particular data uses, a means through which levels of harm could be quantified and calculated would clearly be needed. In this respect, it is worth noting that both UK courts and the CJEU have both recently struggled with the notion of data-related harms and have treated them very differently. For example, in *Driver*, the UK Court of Appeal held that a 'very modest degree of distress' would constitute non-material damage for the purpose of awarding compensation following a data breach.[63] Conversely, in *UI v Österreichische Post AG*, the CJEU concluded that demonstrating 'mere upset' following an infringement of data protection rules would not be sufficient to establish non-material damage had been suffered.[64]

Beyond case law, however, there are multiple examples of regulatory guidance, research projects and other scholarly works from jurisdictions all over the world that have articulated taxonomies of harms that can stem from uses of data. For instance, the UK ICO, the French Commission nationale de l'informatique et des libertés (CNIL) and the US National Institute of Standards and Technology (NIST) have all produced advice on how information-related harms can be calculated in practice.[65] Guidance notes published by all three institutions recognise there are multiple levels of harm that data processing activities can have on individuals. These can, broadly speaking, be separated into four levels of magnitude: negligible; limited; significant; and maximum.[66] The same sources also provide some examples of specific harms that might fall into each category.[67] A collation of these is appended in Table 1.

[63] *Driver v CPS* [2022] EWHC 2500 (KB).

[64] C-300/21 *UI v Österreichische Post AG*.

[65] See CNIL, 'Methodology for Privacy Risk Management' (2012); NIST, 'Guide to Protecting the Confidentiality of Personally Identifiable Information' (2015); NIST, 'Guide for Conducting Risk Assessments' (2012) Special Publication 800-30; NIST, 'An Introduction to Privacy Engineering and Risk Management in Federal Systems' (2017) NISTIR 8062; NIST, 'Risk Management Framework for Information Systems and Organizations: A System Life Cycle Approach for Security and Privacy' (2018) Special Publication 800-37; Trilateral Research & Consulting, 'Privacy Impact Assessment and Risk Management: Report for the Information Commissioner's Office' (2015). See also W Abbass, A Baina and M Bellafkih, 'Using EBIOS for Risk Management in Critical Information Infrastructure' (5th World Congress on Information and Communication Technologies (WICT) 2015); G Milne et al, 'Information Sensitivity Typology: Mapping the Degree and Type of Risk Consumers Perceive in Personal Data Sharing' (2017) 51(1) *Journal of Consumer Affairs* 133.

[66] ibid.

[67] ibid.

Table 1 Data processing harm categories

Negligible	Limited	Significant	Maximum
Minor annoyances, irritations and inconveniences	Prevention of using a service anonymously Denial of non-essential services Social embarrassment Moderate financial losses Moderate stress and anxiety Creation of new data that could be used for adverse purposes	Legal processes becoming unavailable to individuals Vulnerable persons being identified Misappropriation of funds Damage to property Loss of employment Significant but non-permanent/short-term health problems	Major financial losses Inability to work Long-term health problems Permanent injury Death

Given these different levels and types of harms have already been identified and articulated, and play an active role in data protection regulatory guidance worldwide, there seems no good reason why they cannot be directly incorporated into the law itself. However, it is not only the magnitude of harms that would be relevant to a harm-based approach to data protection; the probability of any possible harms would also need to be considered. A harm of a very significant magnitude would, for instance, be of concern to nobody if its probability was nil. By the same token, a harm of very high probability but of negligible magnitude would perhaps also conceivably be considered trifling by many. The true level of the risk of any data processing activity, therefore, would have to be expressed as a function of the risk/probability of a harm occurring multiplied by the magnitude of the harm should it occur. In other words, under a harm-based approach, data controllers would be required to determine the overall level of harm inherent in a data processing activity by measuring and charting the magnitude of a possible harm against the risk or probability of its occurrence. Like harm, probability can also be separated into the four broad categories of negligible, limited, significant and maximum.[68] Factors that would influence probability of harm would likely include:

- whether any security measures (either technological or organisational) were attached/applied to the data (eg access controls/records, audit trails, independent data governance mechanisms and similar);
- the existence of any motivated intruders who may wish to obtain/access the data and use the data for potentially harmful purposes, and the prospect of them achieving their goals;

[68] ibid.

- whether individuals who will have, or are likely to gain, access to the data have received any data protection or information governance training; and
- the existence and identity of any third parties with whom the data will be shared, the security measures these third parties have in place and the purpose(s) for which the data are to be shared.

The determination of both the magnitude and the probability of harm inherent in a particular data processing operation would allow for the calculation of an overall harm score that could be plotted on a risk matrix, an example of which is displayed in Table 2.

Table 2 Risk/harm matrix

4	Moderate	High	Very high	Maximum
3	Low	Moderate	High	Very high
2	Very low	Low	Moderate	High
1	Minimal	Very low	Low	Moderate
	1	2	3	4

The horizontal axis of the matrix charts the potential impact/harm on a scale of 1 to 4, with 1 denoting negligible harm, 2 and 3 denoting limited and significant harm, respectively, and 4 denoting maximum harm. The vertical axis charts the probability of the harm occurring. Similarly, 1 denotes negligible probability, 2 and 3 denote limited and significant probability, respectively, and 4 denotes maximum probability. The combination of risk scores on both axes allows for the calculation of one of seven types of overall harm: minimal, very low, low, moderate, high, very high and maximum. For example, were a data controller to conclude that a data processing operation gave rise to a risk of significant harm (3), but that there was a limited chance of this harm manifesting in practice (2), the overall level of risk associated with the data processing operation would be 'moderate'. Conversely, if a data processing operation was adjudged to have a maximum level of potential harm (4) and the probability of this harm manifesting was adjudged to be significant (3), the overall level of risk associated with the processing would be 'very high'. Whilst data controllers would be required to perform their own risk assessments on their individual data processing operations, some specific data processing activities that are known to be potentially harmful (eg those involving automated decision-making and similar) could be designated to be of a certain harm level (ie moderate, high, very high, etc) by the ICO in published guidance.

Having determined the overall level of risk associated with a data processing operation by placing it on the matrix, the application of data protection rules could then be determined on a spectrum or sliding scale basis. For example, at the lower end of the spectrum, data processing operations with a minimal level of overall harm might not be required to comply with data protection rules and requirements at all. At the other end of the scale, data processing operations with a maximum level of overall harm might be completely prohibited. In between these two extreme ends, where the majority of data processing operations would perhaps be likely to fall (ie data processing operations that had an overall harm level of very low, low, moderate, high or very high), data protection rules and requirements would apply on a sliding scale commensurate with the overall level of harm, ranging from a light-touch application of rules for very-low-harm processing operations, up to a rigorous and extensive application for very-high-harm processing operations. An illustrative harm-based data protection spectrum is set out in Table 3.

Table 3 A prospective harm-based spectrum

Maximum harm		Processing is completely prohibited in all but exceptional circumstances
Very high harm		Processing is prohibited in all but highly controlled/limited circumstances and subject to extensive legal controls
High harm		Processing is prohibited unless data controllers can demonstrate compliance with an intensive range of data protection obligations and principles
Moderate harm		Processing is permissible – data controllers must comply with a broad range of data protection obligations and principles
Low harm		Processing is permissible – data controllers must observe a limited range of data protection obligations and principles
Very low harm		Processing is permissible – data controllers must observe some minor obligations and principles relating to data protection
Minimal harm		Processing is permissible – not subject to any specific legal controls

B. Discussion

The adoption of a more granular approach to regulating data processing activities, as outlined above, whereby the application of legal rules would depend on the contextual peculiarities of specific data uses, would have several notable benefits. Most obviously, it would allow for the law to move beyond the troublesome personal data/anonymous data dichotomy upon which data protection law is currently based. It would allow for the application of data protection rules to be targeted on the basis of real needs and problems, rather than on answers to confusing questions of limited relevance concerning whether or not data are personal. In so doing, it would allow for the semantic and definitional challenges associated with the personal data concept outlined above to be dissolved without weakening or watering down the data protection obligations and responsibilities to which data controllers are currently subject.

Support for non-personal data-based approaches to data protection and information governance more broadly can already be found in a number of locations. For instance, the Proposal for a Regulation on European data governance (Data Governance Act), announced by the European Commission as part of the 2020 strategy for data, outlines a range of rules applicable to public-sector data-handling activities.[69] Personal data, however, is explicitly excluded from the proposed Regulation's scope, thereby tacitly acknowledging the increasing regulatory significance of non-personal data and necessarily implying that personal data should not be the be-all and end-all so far as legal regulation of data processing activities is concerned.[70]

Recognition of the possible merits of a harm-based approach to data protection can also be found in the UK GDPR itself, with some of its articles establishing rules for specific data processing activities, thereby implicitly acknowledging that some types of data processing are likely to be more harmful than others and, thus, that they require more stringent regulation.[71] More generally, various observers have stated their support for risk/harm-based approaches to matters of data protection, with some arguing that, if handled properly, the adoption of such an approach could bring about a valuable shift towards a more substantive protection of fundamental rights and freedoms.[72] Others have noted how risk/harm-based approaches will potentially ease burdens on data controllers, who would know better where to target their regulatory resources, and will provide them with much-needed flexibility in the face of ever-evolving data environments.[73] Others, whilst stopping short of giving risk/harm-based approaches their endorsement, have still explicitly mentioned them as potential alternatives to the current personal data-based approach.[74]

One concern that might be espoused about the harm-based approach proposed here is that it may be incompatible with the EU GDPR, which, as highlighted

[69] Proposal for a Regulation of the European Parliament and of the Council on European data governance (Data Governance Act) COM/2020/767 final, https://eur-lex.europa.eu/legal-content/EN/TXT/?uri=CELEX%3A52020PC0767.

[70] ibid Recital 7.

[71] For instance, Art 22 GDPR and Art 22 UK GDPR provide individuals with rights not to be subject to decisions based solely on automated data processing/decision-making.

[72] See, eg C Quelle, 'Enhancing Compliance under the General Data Protection Regulation: The Risky Upshot of the Accountability- and Risk-Based Approach' (2018) 9(3) *European Journal of Risk Regulation* 502; H Pearce, 'A Proposal for a New Risk-Based Licensing Approach to Disclosing Anonymised Data under the (UK) Freedom of Information Act 2000' (2021) 30 *Information & Communications Technology Law* 108; H Pearce, 'The (UK) Freedom of Information Act's Disclosure Process Is Broken: Where Do We Go from Here?' (2020) 29 *Information & Communications Technology Law* 3540. See also W Kuan Hon, C Millard and I Walden, 'What Is Regulated as Personal Data in Clouds?' in C Millard (ed), *Cloud Computing Law* (Oxford University Press, 2013); H Pearce and S Stalla-Bourdillon; Schwartz and Solove (n 41).

[73] R Gellert, *The Risk-Based Approach to Data Protection* (Oxford University Press, 2020) 245.

[74] See, eg Finck and Pallas (n 42); Purtova (n 31); Koops (n 12).

above, could jeopardise the UK–EU adequacy relationship. For instance, the harm-based approach would apply conditions and restrictions to data processing activities on a granular basis and only in some situations, whereas the EU GDPR applies in its entirety to any processing of personal data. The EU GDPR, therefore, adopts a uniform approach to data protection, whereas the harm-based approach would allow for and encourage variation in the application of legal rules. Accordingly, on the face of things, the harm-based approach might appear to diverge drastically from the EU GDPR and threaten to contravene its goal of providing uniformly high levels of data protection. However, this need not necessarily be the case. There are, in fact, numerous reasons why the harm-based approach would, to some extent at least, be compatible with both the EU GDPR itself and its underlying rationale and objectives.

As noted above, the EU GDPR itself already diverges from its prima facie uniform approach in several significant ways. Most obviously, Article 9 of the EU GDPR explicitly establishes the notion of 'special category' personal data, and subjects the processing of such data to more stringent rules and conditions than supposedly non-special personal data. In a similar vein, Article 11 of the EU GDPR establishes that the full gamut of its provisions will not apply to all types of personal data. Specifically, Article 11(1) specifies that:

> If the purposes for which a controller processes personal data do not or do no longer require the identification of a data subject by the data controller, the controller shall not be obliged to maintain, acquire or process additional information in order to identify the data subject for the sole purpose of complying with this Regulation.

In other words, data controllers are not required to collect more personal data to identify data subjects solely for the purpose of complying with the remainder of the EU GDPR's substantive provisions. In so doing, Article 11 of the EU GDPR recognises that *identifiable* information should not and cannot be regulated in the same manner as *identified* information.[75] Thus, though Article 11 does not explicitly establish a two-tiered system of data protection, according to which different rules and requirements are attached to different classes of personal data and different processing activities, it does permit such an approach.[76] Article 22 of the EU GDPR then provides individuals with a right not to be subject to decisions based on automated processing of personal data, including profiling, thereby necessarily establishing a specific rule for a specific type of data processing. Accordingly, from a consideration of Articles 4(1), 9, 11 and 22 alone, we can discern that the EU GDPR already clearly envisages that some situations, and specific data processing activities, will necessitate the deployment of different levels of protection in order to effectively protect individuals from harm.

Another related possible concern is that the notion of risk that underpins the proposed harm-based approach may be incompatible with the fundamental

[75] Schwartz and Solove (n 41) 914.
[76] ibid.

rights grounding on which the EU GDPR is based.[77] Such concerns, however, are misaligned. There is now a burgeoning body of literature that has convincingly argued not only that risk-based regulatory strategies are compatible with the protection of fundamental rights, but that data protection law is an area where risk-based regulation is already prominent.[78] Gellert, for instance, notes how the proportionality test, a staple of European human rights law, is itself necessarily underpinned by the notion of risk.[79] Similarly, Quelle has convincingly explained how a number of data protection principles are already more or less prohibitive (or perhaps permissive), depending on the foreseeable consequences of data processing operations.[80] To this end, the harm-based approach set out above would, to some extent at least, be consistent with major aspects of the EU GDPR.

There would also likely be practical challenges associated with the harm-based approach. Some have suggested, for instance, that assessing the potential levels of harm inherent in data processing operations may be a highly complicated exercise.[81] However, such difficulties might not be as pronounced as might initially be assumed. As has been argued elsewhere, requiring data controllers to assess the risk of harm associated with their data processing operations should not, in many instances at least, be more burdensome than requiring them to assess whether the data at their disposal are personal or otherwise.[82] And in any event, even if this were to be the case, difficulties in enforcing and applying the law are not, and never have been, a reason to stop trying. This will particularly be the case in situations where the ex post situation following the introduction of a new regulatory framework results in an improvement, relative to regulatory objectives, over the ex ante situation, which, for the reasons provided above, would potentially be the case were the personal data-based approach to data protection be replaced with a harm-based approach.[83]

VI. Conclusion

The Data Protection and Digital Information Bill was purported to refresh and revamp the UK's data protection framework. This chapter has argued that the

[77] On the foundations of data protection law in Europe, see O Lynskey, *The Foundations of EU Data Protection Law* (Oxford University Press, 2015).

[78] See, eg Gellert (n 73). See also M Macenaite, 'The "Riskification" of European Data Protection Law through a Two-Fold Shift' (2017) 8(3) *European Journal of Risk Regulation* 506.

[79] ibid 15.

[80] Quelle (n 72).

[81] See M Gonçalves, 'The Risk-Based Approach under the New EU Data Protection Regulation: A Critical Perspective' (2020) 23(2) *Journal of Risk Research* 139. See also H Pearce, 'Big Data and the Reform of the European Data Protection Framework: An Overview of Potential Concerns Associated with Proposals for Risk Management-Based Approaches to the Concept of Personal Data' (2017) 26(3) *Information & Communications Technology Law* 312.

[82] See Kuan Hon et al (n 72).

[83] On the notion of regulatory effectiveness, see R Brownsword and M Goodwin, *Law and the Technologies of the Twenty-First Century* (Cambridge University Press, 2012).

Bill is unambitious, and it is unwise for UK data protection law to continue to be based around the troublesome concept of personal data. Consequently, the development of alternative models of data protection should be actively pursued. The harm-based approach to date protection sketched in this chapter represents an example of what a new non-personal approach to data protection could look like. Whilst the enactment and operation of a harm-based model of data protection law in this vein would not be without its own challenges, it is a prima facie viable embryonic alternative to the personal data-based model that would benefit further thought and consideration.

PART II

The Precarious Equilibrium of the UK Adequacy Decision: Law Enforcement and National Security

4

Counter-terrorism, Information-Sharing and Law Enforcement Cooperation Post-Brexit

CHRISTINE ANDREEVA

I. Introduction

Despite being an ever-reluctant partner in security matters, the UK made an impact on many important instruments in the field of EU justice and home affairs (JHA), and it benefited substantially from common arrangements in internal security, such as the European Arrest Warrant (EAW), the Schengen Information System (SIS-II) and Prüm databases, Europol and Eurojust.[1] Regrettably, Britain's decision to withdraw from the EU effectively ended some of these arrangements, with no clear replacement on the horizon. However, unlike in other domains of EU cooperation, at the time of the Brexit referendum the added value of instruments and cooperative structures in internal security were not only apparent to both policymakers and practitioners, but proven through their increased usage, especially in handling the increasing jihadist threat. This made participation in internal security instruments a primary topic of discussion in the negotiations between the EU and the UK. In the security domain, the two main stumbling blocks to overcome were the jurisdiction of the Court of Justice of the EU (CJEU) for the UK and the equivalence of data protection standards for the EU.[2] Nevertheless, the bespoke agreement that was stipulated between the parties was a demonstration of ample political will and a clear attempt to retain a maximum access for the UK in EU internal security instruments. As a result, in the Trade and Cooperation Agreement (TCA), the document signed by both parties at the end of the negotiations on 30 December 2020, many of the EU instruments that the UK highly values continue to be available, such as the law enforcement platform Prüm and

[1] H Carrapico, A Niehuss and C Berthélémy, *Brexit and Internal Security. Political and Legal Concerns on the Future UK–EU Relationship* (Palgrave Pivot, 2019) 3, 9, 12.
[2] ibid 21.

the secure police and intelligence exchange information system SIENA, as well as the exchange of passenger name records, while for others alternative arrangements have been made, such as Europol and Eurojust cooperation, the EAW, the exchange of criminal records data and mutual legal assistance. While the TCA clauses discussed in this chapter will enable continued EU–UK engagement in counter-terrorism, law enforcement and judicial cooperation, these information exchanges are conditional on restrictions and subject to longer time frames. Furthermore, losing access to the EU's databases will hamper the added value of immediate exchange in pursuit and investigations of criminality and terrorism, despite the fact that the TCA enables an unprecedented relationship of the EU with a non-EU member and a non-Schengen state, which was clearly perceived as mutually beneficial by the negotiating parties.[3]

This chapter will review the post-Brexit internal security arrangements between the UK and the EU, and will compare them with the ones that the two parties enjoyed while Britain was an EU Member State. In particular, this work will reflect on the likely implications of these new arrangements on cooperative practices in this domain. The chapter begins with an overview of the pre-existent EU–UK internal security relationship, outlining the EU's most beneficial law enforcement and judicial cooperation tools for the UK. It then provides background information into the Brexit and TCA negotiation processes, and discusses the priorities of the negotiating parties. Finally, the chapter details the bespoke EU–UK post-Brexit arrangements in information exchange and law enforcement, and specifically reviews the eight priority areas of cooperation that the two parties deemed it necessary to design new frameworks for. It then concludes by discussing the impact of the new arrangements and the likelihood that under them this field of EU–UK cooperation will remain functional and effective.

II. Background: The EU–UK Internal Security Relationship

Despite its seeming reluctance, Britain was 'heavily involved in and has shaped EU police cooperation', including information exchange and judicial cooperation.[4] The UK has been an influential agenda-setter for EU internal security and has had a direct impact on measures in counter-terrorism and forensics, data collection, sharing and retention, cybersecurity, the development of the EU's police agency

[3] N Ni Loideain, 'Brexit, Data Adequacy, and the EU Law Enforcement Directive' in E Kosta and F Boehm (eds), *The Law Enforcement Directive: A Commentary* (Oxford University Press, forthcoming) 12.

[4] Carrapico et al (n 1) 16; House of Lords Select Committee on the European Union, 'Corrected Oral Evidence: Post-Brexit UK–EU Security Co-operation' (2021) 9, 12, https://committees.parliament.uk/oralevidence/1536/html/.

Europol and intelligence-led policing, as well as in the judicial principle of mutual recognition. Despite its opt-outs[5] and selective participation in the field of JHA, the UK was able to 'deeply influence decision-making', which might not be possible for it anymore after Brexit.[6] Furthermore, the influence of UK security experts and their epistemic communities – which has been extensive – will diminish in Brussels.

Perhaps the most important JHA instrument for the UK was the EU's police agency Europol, as acknowledged by the UK government itself, which claimed that Britain used its tools 'more than almost any other country'.[7] Britain played an important role in Europol's set-up and was 'among the top four contributors' to its main database, Europol Information Systems (EIS).[8] In March 2020, the UK was estimated by the security measures watchdog Statewatch as 'the fifth-largest provider of data to Europol, with over 63,000 "objects" attributed to the country in the agency's main database'.[9] While both sides hinted early on that they were interested in continued cooperation, it would be difficult to draw new terms for this, as the agency is subject to the jurisdiction of the CJEU, whereas its relationships with third countries are based on different degrees of access and bespoke data exchange agreements. A useful tool overseen by Europol is the Joint Investigation Teams (JITs), set up on a case-by-case basis involving the relevant authorities of multiple Member States, and having an increasingly operational role in law enforcement (including its independent data collection and analysis). JITs have been praised by the UK Crown Prosecution Service and the National Crime Agency for the investigation of cross-border cases.[10] Post-Brexit, the UK would only be able to participate in those as a third country and upon invitation of an interested EU Member State.

The second most relevant EU law enforcement instrument for Britain was the EAW, which simplifies and streamlines the extradition of criminals to an unprecedented extent. This mechanism introduced deadlines in the bureaucratic and diplomatic processes regarding extradition from upwards of 10 months to less

[5] The UK secured three opt-outs in EU JHA, covered by Protocols 19 and 21 (Schengen *acquis* and measures on migration, asylum and visas), as well as Protocol 36 (a block opt-out of all pre-Lisbon Treaty JHA measures). All three Protocols allowed selective opt-ins to specific measures, of which the UK has availed. O Garner, 'Part Three of the EU–UK TCA – from a "Disrupted" Area of Freedom, Security and Justice to "New Old" Intergovernmentalism in Justice and Home Affairs?' (2021) Brexit Institute Working Paper Series, No1/2021, https://papers.ssrn.com/sol3/papers.cfm?abstract_id=3778183.

[6] Carrapico et al (n 1) 65; Select Committee on the European Union (n 4) 9.

[7] HM Government, 'The UK's Cooperation with the EU on Justice and Home Affairs, and on Foreign Policy and Security Issues' (2016) www.gov.uk/government/publications/the-uks-cooperation-with-the-eu-on-justice-home-affairs-foreign-policy-and-security-issues-background-note, 4.

[8] T Bunyan and C Jones, 'Brexit: Goodbye and Hello. The new EU–UK Security Architecture, Civil Liberties and Democratic Control' (Statewatch, 2022) www.statewatch.org/media/3050/eu-uk-brexit-goodbye-and-hello.pdf, 1.

[9] Bunyan and Jones (n 8) 2.

[10] European Union Committee, *Brexit: Future UK–EU Security and Police Cooperation* (HL 2016–17, 77) https://publications.parliament.uk/pa/ld201617/ldselect/ldeucom/77/77.pdf.

than three, by operating solely between judicial authorities.[11] According to the UK National Crime Agency, in 2015, 1149 people were extradited by the UK to other Member States, while 123 people were surrendered to the UK.[12] As will be explained below, the UK eventually found a post-Brexit arrangement to replace this mechanism. Falling back on its precursor, the 1957 Council of Europe (CoE) Convention on Extradition would have been a significant downgrade, not only because of longer time frames and more extensive bureaucracy, but also because under this Convention 22 EU Member States could still refuse extradition of their nationals to the UK.[13]

The third most valuable EU resource that the UK is forsaking in information exchange is the Union's law enforcement databases. Except for Europol's EIS database, there are three other important channels for information-sharing in that regard: the SIS-II, the Prüm and the EU Passenger Name Records (PNR) databases. All have been reported as highly valuable to law enforcement agencies from various Member States, including the UK.[14] SIS-II is used in the tracking and pursuit of missing persons, criminals, terrorists, illegal migrants and objects of evidence in their possession. It is the most used law enforcement database, and as such has acquired some features that might in time make the Prüm one obsolete. The latter allows Member States to search each other's databases for DNA (within 15 minutes), vehicle registration (within 10 seconds) and fingerprints (within 24 hours), some of which are now also available on SIS-II through a streamlined procedure (although SIS-II is reserved for serious crime, while Prüm is used in any case of criminality and upon first crime scene inspection). The UK National Crime Agency noted that falling back on the Interpol system would be time-consuming and less effective.[15] The newest of the three, the EU PNR system was modelled after the UK PNR model, which enables the collection of data from airlines regarding air travel.[16]

When it comes to judicial cooperation, the most useful and relevant for the UK among the EU tools were its judicial agency Eurojust and the European Criminal Records Information System (ECRIS), to which the UK lost access. Eurojust is highly valuable in dealing with the prosecution of cross-border criminality within the EU, wherein in 2016, 16 per cent of its workload concerned the UK.[17] Apart from a forum and facilitator of prosecution cooperation, Eurojust is

[11] Carrapico et al (n 1) 21.

[12] National Crime Agency, 'Wanted from the UK: European Arrest Warrant Statistics 2009–May 2016 (Calendar Year)' (2016) https://nationalcrimeagency.gov.uk/who-we-are/publications/72-wanted-from-the-uk-european-arrest-warrant-statistics-2009-may-2016-fiscal-year/file.

[13] Carrapico et al (n 1) 21.

[14] C Andreeva, 'The Evolution of Information-Sharing in EU Counter-terrorism post-2015: A Paradigm Shift?' (2021) 7(5) *Global Affairs*; House of Lords, 'Brexit: The Proposed UK–EU Security Treaty' (2018) https://publications.parliament.uk/pa/ld201719/ldselect/ldeucom/164/16402.htm.

[15] European Union Committee, *Brexit: Future UK–EU Security and Police Cooperation* (n 10) 30.

[16] Carrapico et al (n 1) 20.

[17] ibid 20.

an overseer of the use of the EAW. ECRIS is a useful instrument for prosecutors as (upon request) it presents a suspect's complete criminal record across Member States, speeding up the exchange of information and facilitating the overcoming of prosecution gaps.

III. Brexit and the Bespoke Agreement on Internal Security

The political discourse in the UK both before and after the Brexit referendum implied that Brexit would not affect internal security (or the cooperation therein) much.[18] The 'Leave' campaign seldom mentioned the potential internal security consequences of Brexit, except for conflating freedom of movement and terrorism.[19] This only changed after Theresa May's Lancaster House speech in January 2017, and the subsequent government White Paper and letter triggering Article 50 of the Treaty on the European Union in March, which formally launched the Brexit process. These documents presented the UK government's initial negotiating positions and foreshadowed the difficulty and complexity of the future security negotiations between the UK and the EU. The Brexit letter's harsh tone had supposedly been softened,[20] yet did not signal openness for dialogue – rather, it cautioned the EU that failing to reach an agreement would have serious ramifications for its security cooperation. In parallel, the then UK Prime Minister began speaking of a new bespoke security relationship with the EU, on the basis of a 'toolkit' of cooperation and information-sharing instruments.[21] She also doubled down on the rhetoric of the added value of the cooperation with the EU in this domain, declaring that 'Europe's security is our security'.[22] A key factor in changing the UK's approach were the terrorist attacks in the UK between March and June 2017. These helped to bring internal security to the forefront, with issues of security and counter-terrorism subsequently becoming part of the mainstream national debate, though these were not accompanied by any concrete rhetoric on the implications of Brexit therein.[23] Yet the UK was among the Member States that realised and benefited from the EU's added value in counter-terrorism and law enforcement cooperation, as it opted in to several EU instruments and eventually negotiated continued engagement with EU tools and bodies from a functionalist position.

[18] This was repeated by Theresa May in various speeches in 2017 and 2018. See Carrapico et al (n 1) 43.

[19] Carrapico et al (n 1) 2.

[20] ibid 87.

[21] ibid 43, 87.

[22] T May, 'PM Speech at Munich Security Conference: 17 February 2018' (2018) www.gov.uk/government/speeches/pm-speech-at-munich-security-conference-17-february-2018.

[23] Carrapico et al (n 1) 3.

With the increased and almost symmetrical jihadist threat around the EU, the added value of the EU instruments and of multilateral cooperation in this domain had become clear, which led to the UK fighting for access post-Brexit, while the EU, not wanting to lose a key player in internal security and counter-terrorism, and the massive amounts of useful data coming from the UK, seemed committed to offering alternative arrangements of mutual benefit. This led to negotiations on bespoke arrangements, which, despite leaving some questions to be answered, built a one-of-a-kind cooperation structure, thus demonstrating the commitment of both parties to finding working solutions. In particular, both the UK and the EU were interested in maintaining the ongoing cooperation with Europol for the sake of comprehensive European security and information exchange, which was not feasible, as access to the agency's resources is conditional on EU membership and equivalence of data sharing, retention and protection standards, as well as implying the jurisdiction of the CJEU. Thus, the negotiations on a new UK–Europol relationship were always going to be an exercise in 'damage control' and had to 'make difficult trade-offs between principles and efficiency'.[24]

Politically, the Brexit negotiations were bitter and uncooperative on both sides.[25] The UK was pursuing access to all EU instruments in information exchange without membership, which was not feasible, especially as it refused to recognise the jurisdiction of the CJEU. The Union was trying to play a balancing act, concerned about discriminating against other partners, to which end EU Council President Donald Tusk remarked that the UK should not expect 'the rights of Norway with the obligations of Canada'.[26] In the spirit of compromise, the EU agreed to a bespoke dispute resolution mechanism replacing the jurisdiction of the CJEU. As a result of this compromise, data protection is an aspect wherein Brexit's impact is difficult to estimate. The standardised EU data protection regime enables the high volume of information exchange among European authorities. This is not possible with third countries, because adequate processing of sensitive and personal data cannot be guaranteed. Statewatch expressed concerns over the potential expansion of the Prüm and EU PNR information systems, given the continued access of the UK, which provides 'more grounds for processing and sharing data with other countries than when the UK was an EU Member State'.[27] Further data exchange was conditional upon the EU's adequacy decisions in the commercial and law enforcement sectors, and the UK's willingness to keep up with and adhere to the EU's *acquis* in this regard (including any upcoming changes therein). The EU adequacy decisions enable information exchange with third countries if the Commission's assessment

[24] ibid 95–96; Select Committee on the European Union (n 4) 1,7.

[25] B Farrand and H Carrapico, '"People Like That Cannot Be Trusted": Populist and Technocratic Political Styles, Legitimacy, and Distrust in the Context of Brexit Negotiations' (2021) 17(2) *Journal of Contemporary European Research* 147, www.jcer.net/index.php/jcer/Art/view/1186.

[26] Council of the European Union, 'Statement by President Donald Tusk on the Draft Guidelines on the Framework for the Future Relationship with the UK' (2018) Statements and Remarks 109/18, www.consilium.europa.eu/en/press/press-releases/2018/03/07/statement-by-president-donald-tusk-on-the-draft-guidelines-on-the-framework-for-the-future-relationship-with-the-uk/.

[27] Bunyan and Jones (n 8) 29.

demonstrates 'an adequate level of protection', understood as 'a level of protection for personal data that is essentially equivalent to the level of protection within the EU'.[28] In June 2021, the Commission adopted two adequacy decisions on the UK's data protection regimes for the sake of exchanging information (on both GDPR and law enforcement exchange); however, these can be revoked if the UK diverges too strongly from the EU standards in the future (which might come to be, as the UK is contemplating changes to its data protection regime, as discussed in the first part of this book) and in either case it will expire after four years.[29] The adoption of the adequacy decisions was expected due to the lingering similarity of the UK and EU data protection regimes, yet the temporary access to EU law enforcement data given in the interim to the UK after Brexit was criticised by the European Data Protection Supervisor (EDPS). Moreover, the UK's continued access to this data will remain conditional on the assessments of the EDPS and the CJEU.[30] Thus, as Arnell et al put it: 'while the UK might recoup formal sovereignty via Brexit, its de facto autonomy continues to be curtailed by external influences'.[31]

After the referendum, UK policing engaged quite significantly with EU law enforcement agencies, signalling that the operational world was seeking to 'pragmatically manage any disruption that Brexit might have brought and ensure continued mutual cooperation'.[32] UK law enforcement furthermore re-evaluated its national capabilities in terms of addressing international police requests and cooperation mechanisms, which led to the establishment in 2018 of the International Crime Coordination Centre.[33] Finally, after many years of prioritising Europol, the UK has renewed its investment in Interpol, which was expected to become the EU agency's replacement for British law enforcement recourse.[34] These steps clearly demonstrate that operational staff were eager to maintain an international connection in law enforcement, and were well aware of the gap that would be left by the missing EU mechanisms.

IV. Bespoke EU–UK Arrangements in Information Exchange and Law Enforcement

There is an unspoken consensus in academic and, to a large extent, operational circles that 'the ideal position … from a police cooperation and exchange of

[28] European Commission press release, 'Data Protection: European Commission Launches Process on Personal Data Flows to UK' (2021) https://ec.europa.eu/commission/presscorner/detail/en/ip_21_661.

[29] Bunyan and Jones (n 8) 6; Ni Loideain (n 3) 15.

[30] Ni Loideain (n 3) 13.

[31] P Arnell et al, 'Police Cooperation and Exchange of Information under the EU–UK Trade and Cooperation Agreement' (2021) 12(2) *New Journal of European Criminal Law* 276.

[32] H Ben Jaffel and J Pearson, 'Intelligence, Law Enforcement and Brexit' (UK in a Changing Europe, 2021) https://ukandeu.ac.uk/intelligence-law-enforcement-and-brexit/.

[33] ibid.

[34] ibid.

information perspective was the status quo ante'; nevertheless, it was not feasible for the UK to retain its access as a non-member of Schengen and the EU.[35] Regardless of the arrangements and compromises made, the UK's lack of access to the EU's databases will necessarily mean less information exchange.[36] This may be compensated to an extent by increasing the use of decentralised databases that do not provide interoperability, such as Prüm, PNR and the financial crimes reporting system Fiu.net. Still, the TCA 'maintains a high level of consistency with past arrangements', thus representing 'the best result that could have been achieved in the circumstances', allowing continued access to the Prüm, PNR and Europol's SIENA channel, and establishing new mechanisms to replace other EU instruments, as already explained above.[37] The TCA thus 'enables unprecedentedly close law enforcement and criminal justice cooperation with the UK as a third country'.[38]

A March 2021 House of Lords evaluation of the TCA arrangements in home affairs nevertheless concluded that under this deal the UK had lost 'significant access' to EU law enforcement data, while they qualified the new arrangements as 'complex' and 'untested'.[39] The report underlined the loss of SIS-II as a consequential one for British law enforcement authorities, as the exchange of information therein would require 'hours, not seconds', while it also warned that, as a third country, the EU would hold the UK against a much higher standard on data protection and could interrupt cooperation if the UK 'chooses not to stay aligned with EU data protection rules in the future'.[40]

The next section will review in more detail the institutional and legislative implications of the new bespoke relationship between the UK and the EU in internal security and will compare those to the efficiency and efficacy of the previous arrangements.

A. Institutions Set Up by the TCA

Two new institutional structures consequential for information exchange were introduced by the TCA: the Partnership Council, the high-level body that oversees the agreement's provisions, and the Specialised Committee on Law Enforcement

[35] Arnell et al (n 31) 266; Select Committee on the European Union (n 4) 1; Ni Loideain (n 3) 14.

[36] Carrapico et al (n 1) 91.

[37] Arnell et al (n 31) 267; Select Committee on the European Union (n 4) 1.

[38] C-C Cîrlig, 'Law Enforcement and Judicial Cooperation in Criminal Matters under the EU–UK Trade and Cooperation Agreement' (European Parliamentary Research Service, 2021) www.europarl.europa.eu/RegData/etudes/BRIE/2021/690627/EPRS_BRI(2021)690627_ENpdf.

[39] 'Brexit: UK Lost "significant" Access to EU Policing Data under Deal' (BBC, 2021) www.bbc.com/news/uk-politics-56529359; European Union Committee, *Beyond Brexit: Policing, Law Enforcement and Security* (HL 2019–21, 250) https://committees.parliament.uk/publications/5298/documents/52902/default/.

[40] European Union Committee, *Beyond Brexit* (n 39) 4.

and Judicial Cooperation, which is an expert body, among others in various domains, tasked with overseeing the narrow post-Brexit arrangements in this policy area.

The Partnership Council is composed of EU and UK representatives, co-chaired by an EU Commissioner and a UK government minister, and has executive authority on most Brexit-related decision-making, and the results of its various meetings do not need to be made public.[41] The Council meets in diverse configurations at least once a year, with its first meeting held in June 2021. It can adopt binding decisions regarding the application and interpretation of the TCA or amend it; it can issue non-binding recommendations on all TCA topics; and it can establish, dissolve and mandate Specialised Committees or recommend actions concerning the exchange of personal data.[42] The Specialised Committee on Law Enforcement and Judicial Cooperation is the thematic body that manages the bespoke agreement's application. It is in charge of overseeing and scrutinising the implementation and effective functioning of the TCA and reports to the Partnership Council in that regard, while it also provides a forum for discussion, exchange of information and best practices, including in cases of disagreement and dispute settlement.[43] The Committee can establish, dissolve and mandate thematic working groups, and may issue decisions, recommendations and even amendments upon the TCA, where that is delegated to the Committee by the Partnership Council.[44]

Statewatch has expressed concerns that the institutions established by the TCA 'create supranational policing and security structures that will be even more opaque and unaccountable' than the arrangements under the EU.[45] Another tendency criticised therein is the shift of power towards the executive (political leadership from the Partnership Council and state officials in the Specialised Committees); it is noteworthy that the TCA governing bodies are not required to make their discussions and decision-making public, resulting in lack of transparency and limited accountability.[46]

B. Eight Priority Areas of Cooperation

The bespoke agreement on law enforcement and judicial cooperation between the EU and the UK is covered by Part Three of the TCA, which is subdivided

[41] Bunyan and Jones (n 8) 2.

[42] ibid 21.

[43] T Wilson, 'EU–UK Criminal Justice and Security Cooperation after Brexit: A Perspective' (2021) 3 *Forensic Science International: Synergy* 1, 2, www.sciencedirect.com/science/Art/pii/S2589871X21000127.

[44] European Union Committee, *Beyond Brexit* (n 39) 10; Bunyan and Jones (n 8) 22.

[45] Bunyan and Jones (n 8) 29.

[46] ibid 29.

into 13 titles (the first of which contains solely definitions). This section will analyse the eight main areas of cooperation, while briefly discussing the last three at the end.

(i) Exchange of DNA, Fingerprints and Vehicle Registration Data

The TCA provisions allow for continued automated reciprocal exchange of DNA, fingerprints and vehicle registration data through national contact points, offering a degree of cooperation which is similar to the original arrangements. The main difference in the new arrangements is that there is no real-time exchange and no access to personal data regarding DNA and fingerprints; instead, the decentralised system alerts to a 'hit', or a match of alerts. In such a case, the requesting state is notified, and the exchange of the information is guided by the national law of the state that holds the data. At that point, the UK and the EU Member States are obliged to give access to all categories of data requested by the competent authorities of the partner state. Before all this, however, the UK had to submit an ex ante evaluation and run a pilot for vehicle data (as the UK had not implemented the cooperation system for that type of data)[47] in order for the EU to decide that personal data could be exchanged. In the interim, such exchanges could occur for a period of nine months after the adoption of the TCA (ie until 29 September 2021).[48] The evaluation report was not published until 14 June 2022;[49] however, the UK and the EU extended the interim period of exchange until then, so as not to interrupt the information flow. This caused concern in some observers that, in the interest of continued information-sharing between the parties, less safeguards would be provided, leading to a patchy data protection regime.[50] The evaluation report points out that the assessment of the UK's suitability as a partner for sharing data was successful and the Union may exchange personal data with it.[51]

[47] T Wahl, 'Brexit: EU–UK Trade and Cooperation Agreement – Impacts on PIF and JHA in a Nutshell' (The European Criminal Law Associations' Forum, 2021) https://eucrim.eu/media/issue/pdf/eucrim_issue_2020-04.pdf.

[48] Garner (n 5) 5.

[49] Council of the European Union, Council Decision on the position to be taken on behalf of the Union vis-à-vis the United Kingdom of Great Britain and Northern Ireland regarding the determination under Article 540(2) of the Trade and Cooperation Agreement between the European Union and the European Atomic Energy Community, of the one part, and the United Kingdom of Great Britain and Northern Ireland, of the other part, of the date from which personal data relating to DNA profiles and dactyloscopic data as referred to in Articles 530, 531, 534 and 536 of that Agreement may be supplied by Member States to the United Kingdom (14 June 2022) 9539/22, www.statewatch.org/media/3383/eu-council-prum-uk-dna-fingerprints-decision-9539-22.pdf.

[50] Statewatch, 'Policing: EU and UK to Extend Post-Brexit Biometric Data Exchange Agreement' (2021) https://webcache.googleusercontent.com/search?q=cache:EMkHDkmXF8kJ:www.statewatch.org/news/2021/september/policing-eu-and-uk-to-extend-post-brexit-biometric-data-exchange-agreement/+&cd=1&hl=en&ct=clnk&gl=de.

[51] Council of the European Union (n 49).

Statewatch notes that the EU is planning to extend the Prüm system to include biometrics and facial recognition, and this might also involve the (voluntary) exchange of police records.[52] Should this proposal pass, the upgrade would enable the 'cross-border comparison of facial images and data stored in police files'.[53] The UK could potentially join this system without parliamentary debate; however, as the system would substantially change, the Prüm cooperation between the UK and the EU could also be suspended.[54]

(ii) Transfer and Processing of Passenger Name Record Data

The TCA provides for continued exchange of PNR data to flights originating from the UK and the EU via the British national PNR system. The exchange was conditional on the EU adequacy decisions and on data safeguards. The UK is in principle limited in its use of PNR data for the purposes of preventing and prosecuting serious crimes or terrorist plots, or when necessary (on a case-by-case basis) for the protection of vital interests of specific persons or as evidence in criminal proceedings (thus introducing purpose limitation). The TCA obliges the UK to share their analysis of PNR data with Europol, Eurojust and national Passenger Information Units (PIUs) at their request. The reciprocal obligation is imposed on national PIUs towards UK authorities. The TCA also introduces safeguards in the treatment of PNR data by the UK: non-discrimination, forbidding the establishment of special categories of personal data, ensuring data security and integrity, informing passengers of the purposes of the PNR data collection, processing data on the basis of 'non-discriminatory, specific and reliable pre-established models and criteria'.[55] The UK is obliged to depersonalise data, ie remove elements that could identify the person, and is not allowed to share it with third countries without authorisation. The purposes for use of PNR data are the same in the TCA as they were in the EU PNR Directive, while the type of data collected includes the same elements.[56]

In terms of retention, the UK is forbidden from keeping the data for more than five years, and is obliged to delete PNR data once the passenger has departed the country. To enable the UK to introduce the new data safeguards, it was granted an interim period of nine months after the adoption of the TCA (extendable for one year) in which the exchange could still occur, at the end of which it had to report back to the Specialised Committee. The third extension period is currently ongoing and expires at the end of December 2023.

[52] Bunyan and Jones (n 8) 9.
[53] ibid 9.
[54] ibid 9; Wahl (n 47).
[55] Trade and Cooperation Agreement between the European Union and the European Atomic Energy Community, of the one part, and the United Kingdom of Great Britain and Northern Ireland, of the other part of 30 April 2021, [2021] OJ L444/14, 31 (TCA).
[56] Arnell et al (n 31) 269.

The European Data Protection Supervisor has expressed concerns over this derogation, as the UK is not obliged to delete data in that period. The UK's Home Office noted in a report for the Specialised Committee the 'highly complex' and expensive infrastructure that needs to be introduced to fulfil the obligation and invoked the extension in October 2021, approved in December 2021.[57]

While the new arrangements are largely similar to the old ones, there are some differences with potentially long-term consequences. Unlike the PNR Directive (which made it voluntary), the TCA obliges the exchanges of PNR data, conditional on certain safeguards, which might disproportionally affect the volume of data exchanged inside the EU versus the the volume shared between the EU and the UK.[58] Statewatch expresses concern over the likely extension of the PNR system to other forms of travel; for example, the UK is said to be taking part in a pilot project on railway transport.[59] Both the UK and the EU have expressed the desire to extend the PNR, which is reflected in the TCA, obliging the partners to discuss and consider this (not conditional on domestic parliamentary debate).[60]

(iii) Cooperation on Operational Information

The TCA describes cooperation between the parties on operational information, without delimiting the definition of what such information entails or by which bodies it may be exchanged, only stipulating that it is outside the remit of judicial authorities.[61] Thus, it can be considered that the objective of this title is to emphasise the continued operational exchange in law enforcement and customs. The purposes specified in the TCA are:

(a) the prevention, investigation, detection or prosecution of criminal offences;
(b) the execution of criminal penalties;
(c) safeguarding against, and the prevention of, threats to public safety; and
(d) the prevention and combating of money laundering and the financing of terrorism.[62]

The provision also makes it clear that data can be spontaneously provided and requested when it regards criminal or terrorist offence, if it does not involve the judicial system, in which case the state providing the information needs to approve the exchange.[63] The providing state must also authorise the data's usage in judicial procedures and may impose conditions. These exchanges can occur

[57] Bunyan and Jones (n 8) 13.
[58] Arnell et al (n 31) 269.
[59] Bunyan and Jones (n 8) 13.
[60] ibid 13.
[61] ibid 14.
[62] TCA, 48.
[63] ibid 48; The Law Society, 'Law Enforcement and Judicial Cooperation in Criminal Matters after Brexit' (2021) www.lawsociety.org.uk/en/topics/brexit/law-enforcement-and-judicial-cooperation-in-criminal-matters-after-brexit.

through any communication channel, including SIENA and Europol, while the UK can also conclude bilateral agreements on this with individual Member States, in compliance with EU law.[64]

For the uninformed reader, the vagueness of this mandate of information exchange might mask the 'significant discontinuity' represented by the interrupted access to SIS-II, which enabled a real-time information exchange between competent authorities, especially useful (and praised by law enforcement agencies) in cases of hot pursuit or discreet surveillance.[65] The EU cannot legally allow the UK continued access to SIS-II as a non-Schengen, non-EU country. Interpol's databases are the only current replacement for SIS-II, and their reliability will be conditional on EU Member States' willingness and diligence in passing alerts from SIS-II to Interpol in order for the UK to have a potential involvement in a cross-border case. The UK has been developing a new 'International Law Enforcement Alert Platform' (I–LEAP), approved in November 2021 and expected by 2025.[66] It will provide nominal data and criminal history on suspects subject to international police jurisdiction, while the Home Office's intention is to have

> a single mechanism for UK Law Enforcement users to access and share alerts related to people, documents and objects with International partners on a reciprocal basis at the point of need, thereby enabling UK and International Law Enforcement to better protect citizens.[67]

Intended as a substitute for SIS-II and as an alternative (or perhaps replacement) to the much-slower Interpol, it is supposed to provide real-time access to the Fixed Interpol Network Database (FIND), and in the future it might enable bilateral partners to gain access to the National Crime Agency and UK border authorities (depending on the agreements the UK government can secure).

(iv) Cooperation with Europol

The TCA establishes the conditions for continued cooperation between the UK and the EU's main JHA agencies – Europol (dealing with law enforcement) and Eurojust (coordinating criminal justice). Europol will post one or more liaison officers to the UK, while the UK will post its own liaison officer(s) to the agency, who may be invited to operational meetings on a case-by-case basis. Since the beginning of the transition period on 1 February 2020, the UK lost a say in the agency's management, while on 1 January 2021 it also lost direct access to Europol's databases EIS and Analysis Work Files (AWF). Access to the secure communication channel SIENA is, however, still available to the UK through a designated national contact point, who will act as a liaison officer between Europol

[64] The Law Society (n 63).
[65] Wilson (n 43) 1.
[66] Bunyan and Jones (n 8) 7.
[67] ibid 7.

and the UK's competent authorities (as was done previously with third countries) and will be responsible for the 'review, correction and deletion of personal data'.[68] The exchange of personal information was made conditional on the EU adequacy decisions, as well as on the principle of purpose limitation (including deleting the data when no longer necessary and reviewing its relevance after six months), restrictions on the access/use of such data and its transfer to third parties (wherein the UK would be liable for violations). The relationship between Europol and its British counterparts is further stipulated in the September 2021 Working and Administrative Arrangements,[69] which cover such issues as exchanges of classified information and purpose limitation, the obligations of liaison officers and involving the UK in operational analysis projects.[70] The European Parliament's research centre points out that such arrangements 'may provide much leeway in giving the UK broad access to Europol resources currently limited to EU Member States and risk impacting existing data exchange and information systems in the EU by adding a specific UK-related system'.[71]

The scope of cooperation between the UK and Europol is defined by the TCA as:

(a) the exchange of information such as specialist knowledge;
(b) general situation reports;
(c) results of strategic analysis;
(d) information on criminal investigation procedures;
(e) information on crime prevention methods;
(f) participation in training activities; and
(g) the provision of advice and support in individual criminal investigations as well as operational cooperation.[72]

With access to common operations, JITs, analysis projects and the SIENA network, the UK seems to have gained disproportionally extensive access to Europol-led instruments compared to other EU partner countries.[73] Furthermore, the bilateral agreement concerns specific UK agencies, which might incur chaos in the relationships between Europol and British law enforcement and judiciary bodies, while 'This multiplicity of rules may in turn affect data protection' because of these bodies' different regimes.[74] Still, the TCA arguably provides 'very strict data protection and management terms and rel[ies] on human rights law', which is encouraging in terms of the treatment of law enforcement data between the

[68] TCA, Art 568.
[69] Required by Arts 23(5) and 25(1) from the Europol Regulation.
[70] Europol, 'Working and Administrative Arrangement Establishing Cooperative Relations between the Competent Authorities of the UK and Europol' (2021) www.europol.europa.eu/partners-collaboration/agreements/working-and-administrative-arrangement-establishing-cooperative-relations-between-competent-authorities-of-uk-and-europol#downloads.
[71] Cîrlig (n 38) 7.
[72] TCA, Art 567.
[73] Arnell et al (n 31) 273.
[74] ibid 273.

two parties.[75] Finally, the proposal to update Europol's legal basis will surely have implications on the UK–Europol relationship and data exchange in the future, as well as the UK's access to Europol's tools, though this remains to be seen and will largely depend on what the upgraded mandate will entail.[76]

(v) Cooperation with Eurojust

Similarly to Europol, the TCA specifies that the UK is to post at least one liaison magistrate at Eurojust, while the agency will designate a magistrate to the competent UK authority. The liaison magistrates might be invited to strategic or operational meetings at Eurojust if Member States agree.[77] The transfer of personal data concerning witnesses, victims, minors, etc to third countries or international organisations is forbidden unless strictly necessary in specific cases or authorised by the providing country.[78] PNR data can be shared with Eurojust, while the agency can advise the UK or Member States on existing EAWs or facilitate requests for assistance or spontaneous information exchange between the parties.[79] As with Europol, the UK needed to further negotiate bilateral Working and Administrative Arrangements with Eurojust (signed on 20 December 2021), which stipulate administrative and data usage conditions.[80] Both the Europol and Eurojust Arrangements contain clauses on dispute settlement, penalties, liability and termination. As Eurojust's counter-terrorism role has increased since 2016 (including through its Judicial Counter-Terrorism Register), the TCA requires that one of its contact points in the UK will be the UK's 'Domestic Correspondent for Terrorism Matters'.[81]

(vi) Surrender Procedure

One of the more substantial losses from the JHA apparatus for the UK is the EAW. While no worthy replacement for the EAW, the TCA establishes a new surrender procedure, which in practice serves as a middle ground between the old procedure under the 1957 CoE Convention and the streamlined EAW procedure, and is modelled after the EU's Surrender Agreement with Norway and Iceland.[82]

[75] ibid 273.

[76] Proposal for a Regulation of the European Parliament and of the Council, amending Regulation (EU) 2016/794, as regards Europol's cooperation with private parties, the processing of personal data by Europol in support of criminal investigations, and Europol's role on research and innovation; Arnell et al (n 31) 273.

[77] Cîrlig (n 38) 7.

[78] The Law Society (n 63).

[79] Cîrlig (n 38) 8.

[80] Eurojust, 'Eurojust and UK Home Office Sign Working Arrangement' (2021) www.eurojust.europa.eu/news/eurojust-and-uk-home-office-sign-working-arrangement.

[81] TCA, Art 584; Bunyan and Jones (n 8) 16.

[82] Wahl (n 47).

An arrest warrant can be issued for a criminal act punishable in the issuing state with detention for a maximum period of at least 12 months, while the strict time limits and the content and form of the warrant are modelled after those of the EAW.[83] The deadline for operationalising an arrest warrant where the suspect consents to extradition is rather short, at 10 days, whereas in case of refusal it increases to 60 days; in both cases, the deadline can be extended by an extra 30 days by request.[84] The surrender procedure retains the key features of the EAW, while it has two fundamental differences:

1. The nationality exemption: due to the divergence of legal systems, each party (the UK or an EU Member State) can ex ante (through the Specialised Committee) refuse to extradite its own nationals to the other party, or make extradition conditional on a specific requirement or requirements (Article 603, TCA); in this case, the other party can declare reciprocity.[85] The TCA specifies that where this concerns refusal by a Member State, the latter is obliged to consider criminal proceedings against its national (or else provide a judicial justification); however, it does not clarify if the same is true if the UK refuses to extradite to an EU country. The exemption should be related to issues of respect of fundamental freedoms and the legal procedures in the receiving state (such as the suspect's rights during detention). There are reportedly 12 EU Member States that have already notified the use of this exemption (among which are Croatia, Finland, France, Germany, Greece, Latvia, Poland, Slovakia, Slovenia and Sweden), while the Czech Republic and Austria notified that they would only extradite citizens with their consent.[86]
2. The political offence exemption: as with the EAW, the TCA specifies that the execution of the surrender procedure may not be refused on grounds that the offence might be regarded by the executing state as a political offence.[87] The difference is that there is a new safeguard introduced by the TCA that allows either an EU Member State or the UK to notify the Specialised Committee that they would like an exemption (unless it concerns terrorist offences, as defined by the European Convention on the Suppression of Terrorism, where the TCA does not provide possibility for exemption). In the case of such notification, the other party can apply reciprocity. Twelve EU Member States have already notified their use of this exemption (Belgium,

[83] Select Committee on the European Union (n 4) 6; Cîrlig (n 38) 8.
[84] Bunyan and Jones (n 8) 17.
[85] Wahl (n 47).
[86] The notification expires after five years, thus must be reviewed and resubmitted at that time. The Law Society (n 63); Bunyan and Jones (n 8) 17.
[87] The Law Societies, 'Surrender Provisions – Refusal to Surrender under the EU–UK TCA' (2021) www.lawsocieties.eu/news/surrender-provisions-refusal-to-surrender-under-the-eu-uk-tca/6001810. Art.

Czech Republic, Denmark, France, Croatia, Italy, Cyprus, Poland, Portugal, Slovakia, Finland and Sweden).[88]

The surrender procedure further stipulates conditions of respect for fundamental rights (legal and interpretation assistance, information on the individual's rights and conditions of the warrant, terms and length of detention), as well as the proportionality principle (not part of the EAW and introduced at the UK's request), which requires that extradition be necessary and proportionate, taking stock of the suspect's rights, the victims' interests and the severity of the offence, and aiming to avoid long pre-trial detentions.[89] Furthermore, the TCA reintroduces the requirement of double criminality, which was not in the EAW and requires that the criminal offence is considered such by both the extraditing and the receiving state, for which a list of exceptions is provided. Similar to the exemptions listed above, this requirement can be waived by individual Member States or the UK via notification of the Specialised Committee – in such a case, it would suffice that the offence be listed in Article Law.SURR.79(5) of the TCA (corresponding to the list in the EAW Framework Decision) and that it be punishable with at least three years' detention in the extraditing state.[90] Fifteen countries have waived that requirement already (Belgium, Ireland, Greece, Spain, France, Italy, Cyprus, Lithuania, Luxembourg, Hungary, the Netherlands, Austria, Poland, Portugal and Romania).[91] The non-compliance with the conditions of respect for fundamental rights and the proportionality principle, along with the conditions stipulated by the EAW, constitute grounds for non-execution of the arrest warrant, while discriminatory prosecution regarding an arrest warrant would also be considered grounds for refusal.[92]

The TCA provisions will apply also to EAWs that were issued before the end of the transition period but where the suspect had not been arrested by the end of that period.[93] Overall, it is considered that the pursuit of continuity and compromise in this new arrangement is 'unprecedented with regard to a non-EU and non-Schengen third country'.[94] Nevertheless, the loss of access to SIS-II and the reliance on Interpol's databases will severely restrict the effectiveness of extradition and law enforcement across the two parties, especially in terms of the lack of real-time information exchange.[95] As is the case in other JHA arrangements, the drawbacks result not from the new arrangement itself, but from a communication channel or mechanism that can no longer be accessed by the UK. Without access to SIS-II, it is expected that arrest warrant exchanges will be 'materially less

[88] ibid.
[89] Cîrlig (n 38) 8; Bunyan and Jones (n 8) 17.
[90] The Law Societies (n 87).
[91] Cîrlig (n 38) 9.
[92] ibid 8; The Law Society (n 63).
[93] The Law Society (n 63).
[94] Cîrlig (n 38) 9.
[95] Select Committee on the European Union (n 4) 7; Cîrlig (n 38) 9.

efficient and effective', as the EAW's operation is to an extent conditional upon the real-time exchange through the database.[96]

(vii) Mutual Legal Assistance

In place of the EU's Mutual Assistance in Criminal Matters, the TCA facilitates and supplements the application of three CoE Conventions and Protocols: the 1959 European Convention on Mutual Assistance in Criminal Matters, the 1978 Additional Protocol to the European Mutual Assistance Convention and the 2001 Second Additional Protocol to the European Mutual Assistance Convention.[97] The TCA also incorporates elements from the European Investigation Order Directive, another unfortunate loss for the UK.[98] Mutual Legal Assistance (MLA) is an important principle whose inclusion in EU law was largely influenced by the UK; it entails competent judicial or legal authorities making requests for assistance in criminal investigations and the ensuing prosecution. The condition for requesting MLA is that the measure requested be necessary, proportionate and available under similar conditions and circumstances in the requested state, while MLA cannot be refused in obtaining evidence from police and judicial databases, in other non-coercive investigative measures aimed at criminal proceedings or in the hearings of witnesses and victims.[99]

The competent authorities of the requested state are obliged to inform their counterparts if the request is incomplete (thus making it impossible to execute) or if, in the course of executing the request, it is established that further investigative measures not initially foreseen are necessary.[100] A request may be refused when it comes to double criminality (*ne bis in idem*), ie if a person has been prosecuted by another state on the same acts, thus not allowing a second trial on the same subject in a different state.[101] The grounds for refusal from the CoE Convention still apply, namely political or fiscal offences, likely prejudice to sovereignty, security, public order or the essential interests of the state.[102]

The TCA stipulates that at the latest 45 days after receipt of an MLA request a decision must be communicated and the action therein must be executed within 90 days of that communication.[103] These tight time limits might become unrealistic due to the UK's third-country status, lack of a standardised procedure and the vague interpretation on the adherence to the European Convention on Human Rights.[104] The TCA further provides that the UK may keep on participating

[96] Arnell et al (n 31) 267.
[97] The Law Society (n 63).
[98] Wilson (n 43) 1; Cîrlig (n 38) 9.
[99] TCA, Art 637.
[100] ibid Art 638.
[101] ibid Art 639; Garner (n 5) 12.
[102] Cîrlig (n 38) 9.
[103] The Law Society (n 63).
[104] Cîrlig (n 38) 10.

in JITs, though only by invitation from an EU Member State, as this is regulated by EU *acquis*. Requests for MLA can be transmitted by the competent authorities designated by EU Member States or by UK public prosecutors, or in cases of urgency by Eurojust or Europol.[105]

(viii) Exchange of Criminal Record Information

The TCA provides for continued exchange of information contained in criminal records held by the UK and EU Member States (with changes in terms of time frames, scope of information exchanged and communication channels used). The new arrangement mostly corresponds to the ECRIS decisions, and it would take precedence over MLA provisions. Each state must designate one or more central authorities, who would be responsible for the exchange of information on criminal records (as was the case with ECRIS). The central judicial authorities are required to inform one another of the convictions made against their respective citizens once a month (whereas the timeline was 'as soon as possible' in the ECRIS decisions) and requests must be addressed within 20 working days (versus 10 days within the ECRIS framework). Whereas the EU is setting up an ECRIS-TCN providing for the exchange of third-country nationals' criminal records (which will now include UK citizens too), the TCA does not provide for such exchange with the UK.[106] As EU Member States will continue to use ECRIS (a secure, decentralised, encrypted network providing infrastructure for criminal justice information exchange), the UK will be expected to build its own infrastructure compatible with it, namely UKRIS.[107] The TCA also sets the conditions for the use and processing of personal data, such as purpose limitation 'within the limits specified by the requested state', wherein an exception could be made 'to prevent an immediate and serious threat to public security'.[108] Furthermore, states are allowed to pass personal data received via this cooperation scheme to a third country under certain conditions: that data is disclosed (on a case-by-case basis) only by the competent authority, for the purposes of criminal proceedings or prevention of security threat, only if appropriate safeguards are identified and only if the receiving authority uses the data within the scope and time frame specified ex ante.[109] These conditions are less restrictive than the ECRIS legislation, which only allows such exchanges for the sake of criminal proceedings.[110] Exchanges of criminal record data will take place virtually via the common encrypted communication infrastructure TESTA (Trans-European Services for Telematics between Administrations), whereas the UK will be responsible for developing its own interconnection software.[111]

[105] The Law Society (n 63).
[106] Cîrlig (n 38) 10.
[107] ibid 10; Arnell et al (n 31) 274.
[108] TCA, Art 651.
[109] ibid Art 651.
[110] Bunyan and Jones (n 8) 19.
[111] The Law Society (n 63).

It is expected that the UK's lack of access to such data on third-country nationals will negatively affect the fight against international crime and terrorism over the long term, and it is speculated that the lack of exonerating information may affect the fairness to suspects on trial.[112] However, the TCA provides guarantees that Member States will inform each other of national deletion of criminal records data in the context of the exercise of the so-called 'right to be forgotten'.[113]

(ix) Other Areas of Justice and Home Affairs' Cooperation

The TCA provides for continued cooperation on anti-money laundering and anti-terrorist financing measures. The two parties commit to information exchange and support of international efforts in tackling these crimes, while aiming to go beyond the Financial Action Task Force's standards in line with advancements in EU law.[114] Both parties are obliged to establish central registers for competent authorities and to guarantee that legal entities in the respective state provide up-to-date and accurate data on their activities.[115] The TCA does not specify a channel for information exchange, which can occur via operational information channels. It is unclear how cooperation between the EU Financial Information Units (FIUs) and the UK FIU would be impacted by Brexit; nevertheless, it is expected that it will be affected by further EU legislative changes.

The TCA replaces the CoE conventions and EU instruments (eg Regulation 2018/1805) on freezing and confiscation of assets with a new mechanism, aimed at deeper cooperation. Both parties must comply with requests (with limited grounds of refusal) concerning confiscation and freezing of assets, the procedures of which will follow the requested state's national law, and the latter must give such requests the same priority as domestic ones.[116] Confiscation is conditional on a court order from the requesting state (while the requested state could also obtain one). The persons subject to such orders must be ensured their rights to adequate legal representation and fair judicial treatment, while the TCA also details what happens with the confiscated asset post hoc.[117]

The bespoke dispute settlement mechanism is also covered by this title, replacing the jurisdiction of the CJEU. If a dispute should occur, the parties will carry out consultations either bilaterally or within the Specialised Committee or the Partnership Council. If no agreement is reached within the set time frame, the party that deems the other to have been in serious breach of an obligation may suspend cooperation under that title, following a written notification.[118]

[112] Arnell et al (n 31) 274.
[113] ibid 274.
[114] Garner (n 5) 13; Select Committee on the European Union (n 4).
[115] Cîrlig (n 38) 10.
[116] ibid 11.
[117] ibid 11.
[118] ibid 11.

The other party may then suspend cooperation under the remaining titles, again after notification, and with three months' notice. The Specialised Committee must decide how the cooperation can end adequately, while if the breach is no longer present, the parties must reinstate the interrupted cooperation mechanisms.[119]

V. Conclusion

As the TCA could never match the extent of law enforcement and judicial cooperation of the UK with the EU at the time of its membership, the new arrangements 'inevitably represent a "security downgrade"' when it comes to information-sharing.[120] Still, the TCA provides for the closest possible relationship between the two parties, and seeks to balance out continued information exchange with adequate data protection, specifically in relation to EU data vis-à-vis a now third country. The EU and the UK managed to find cooperative arrangements that were as close as possible without compromising each other's red lines while simultaneously preserving a spirit of partnership in pursuit of mutually beneficial security cooperation. The eight priority areas discussed in this chapter were clearly of key significance to both parties, as the arrangements in these come as close as possible to those available to EU Member States, wherein the UK maintains a maximum amount of privileges and access to EU instruments in this domain. Still, the absence of real-time data exchange is likely to hamper both the law enforcement and judiciary aspects of fighting crime and terrorism, and many of the new arrangements' functioning will depend on the goodwill of both parties. This is especially the case in terms of the use of Interpol in place of SIS-II and the circulation of national arrest warrants to enable the surrender procedure, whereas some channels have been replaced by others and some obligations and deadlines have been altered, requiring the goodwill and 'soft cooperation' of participating actors for smooth functioning. Finally, on top of losing influence over European security, the UK has also lost the trust of some of its EU partners. Both sides would be wise to invest in a renewed EU–UK security relationship, as the fragmentation of cooperation indicates divisions among European partners and divergence in their priorities, which arguably can empower global rivals wishing to undermine security in Europe.[121]

[119] ibid 11.
[120] Arnell et al (n 31) 275.
[121] ibid 275.

5

An (In)adequate Data Protection Regime after Brexit? Bulk Surveillance Powers, National Security and the Future of EU–UK Data Transfers

SOTIRIOS SANTATZOGLOU AND MARIA TZANOU*

I. Introduction

On 28 June 2021, the European Commission (the Commission) adopted two adequacy decisions – one under the General Data Protection Regulation (GDPR)[1] and one under the Law Enforcement Directive (LED)[2] – confirming that the UK ensures a level of protection for personal data transferred from the EU that is 'essentially equivalent' to the one guaranteed by EU data protection law.[3] In its UK adequacy decision on the GDPR, the Commission included a discussion entitled 'Access and use of personal data transferred from the European Union by public

* The drafting of s II of this chapter is attributed to Sotirios Santatzoglou, and that of s III to Maria Tzanou. Sections I and IV were co-drafted. The whole manuscript was shaped by both authors.

[1] Regulation (EU) 2016/679 of the European Parliament and of the Council of 27 April 2016 on the protection of natural persons with regard to the processing of personal data and on the free movement of such data, and repealing Directive 95/46/EC (General Data Protection Regulation) [2016] OJ L119 (GDPR); European Commission, Commission Implementing Decision of 28 June 2021 pursuant to Regulation (EU) 2016/679 of the European Parliament and of the Council on the adequate protection of personal data by the United Kingdom, C(2021) 4800 final.

[2] Directive (EU) 2016/680 of the European Parliament and of the Council of 27 April 2016 on the protection of natural persons with regard to the processing of personal data by competent authorities for the purposes of the prevention, investigation, detection or prosecution of criminal offences or the execution of criminal penalties, and on the free movement of such data, and repealing Council Framework Decision 2008/977/JHA (Law Enforcement Directive) [2016] OJ L119/89 (LED); Commission Implementing Decision of 28 June 2021 pursuant to Directive (EU) 2016/680 of the European Parliament and of the Council on the adequate protection of personal data by the United Kingdom, C(2021) 4801 final.

[3] LED (n 2) Art 1.

authorities in the United Kingdom', which analysed the UK's legal framework for government access to personal data collected by business operators for criminal law enforcement and national security purposes.

Nevertheless, despite the Commission's adequacy findings in this respect, significant uncertainty still exists regarding the UK surveillance framework, which risks jeopardising the future of the EU–UK data privacy relations. Indeed, there are important concerns and doubts as to whether the UK's national security regime is actually 'essentially equivalent' to the EU's standards, despite the Commission's positive findings in this regard. The inadequateness of this regime is not a new issue; rather, it is deeply rooted in the UK's broader socio-political choices, which prioritise security over fundamental rights concerns. The historical examination presented in the first part of this chapter reveals that this trend emerged long ago, within the broader context of law enforcement and with the in-principle agreement of the two main UK political parties.

Drawing on this historical examination of the UK political setting, this chapter argues that the UK approach follows an established, irreversible (primary political) path, dictating expansionism as the main direction in crime prevention and national security policy. Bulk surveillance powers are at the centre of this expansionist approach as they figure prominently in the UK's regulatory architecture in the contexts of both law enforcement and national surveillance despite a series of critical decisions by the Court of Justice of the European Union (CJEU) and the European Court of Human Rights (ECtHR). At the same time, bulk surveillance powers are one of the main concerns of EU institutions regarding EU–UK data protection relations in the post-Brexit era. Indeed, such concerns open up the post-Brexit EU–UK data privacy relationships to significant uncertainty and volatility that might undermine trust, resulting in a future finding of inadequacy. Regrettably, they also erode the standards of fundamental rights protection in the UK as a whole – an unwelcome further consequence of Brexit.

Following this introduction, the chapter is structured as follows: section II undertakes a historical examination of the bulk powers regulatory framework in the UK by exploring its peculiar trajectory (section IIA), its underpinning rationale (section IIB) and its established broader use in the context of law enforcement (section IIC). It then turns to the current UK national security framework, the Investigatory Powers Act 2016 (IPA), and examines in detail the political debate that preceded its adoption (section IID). Section III focuses on the EU–UK post-Brexit data protection regulatory environment, pointing out the unique position of the UK (section IIIA) and the interesting issues that arise regarding the extraterritorial application of EU fundamental rights in the post-Brexit context (section IIIB). It then explores the main vulnerabilities of the UK's national security regime (section IIIC). The final part offers brief conclusions (section IV).

II. UK Bulk Surveillance and the Determining Impact of the Political Setting

A. The Peculiar Regulatory Trajectory of Surveillance Powers

The legislative process concerning the regulation of surveillance powers in the UK has followed a peculiar trajectory fraught with complexities. The saga commenced from the invalidation by the CJEU of the EU Data Retention Directive,[4] which was the basis for the Regulation of Investigatory Powers Act 2000 (RIPA). At the same time, following the Snowden revelations of the hitherto unknown Government Communications Headquarters (GCHQ) surveillance practices,[5] the existence of a 'questionable' legal basis concerning the exercise of state surveillance activities had become apparent,[6] raising the need to reconsider the RIPA regime.[7]

The enactment of the Data Retention and Investigatory Powers Act 2014 (DRIPA) was supposed to address the serious issues arising from its predecessor, RIPA. DRIPA was 'quickly passed' in Parliament,[8] aiming to cure the RIPA pathologies. However, following the CJEU's *Tele2 and Watson* judgment,[9] DRIPA was also deemed to be 'not fit for purpose'.[10] In the domestic 'Davis' (later 'Watson') judicial review, which was brought against the Secretary of State from a group of five (all-party) parliamentarians, the High Court[11] concluded that DRIPA was incompatible with EU law as set out in *Digital Rights Ireland*.[12] This was because the CJEU had found communications data retention only permissible if the objective

[4] Directive 2006/24/EC of the European Parliament and of the Council of 15 March 2006 on the retention of data generated or processed in connection with the provision of publicly available electronic communications services or of public communications networks and amending Directive 2002/58/EC [2006] OJ L105/54.

[5] C Walker, 'Case Comment *R (on the application of Davis) v Secretary of State for the Home Department* Divisional Court' [2016] *Crim LR* 1, 50.

[6] B Schafer, 'Surveillance for the Masses: The Political and Legal Landscape of the UK Investigatory Powers Bill' [2016] *Datenschutz und Datensicherheit* 592.

[7] L Woods, 'United Kingdom: Draft Investigatory Powers Bill' (2016) 2 *European Data Protection Law Review* 103.

[8] M White, 'Data Retention: Serious Crime or a Serious Problem?' [2019] *PL* 633.

[9] Joined Cases C-203/15 and C-698/15 *Tele2 Sverige AB v Post- och telestyrelsen; Secretary of State for the Home Department v Watson* ECLI:EU:C:2016:970.

[10] MW Jones, 'Double-Lock or Double-Bind? The Investigatory Powers Bill and Freedom of Expression in the United Kingdom' in RL Weaver, SI Friedland, A Raynouard and D Fairgrieve (eds), *Cybersurveillance in a Post-Snowden World: Balancing the Fight Against Terrorism Against Fundamental Rights* (Carolina Academic Press, 2017).

[11] *R. (on the application of Davis) v Secretary of State for the Home Department* [2015] EWHC 2092 (Admin).

[12] Joined Cases C-293/12 and C-594/12 *Digital Rights Ireland Ltd v Minister for Communications, Marine and Natural Resources and Others and Karntner Landesregierung and Others* ECLI:EU:C:2014:238.

is to fight serious crime,[13] a threshold not provisioned in DRIPA. At the appeal stage of the 'Davis/Watson' judicial review, the Court of Appeal referred the case to the CJEU,[14] but by then it had already become clear that (again) new legislation was needed to correct and expand upon DRIPA, as the UK legal framework regulating surveillance was 'in tatters'.[15]

One would reasonably expect that by then the UK government would have learned from the judicial lessons. The Investigatory Powers Bill (IPB) was announced in May 2015, introduced to the House of Commons in March 2016 and received royal assent on 29 November 2016. During the parliamentary debates, it was evident that MPs (and the government) understood well that the Bill was legalising 'excessive powers', whilst the 'Watson/Davis' case was 'midway between the CJEU and the Court of Appeal', with the expectation to confirm the CJEU's approach restricting data retention to serious crime purposes.[16] Indeed, in December 2016, the CJEU issued its decision in *Tele2 and Watson*, confirming 'the fight of *serious* crime' as the threshold for the retention of communications data.[17]

The UK government conceded the incompatibility of the newly enacted IPA with EU law and planned its amendment[18] to address (among other things) the missing 'serious crime' threshold. In the meantime, following a challenge from the *National Council for Civil Liberties*, the High Court[19] ruled the IPA to be incompatible with EU law – 'partially because access to retained data was not limited to the purposes of fighting serious crime'.[20] The judgment set 1 November 2018 as the deadline for amending legislation to draw up 'an alternative scheme'.[21] Indeed, as a commentator noted, while the IPA 'was meant to clarify and settle electronic surveillance powers, it [was] itself unsettled'.[22] In 2018, the Court of Appeal confirmed that DRIPA was incompatible with EU law.[23] On 31 October 2018, the Data Retention and Acquisition Regulations Act was enacted, addressing the contentious issues arising from RIPA and the IPA, including the introduction

[13] White (n 8).

[14] *R (on the application of Davis) v Secretary of State for the Home Department* [2015] EWCA Civ 1185, [2016] 1 CML Rev 48. The Court of Appeal disagreed with the High Court and referred to the CJEU: J Cobbe, 'Casting the Dragnet: Communications Data Retention under the Investigatory Powers Act' [2018] *PL* 10, 11; White (n 8) 633.

[15] Schafer (n 6).

[16] Investigatory Powers Bill, HC Deb 6 and 7 June 2016, vol 611; see in particular Sir Keir Starmer, col 1067.

[17] Above n 9; see also the discussion in White (n 8) 633.

[18] White (n 8) 633–34.

[19] *The National Council for Civil Liberties (Liberty) R (on the Application of) v Secretary of State for the Home Department & Anor* [2018] EWHC 975.

[20] White (n 8) 633, 34.

[21] ibid.

[22] C Boukalas, 'Overcoming Liberal Democracy: "Threat Governmentality" and the Empowerment of Intelligence in the UK Investigatory Powers Act' in A Sarat and P Ewick (eds), *Studies in Law, Politics, and Society* (Emerald, 2020) 1.

[23] White (n 8) 633, 34.

of a serious crime threshold, especially when indiscriminate bulk surveillance practices were involved.

B. Underlying Reasons

The above saga is explained by the political hastiness in preparing and voting the relevant laws, an unwelcome practice for legislation of such significance.[24] This peculiar legislative trend primarily demonstrates the distancing of policy from judicially established standards – both at the national and the EU level – on matters of communications surveillance. This distancing reflects a policy direction leaning favourably towards the legitimisation of extended state surveillance by intelligence services and the police. The granting of extended surveillance powers to intelligence agencies sets the UK policy in distancing not only with judicial values, but also with the policy practice of major EU continental states. As Brants indicated, unlike the UK, in the Netherlands, 'intrusive police investigation is a primary concern', and the policy emphasis is on the adherence of agencies to the rules of proportionality and necessity, as required by European courts.[25] Indeed, the British differentiation in the regulation of surveillance powers can be attributed to the UK's 'historical and political context'.[26] It can be linked to the Tories as an 'increasingly surveillance and police friendly' party,[27] and to the Labour Party broadly failing to exercise effective opposition on these matters.[28] Regrettably, it has resulted in accepting the intelligence sector as 'determining the law' governing surveillance.[29]

These political hermeneutics form an appropriate appreciation of the British regulatory landscape concerning surveillance powers. In particular, the risk of asymmetrical terrorist threats has been proffered as a reason behind this political approach and hence the need to develop 'total intelligence' to fight this 'new type of enemy'.[30] Nevertheless, it should be noted that this explanatory perspective is limited. As the then Home Office Secretary, Theresa May, stated in the foreword of the draft IPB, surveillance powers are also essential to the fight against wider crime, such as tackling child sexual exploitation, dismantling serious crime cartels, and taking drugs and guns off the streets.[31] The roots of this permissive regulation can

[24] Case Comment, 'Data Protection Law to Be Rewritten following Court Ruling' (2015) 4(4) *Compliance & Risk* 17.
[25] C Brants, A Jackson and T Wilson, 'A Comparative Analysis of Anglo-Dutch Approaches to "Cyber Policing": Checks and Balances Fit for Purpose? [2020] *Journal of Criminal Law* 451, 467.
[26] Schafer (n 6).
[27] ibid.
[28] C Murphy, 'State Surveillance and Social Democracy' in A Bogg, J Rowbottom and AL Young (eds), *The Constitution of Social Democracy: Essays in Honour of Keith Ewing* (Hart Publishing, 2020).
[29] Boukalas (n 22) 2–4.
[30] ibid 9, 10.
[31] *Draft Investigatory Powers Bill* (Cm 9152, 2015).

be traced to the nature of British criminal policy, which goes beyond the evolution of terrorism legislation. It is, thus, crucial to place the UK national security regulation within the broader context of the country's criminal policy. The following section examines the historical evolution of this policy approach.

C. A Criminal Policy Leaning to Authoritarianism

The crime rhetoric had 'played a prominent role' in Thatcher's 1979 election, but during her premiership criminal policy was marked by 'principled pragmatism', as it was 'broadly "liberal" in its intentions and effects'.[32] A policy shift towards authoritarian solutions became evident in the early 1990s, during John Major's Conservative government. The appointment of Michael Howard as home secretary in 1993 signified a 'turning point' for the British criminal policy.[33] What was called the 'moment of Howard' embodied both a rhetoric and commitment rejecting 'the long-standing policy of prison as a last resort'.[34] Howard's U-turn was summarised in his catchphrase 'Let us be clear – prison works'.[35] This political move aimed to bring a weakening Conservative government in touch with the public,[36] the 'silent majority'[37] and their common sense logic. This political choice shifted criminal policy, gradually, towards an authoritarian formula.[38]

From 1997 onwards, the subsequent New Labour governments, faithful to the electorally successful Blair's credo of 'Tough on crime', clearly endorsed, strengthened and widened this criminal policy transition in terms of both rhetoric and commitment. In this way, the successive New Labour governments ensured that the law-and-order territory was not a Tory-dominated political arena as they listened to the 'ordinary people's' concerns over crime and their common-sense solutions.[39]

Hence, Howard's moment marked the start of an era of politicisation linking crime policy to electorate interests, as the main political parties argued over their competence to fight crime through the greater use and enactment of criminal laws.[40] Crime prevention, law enforcement and punishment became distant from

[32] D Faulkner, 'The End of the Beginning of an Era? Politics and Punishment under Margaret Thatcher's Government' in M Wasik and S Santatzoglou (eds), *The Management of Change in Criminal Justice: Who Knows Best?* (Palgrave Macmillan, 2015) 34.

[33] S Santatzoglou and M Wasik, 'Who Knows Best? in Wasik and Santatzoglou (n 32) 14.

[34] J Sim, *Punishment and Prisons: Power and the Carceral State* (Sage, 2009).

[35] Speech to the Conservative Party conference, 6 October 1993, www.michaelhoward.org, Prison_Works.

[36] Santatzoglou and Wasik (n 33) 15.

[37] C Brown, 'Howard Seeks to Placate "Angry Majority": Home Secretary Tells Party that Balance in Criminal Justice System Will Be Tilted towards Public' *The Independent* (6 October 1993).

[38] L Radzinowicz, 'Penal Regressions' [1991] *CLJ* 428.

[39] A Rutherford, 'An Elephant on the Doorstep' in P Green and A Rutherford (eds), *Criminal Policy in Transition* (Hart Publishing, 2000); Santatzoglou and Wasik (n 33) 17.

[40] Santatzoglou and Wasik (n 33) 17.

the less appealing (to the electorate) concepts of proportionality and necessity. Criminal policy became integral to the political readiness to respond with immediate legislative action to the populist press's headlines concerning crime and public safety. As Ashworth observed, this politicisation trend resulted in an unprincipled and chaotic overgrowth of criminal laws and policy: '[criminal law] … is a multi-purpose tool, often creating the favourable impression that certain misconduct has been taken seriously and dealt with appropriately'.[41]

Notably, a further feature of this trend was the occurrence of a political soft consensus between the two major UK political parties concerning the adoption of conservative, social authoritarian formulas of criminal policy.[42] As Downes and Morgan put it: 'In the twenty-first century we may be witnessing some underlying agreement in law and order' where 'political squabbles … are largely about relative levels of expenditure on law and order services, police numbers and the like'.[43] Indeed, the politicisation trend has been characterised by the absence of political argumentation over issues of principle concerning the shaping of the boundaries of criminal law and criminal justice. A crude statistical example of this trend is evidenced in the growth of imprisonment in the UK. In 2016, the rate of imprisonment in England and Wales was 'the 8th highest among EU countries and the highest amongst western European jurisdictions'[44] (the countries with a higher rate coming from the former Soviet bloc).

The direction towards the expansion of control measures in the UK has been particularly evident through the extended use of modern technologies.[45] The strong political attraction in the UK to science and emerging technologies was demonstrated as early as 1999 with the additional funding from the incoming New Labour government – over £300 million over five years – for the rapid expansion of the National DNA Database, which ended as the largest genetic information database in the world.[46] The database was seen as 'Tony Blair's flagship scheme to store the genetic fingerprints of every criminal in Britain'.[47] Within the political (and law enforcement) chambers, the storing of six million profiles was considered an 'uncomplicated success story' of crime detection and

[41] A Ashworth, 'Is the Criminal Law a Lost Cause?' [2000] *LQR* 225, 226.

[42] Santatzoglou and Wasik (n 33) 25,26. This was the case even during the coalition government period, despite the participation of the Liberal Democrats, as the case of the government's youth crime control policy demonstrated; see for example, Roger Smith, 'Troubling Troubled or Troublesome?' in Wasik and Santatzoglou (n 32).

[43] D Downes and R Morgan, 'Overtaking on the Left?' in M Maguire, R Morgan and R Reiner (eds), *The Oxford Handbook of Criminology*, 5th edn (Oxford University Press, 2012).

[44] G Sturge, *UK Prison Population Statistics*, Commons Library Research Briefing (29 October 2021) 30.

[45] Importantly, critics of the IPA extended use of bulk surveillance also stress the largeness of DNA databases and/or the wide use of CCTV sets; see, eg Jones (n 10).

[46] Home Office 2005 DNA Expansion Programme 2000–2005: Reporting achievement. Forensic Science and Pathology Unit.

[47] M Bright and G Hinsliff, 'Police Snub Blair's DNA Bank' *The Observer* (3 September 2000).

reduction, justifying the uncritical disregard of questions of civil liberties and human rights.[48]

This pattern of politically driven bulk expansion of crime control biotechnology can also be observed in the UK's use of CCTV. Indeed, the extensive use of CCTV by public authorities for the purpose of crime prevention is closely linked with the 'looking-for-the- needle-in-the-haystack' approach that followed RIPA.[49] The use of CCTV as a mainstream crime prevention measure can be traced to UK Conservative government policy choices in 1996.[50] The subsequent 'dramatic increase' of these systems following governments' generous funding reflected the public popularity of the measure, and the political belief in potential benefits of 'being seen to be doing something visible' against crime.[51] Nevertheless, despite the generation of large data sets from CCTV records, there was 'rather little serious debate' regarding civil liberties issues or scientific evidence concerning the effectiveness of these systems.[52] In fact, in the early days of CCTV bulk expansion, 'political parties … raised few critical questions',[53] focusing instead on the 'apparent plausibility [that CCTV] (must work)'[54] as a crime solution. This approach disregarded crucial issues, such as that CCTV could also 'capture not only what individuals do, but also whom they meet … whether it be with potential business partners, lovers, political allies, or (non-criminal) friendship with offenders'.[55]

This long-ongoing – since the mid-1990s – bipartisan UK government obsession with extensive crime prevention and control measures is the main reason for the adoption of a bulk-oriented political logic regarding the use of control measures. From the growth of imprisonment to the CCTV expansion, the logic is the same: the use of bulk measures. Within this political setting, considerations of a measured and ethical use of interventions are not sufficiently discussed or are faced with indifference during the political legislative process. The political soft consensus of social authoritarianism across the two main UK political parties has upheld the sanctity of bulk crime prevention and control without much criticism, and arguably has also defined the legislative process of national security bulk surveillance powers. It was exactly against this ongoing broader socio-political and historical background that the IPA was negotiated in the UK Parliament.

[48] AO Amankwaa and C McCartney, 'The Effectiveness of the UK National DNA Database' [2019] *Forensic Science International: Synergy* 45, 46–47.

[49] Schafer (6).

[50] EL Piza, BC Welsh, DP Farrington and AL Thomas, 'CCTV Surveillance for Crime Prevention – A 40-Year Systematic Review with Meta-analysis' [2019] *Criminology and Public Policy* 136.

[51] KA Painter and N Tilley, 'Seeing and Being Seen to Prevent Crime' in KA Painter and N Tilley (eds), *Surveillance of Public Space: CCTV, Street Lighting and Crime Prevention* (Crime Prevention Studies, 1999); R Armitage, 'To CCTV or not to CCTV? A Review of Current Research into the Effectiveness of CCTV Systems in Reducing Crime' (Narco, 2002) 8.

[52] ibid.

[53] ibid.

[54] Armitage (n 51) 8.

[55] Painter and Tilley, 'Seeing and Being Seen' (n 51).

D. The IPA and the Surveillance Bulk Powers Debate

The enactment of the IPA was seen as 'an improvement to the previous situation'.[56] This is, in particular, because of the introduction of the so-called 'double lock' procedure, under which a surveillance warrant issued by the Secretary of State must be subject to review by a 'judicial commissioner',[57] providing – according to the UK government – a 'fundamental safeguard'.[58]

However, the IPA was criticised for its 'ambivalence',[59] and was strongly opposed by civil liberties groups.[60] Bulk surveillance powers were seen as the major controversy of the legislation.[61] The IPA legalised the employment of bulk powers, placing an obligation on companies to assist in such operations and 'bypass encryption',[62] thus resulting in a form of mass state surveillance.[63] During the bill consultation, David Anderson KC, as Independent Reviewer of Terrorism Legislation, warned of the controversial nature of bulk powers, which 'may be seen as placing control in the hands of the state'.[64] Early critics pointed out that the bulk practice is indiscriminate in nature, with the apparent potential of 'bringing individuals who are not of interest to the authorities under a form of surveillance'.[65] In the context of communications data surveillance, the IPA established bulk retention as the rule rather than the exception, thereby permitting general and indiscriminate data retention with no legitimate aim.[66]

The UK Parliament debate provides a telling case study of the bipartisan soft consensus legitimising the use of bulk powers. During the Report-stage debate of the IPB that took place in Parliament on 6 and 7 June 2016, small opposition parties (such as the Liberal Democrats and the Scottish National Party (SNP)), along with Harriet Harman MP, chair of the Joint Committee on Human Rights, and a few Conservative and Labour backbenchers, raised a number of criticisms regarding bulk powers. It was pointed out that a Bill 'of huge constitutional significance' was allocated 'fewer than two full working days to debate it on Report'.[67] Conservative MP Stephen McPartland noted that 'the carte blanche on bulk

[56] L Woods, 'The Investigatory Powers Act 2016' [2017] 3 *European Data Protection Law Review* 13.
[57] IPA, s 227.
[58] Jones (n 10).
[59] ibid 8, 11.
[60] Cobbe (n 14) 11.
[61] ibid.
[62] Jones (n 10) 10.
[63] V Chadha, 'Balancing the Privacy v Surveillance Argument: A Perspective from the United Kingdom' [2022] *European Journal of International Relations* 190, 196.
[64] D Anderson, *A Question of Trust: Report of the Investigatory Powers Review* (HM Government, 2015) para 2.7.
[65] Woods, 'United Kingdom' (n 7) 104.
[66] Schafer (n 6); Cobbe (n 14) 18; White (n 8) 642; Boukalas (n 22); G Davies, 'Shining a Light on Policing of the Dark Web: An Analysis of UK Investigatory Powers' [2020] *Journal of Criminal Law* 407, 425.
[67] Investigatory Powers Bill (n 16) Joanna Cherry, col 1148.

powers should not be the first resort; it should always be the last resort';[68] whilst Conservative MP Ken Clarke indicated the expansionist character of the Bill, noting that a serious threshold is required for all bulk surveillance powers.[69] SNP MP Ann McLaughlin stressed that the regulation of bulk powers was 'perhaps one of its most controversial parts',[70] noting that:

> At the heart of the matter is the retention of intimate personal details regarding the tens of millions of ordinary citizens of this country who do not merit such information being held by the state … The offline analogy is instructive. If we were asked by the state to deposit our membership forms for various organisations – political parties, campaign groups, golf clubs – or forms with our direct debit details, health records and other such bulk information into a big safe on the understanding that only the security services would have access to it, we would rightly baulk at such a proposal. Just because such a system is being proposed online and without the consent of the individuals concerned does not make it acceptable – in many ways, it makes it much worse.[71]

However, these arguments demonstrating the problematic expansion of surveillance powers were ignored during the two days parliamentary debate. Instead, a bipartisan soft consensus between the Conservative Party and the Labour Party emerged as the 'Opposition and the Government … worked together on the Bill'[72] and 'made good progress'.[73] In this regard, the Labour Party stated that it had adopted 'a responsible and pragmatic approach' to the Bill,[74] evident in 'the very constructive way' in which Labour dealt with the government's proposals.[75] This alignment between the two main UK political parties demonstrated a consensus on the necessity of bulk powers for intelligence agencies.

Among the Conservatives, the endorsement of bulk powers was accepted from the Eurosceptic right-wing end of the party to its centre-right Europhile side. The former justified the indiscriminate surveillance on the 'constant state of threat' and the 'international security war … [and the] war on the online fraudsters and the paedophiles' that the government was waging,[76] whilst the latter argued for the significant utility of 'the needle in the haystack' approach.[77] In fact, it was pointed out that although what is searched for is indeed 'a needle in a haystack', 'bulk powers are essential for building up that network in order to be able to search'[78] and thereby to 'discover new threats from people who were previously unknown and identify patterns of behaviour'.[79] In this way, the Conservative Party presented

[68] ibid Stephen McPartland, col 1092.
[69] ibid Ken Clarke, col 1122.
[70] ibid Ann McLaughlin, col 1053.
[71] ibid Ann McLaughlin, col 1058.
[72] ibid J Hayes, Minister for Security, col 981.
[73] ibid Keir Starmer, col 1065.
[74] ibid Andy Burnham, col 952.
[75] ibid James Berry, col 1135.
[76] ibid Suella Fernandes, col 1085.
[77] ibid Dominic Grieve, Chair of the Intelligence and Security Committee, col 1059.
[78] ibid Tom Tugendhat, col 1082.
[79] ibid Seema Kennedy, col 1082; Stephen Hammond, col 1087.

the bulk approach to surveillance as necessary, reflecting, as one (pro-European) Conservative MP put it, 'the reality' despite its controversial nature,[80] which shows that none of these powers are 'unnecessary or disproportionate'.[81]

Moreover, Dominic Grieve, the Chair of the Intelligence and Security Committee (ISC), stated that although people can be 'legitimately anxious' about the potential misuse of bulk powers, 'the ethical standards of the agencies are very high' and the ISC has been reassured that 'those ethical standards are at the heart of what they do'.[82] It is worth noting that, in a recent judgment delivered in 2023 in a case concerning the use of bulk powers,[83] the Investigatory Powers Tribunal concluded that there were 'serious failings in compliance with the statutory obligations of MI5 from late 2014 onwards'.[84] In particular, the IPC found that the holding and handling of data was 'unlawful' on the basis that under the relevant provisions of RIPA and IPA satisfactory safeguards relating to retention, review and disposal of personal data were not in place.[85] Indeed, MI5 accepted that it was in breach of its safeguarding obligations from 2016.[86] Notwithstanding this, ironically, a recent Home Office report on the operation of the Investigatory Powers Act asserted that the IPA 'introduced world leading oversight arrangements that strengthened the safeguards that apply to the use of investigatory powers'.[87] This demonstrates once again the state of political apathy regarding the serious risks of misuse inherent in the embedded bulk culture of national security and crime control as evidenced in the Report-stage debate. The Labour opposition, in line with the soft consensus approach on the expansionism of criminal policy, adopted a 'sitting on the fence' approach, otherwise minimally questioning the bulk surveillance powers. A characteristic example of the former was the Labour's twofold suggestion: (i) to set an overarching privacy clause and (ii) to set an independent review of 'the operational case for the bulk powers'.[88] Unsurprisingly, the government accepted both 'demands'. Ironically, the suggested clause did not set any binding effect on the decision-makers[89] – which indicates its toothless effect. Also, ironically, the latter 'demand' led to David Anderson QC's 'Report of the Bulk Powers Review', which concluded with the operational vitality of bulk powers.[90] Regarding the Labour amendments aiming at minimal limitations to

[80] ibid Dominic Grieve, Chair of the Intelligence and Security Committee, col 1059.

[81] ibid Stephen Hammond, col 1087.

[82] ibid col 1060.

[83] *Liberty and Privacy International v Security Service and Secretary of State for the Home Department* [2023] UKIPTrib1.

[84] ibid para 160.

[85] ibid.

[86] ibid.

[87] Home Office, *Report on the operation of the Investigatory Powers Act 2016*, www.gov.uk/government/publications/report-on-the-operation-of-the-investigatory-powers-act-2016/home-office-report-on-the-operation-of-the-investigatory-powers-act-2016-accessible-version.

[88] ibid Sir Keir Starmer, col 883.

[89] Woods, 'The Investigatory Powers Act 2016' (n 56).

[90] D Anderson QC, *Report of the Bulk Powers Review* (HM Government, 2016) 119–28. Anderson acted in his capacity as Independent Reviewer of Terrorism Legislation.

bulk powers, their proposed definition of 'serious crimes' was to cover offences with a provisioned imprisonment of more than six months. As Labour MPs stated, 'we felt that that was proportionate'.[91] Ironically, two years later, during the consultation to amend the IPA, the government conceded that Labour's proposed six-month imprisonment threshold concerning the retention of communication data[92] did not sufficiently reflect the notion of 'serious crime' as established by the CJEU, and increased it to 12 months.[93]

This non-conflictual debate of the IPB Report provides further evidence of the politicisation of criminal and national security policy in the UK and the interrelated bipartisan soft consensus to embedding bulk powers in the IPA. The centrality of bulk powers within the IPA's architecture demonstrates the 'legal buttressing' of the 'anti-legal logic' of indiscriminate surveillance within the rule-of-law framework.[94] Nevertheless, it should be stressed that this is the outcome of a long-established bipartisan political consensus in the UK rooted in expansive law enforcement powers. Importantly, the boundaries of this setting are not limited to the extreme sides of the political spectrum but, rather, include the critical political zone in the UK, which extends from the centre-right to the centre-left. That is why this soft authoritarian direction legitimising bulk powers appears irreversible. The question then is about its consequences within the EU–UK data protection regulatory space.

III. Surveillance in the Post-Brexit EU–UK Data Protection Relations

A. International Data Transfers and the UK Uniqueness

In many ways, the UK occupies a unique position among the third countries engaging in international data transfers with the EU. The UK is the only third country enjoying former EU Member State status[95] and has, therefore, for decades implemented EU primary and secondary law in general and data protection law in particular. The UK was also subject to the CJEU's jurisprudence

[91] Investigatory Powers Bill (n 16) Andy Burnham, col 1120.

[92] Home Office, *Investigatory Powers Act 2016 Consultation on the Government's proposed response to the ruling of the Court of Justice of the European Union on 21 December 2016 regarding the retention of communications data* (November 2017).

[93] Home Office, *Investigatory Powers Act 2016: Response to Home Office Consultation on the Government's proposed response to the ruling of the Court of Justice of the European Union on 21 December 2016 regarding the retention of communications data* (June 2018); White (n 8) 635, 636.

[94] Boukalas (n 22) 9, 16.

[95] See also EDPB, Opinion 14/2021 regarding the European Commission Draft Implementing Decision pursuant to Regulation (EU) 2016/679 on the adequate protection of personal data in the United Kingdom, adopted on 13 April 2021, para 35.

until 31 January 2020. The European Union Withdrawal Act 2018 (EUWA) directly incorporated applicable EU legislation into the UK's legal order.[96] Hence, the GDPR is considered 'retained EU law'[97] in the UK, and Part 3 of the Data Protection Act 2018 (DPA)[98] – which transposes the LED – constitutes 'EU-derived domestic legislation'.[99]

Besides the previous Member State status, the UK is also subject to the international human rights law commitments shared by the EU as a member of the Council of Europe, the European Convention on Human Rights (ECHR), the Convention for the Protection of Individuals with regard to the Processing of Personal Data (Convention 108+) and its submission to the jurisdiction of the European Court of Human Rights (ECtHR).[100] Hence, the ECtHR case law has had a significant positive effect on the compliance of UK surveillance frameworks and mechanisms with the ECHR's rights. For instance, the UK Investigatory Powers Tribunal (IPT), considered by the ECtHR in 2010 as providing inadequate remedies, was found in 2018 to provide 'a robust judicial remedy to anyone who suspected that his or her communications had been intercepted by the intelligence services'.[101] Indeed, the IPT has progressively evolved over the years from 'passively reviewing the law to actively intervening in it',[102] with the European Data Protection Board noting that it 'functions as a proper court in the meaning of Article 47 Charter of Fundamental Rights of the European Union'.[103]

Compliance with data protection rules and enforcement in the UK is carried out by an independent supervisory authority, the Information Commissioner's Office (ICO), although the ICO's role in the area of national security processing is limited.[104] For instance, according to Schedule 11 of section 110 DPA, intelligence services are not obliged to communicate personal data breaches to the ICO.

Against this background, a Commission adequacy finding appeared relatively easy in the UK case as its 'data protection rules … in many aspects closely mirror the corresponding rules applicable' within the EU.[105] Indeed, the UK did not seem to pose the challenges that the Commission faces when encountering the

[96] European Union Withdrawal Act 2018, www.legislation.gov.uk/ukpga/2018/16/contents. See also J Savirimuthu and M Tzanou, 'The United Kingdom' in J Dumortier, P Gryffroy, R Roex and YS Van Der Sype (eds), *International Encyclopaedia of Laws: Privacy and Data Protection* (Kluwer Law International, 2022).

[97] EUWA, s 6.

[98] Data Protection Act 2018 www.legislation.gov.uk/ukpga/2018/12/contents.

[99] EUWA, s 6.

[100] Commission adequacy decision on GDPR, para 19.

[101] ECtHR (Chamber, First Section) *Big Brother Watch et al v United Kingdom* [2018] ECHR 722, para 265; ECtHR (Grand Chamber) *Big Brother Watch et al v United Kingdom* App nos 58170/13, 62322/14 and 24960/15, 25 May 2021, Grand Chamber, para 415.

[102] B Keenan, 'The Evolution of Elucidation: The Snowden Cases before the Investigatory Powers Tribunal' (2022) 85(4) *MLR* 906, 933.

[103] EDPB, Opinion 14/2021 (n 95) para 25.

[104] See Savirimuthu and Tzanou (n 96) para 241 and references therein.

[105] Commission adequacy decision on GDPR (n 1) para 16.

US legal framework and surveillance regimes.[106] That being said, a flexible approach to allow the swift operation of international data transfers seems to have been adopted in the case of the UK as well. As the Commission confirmed,

> the adequacy standard … does not require a point-to-point replication of Union rules. Rather, the test lies in whether, through the substance of data protection rights and their effective implementation, supervision and enforcement, the foreign system as a whole delivers the required level of protection.[107]

This appears to be in accordance with the CJEU's recently developed flexible approach when reviewing foreign law. Under this, the Court has fleshed out an amended test on the merits for assessing external surveillance interferences. This test requires that: (i) limitations to fundamental rights must be provided for by law; (iii) their legal basis must itself define the scope of the limitation on the exercise of the right concerned; (iii) to satisfy the requirement of proportionality, the legislation in question must lay down clear and precise rules governing the scope and application of the relevant measures and impose 'minimum safeguards, so that the persons whose data has been transferred have sufficient guarantees to protect effectively their personal data against the risk of abuse'; and (iv) the third country must provide 'effective and enforceable data subject rights' for persons whose personal data is transferred.[108]

Overall, the UK as a third country comes from the starting point of close alignment with the EU, which puts it at a clear advantage compared with other third countries with which the EU has or is pursuing data transfer agreements. As one commentator has noted, 'the UK will have the strongest personal data relationship with the EU outside of the EEA and Switzerland'.[109]

B. Brexit, National Security and the Extraterritorial Application of EU Fundamental Rights

Data flows post-Brexit raise two main sets of issues concerning the interrelationship of national security and the extraterritorial application of

[106] See M Tzanou, '*Schrems I* and *Schrems II*: Assessing the Case for the Extraterritoriality of EU Fundamental Rights' in F Fabbrini et al (eds), *Data Protection beyond Borders Transatlantic Perspectives on Extraterritoriality and Sovereignty* (Hart Publishing, 2020).

[107] Commission adequacy decision on GDPR (n 1) para 4.

[108] Case C-311/18 *Data Protection Commissioner v Facebook Ireland Limited and Maximillian Schrems* ECLI:EU:C:2020:559 (*Schrems II*); Tzanou (n 106) 114. It should be noted that under this flexible approach, the CJEU avoids applying directly to external situations the analytical framework of Art 52(1) CFR. See also EDPB, Recommendations 02/2020 on the European Essential Guarantees for surveillance measures, para 24.

[109] D Erdos, 'The UK and the EU Personal Data Framework after Brexit: Another Switzerland?' (University of Cambridge, March 2021) Faculty of Law Research Paper No 15/2021, 2, https://papers.ssrn.com/sol3/papers.cfm?abstract_id=3811296.

EU fundamental rights: (i) the scope of review when national security is at stake; and (ii) the extraterritorial application of EU fundamental rights in this context.

The two matters are closely interlinked, but we will approach them separately here, before pointing out their various interconnections. First, the question of applicability of EU law in the context of national security measures in general and international data transfers in particular raises a number of issues. In *Privacy International*,[110] a seminal case decided after the Brexit referendum but before the UK's formal departure from the EU, on a preliminary reference question received by the IPT, the CJEU clarified an issue of particular importance to the UK (and all Member States) once and for all: the applicability of EU law to domestic national security legislation.[111] The issue had arisen in several cases over the past few years,[112] with Member States insisting that intelligence services' activities relating to the maintenance of public order and the safeguarding of internal security and territorial integrity are part of their essential functions and, consequently, fall within their exclusive competence pursuant to Article 4(2) of the Treaty on European Union (TEU).

The CJEU took the opportunity in *Privacy International* to put the debate to bed by introducing a fundamental distinction: national laws that require electronic communications service providers (ECSPs) to retain or grant access to data to national authorities for the purpose of safeguarding national security fall within the scope of the ePrivacy Directive and, therefore, the Charter of Fundamental Rights of the European Union (CFR) and EU law more broadly.[113] By contrast, national laws that do not impose any obligations on ECSPs but directly implement national security measures fall outside the scope of the ePrivacy Directive (and EU law) even if these derogate from the principle of confidentiality of electronic communications established in the ePrivacy Directive.[114] The crucial aspect of the distinction concerns the involvement of ECSPs and the allocation of data processing obligations to these.[115] Any obligations imposed on ECSPs trigger the application of the ePrivacy Directive no matter the purpose for the access to the data. If, however, the data is directly retained by national authorities without

[110] Case C-623/17 *Privacy International v Secretary of State for Foreign and Commonwealth Affairs and Others* ECLI:EU:C:2020:790.

[111] The Court defined national security as 'the primary interest in protecting the essential functions of the State and the fundamental interests of society [which] encompasses the prevention and punishment of activities capable of seriously destabilising the fundamental constitutional, political, economic or social structures of a country and, in particular, of directly threatening society, the population or the State itself, such as terrorist activities'. See Joined Cases C 511/18, C 512/18 and C 520/18 *La Quadrature du Net and Others v Premier Ministre and Others* ECLI:EU:C:2020, para 135.

[112] *Tele2* (n 9); Case C-207/16 *Ministerio Fiscal* ECLI:EU:C:2018:788.

[113] *Privacy International* (n 110) para 39.

[114] *La Quadrature du Net* (n 111) para 103. The Court recognised, however, that these rules may be subject to the application of the LED.

[115] M Tzanou and S Karyda, 'Privacy International and Quadrature du Net: One Step Forward Two Steps Back in the Data Retention Saga?' (2022) 28(1) *European Public Law* 123.

the compelled cooperation of ECSPs, the ePrivacy Directive is not applicable – in this case, such measures must comply with national constitutional law requirements and the ECHR.

However, national security raises a particular paradoxical situation in the context of international data transfers. Pursuant to Article 4(2) TEU, national security remains the sole responsibility of each Member State, but, as clarified in *Privacy International*, Member States' national security measures do fall within the scope of EU law when personal data is retained by service providers. However, when assessing the adequacy of a third country, the Commission is obliged under Article 45(2)(a) to take account of 'the rule of law, respect for human rights and fundamental freedoms, relevant legislation, both general and sectoral, *including concerning public security, defence, national security* and criminal law *and the access of public authorities to personal data*' (emphasis added). Hence, the UK finds itself in an unusual position: if it were still an EU Member State, it could in principle benefit from the exception under Article 4(2) TEU, which, following *Privacy International*, would allow it to avoid scrutiny of its national security framework – at least when data retention through service providers is not at stake; but, ironically, by leaving the EU, hence as a third country, such scrutiny is unavoidable as the UK became subject to the GDPR's adequacy regime.[116]

In fact, in the 2021 Commission's decision on the adequate protection of personal data by the UK on the basis of the GDPR, the discussion on 'access and use of personal data transferred from the EU by public authorities in the UK' is longer that the actual analysis of the UK's general data protection regime, spanning over 57 pages[117] – while the discussion of the UK's overall data protection framework is actually only 31 pages.

Second, the application of EU fundamental rights raises interesting issues in the Brexit context – even more than before. Indeed, the use of EU fundamental rights to review domestic measures has always been 'controversial' in the UK.[118] This controversy had already commenced long before Brexit, when the UK was still a Member State.[119] For instance, prior to the signing of the Lisbon Treaty, the UK government was eager to secure a protocol stating that the CFR did not 'extend' the ability of the CJEU to declare any UK practice or law invalid,[120] with the then UK Prime Minister declaring that he would 'not accept a treaty that allows the Charter of Fundamental Rights to change UK law in any way'.[121] After Brexit,

[116] This paradox was not lost by commentators. See, eg E Celeste, 'Data Protection' in F Fabbrini (ed), *The Law & Politics of Brexit. Volume 3. The Framework of Future EU–UK Relations* (Oxford University Press, 2021) 197, 209.

[117] From p 31 to p 88, from para 112 to para 272.

[118] See D Chalmers et al, *European Union Law*, 4th edn (Cambridge University Press, 2019) 281; AD Murray, 'Data Transfers between the EU and UK post Brexit?' [2017] *International Data Privacy Law* 149.

[119] See European Scrutiny Committee, *The Application of the EU Charter of Fundamental Rights in the UK: A State of Confusion* (HC 2013–14, 979) 13.

[120] Protocol on the Application of the Charter to Poland and the United Kingdom, Art 1(1).

[121] G Jones, 'Blair's EU Safeguards "May Not Be Watertight"' *The Telegraph* (26 June 2007).

unsurprisingly, the CFR ceased to have an independent existence in UK law,[122] was no longer relevant to the interpretation of other retained EU law and no longer formed part of UK law as it has not been classified as retained EU law.[123]

Yet, while the CFR is no longer applicable to the UK since its departure from the EU, the potential 'extraterritorial' application of the Charter in the context of international data transfers is still very much on the table. The dominant position seems to be that the Charter applies regardless of territorial criteria[124] – what matters is whether a situation is covered by an EU competence.[125] In international data transfers, said applicability derives from the Commission's powers to act in the context of adequacy decisions.[126] This approach is closely linked to the elevation of data protection to the level of a fundamental right that makes the EU's exercise of jurisdiction 'not just … permissive (discretionary), but also mandatory'.[127] This means that transborder data flows could be regarded as part of the EU institutions' fundamental rights protective duty'.[128] It is now established case law that data subjects whose personal data are transferred to a third country should be afforded a level of protection 'essentially equivalent' to that guaranteed within the EU by 'the GDPR, *read in the light of the Charter*' (emphasis added).[129]

The UK, therefore, finds itself in a second paradoxical situation. While, as an EU Member State, it tried to secure an opt-out from the CFR, currently, as a third country, it cannot escape the extraterritorial application of the CFR in the context of data transfers with the EU. In fact, the external, EU scrutiny of the UK legal framework on the basis of EU fundamental rights will intensify and focus mainly on the UK public authorities' access to personal data in the fields of law enforcement and national security, rather than the general data processing in the commercial context – where, conversely, the UK broadly aligns with the EU requirements.[130]

Thus, paradoxically, since Brexit, national security matters have become the rationale for an increased EU review of the UK legal framework in the context of

[122] EU Withdrawal Act 2018.

[123] See also Data Protection, Privacy and Electronic Communications (Amendments etc) (EU Exit) Regulations 2019 ('DPPEC Regulations'). For a detailed analysis of the UK legal framework, see Savirimuthu and Tzanou (n 96).

[124] See, among others, A Ward, 'Article 51 – Field of Application' in S Peers et al (eds), *The EU Charter of Fundamental Rights: A Commentary* (Hart Publishing, 2014); V Moreno-Lax and C Costello, 'The Extraterritorial Application of the EU Charter of Fundamental Rights: From Territoriality to Facticity, the Effectiveness Model' in Peers et al (idem); E Kassoti, 'The Extraterritorial Applicability of the EU Charter of Fundamental Rights: Some Reflections in the Aftermath of the Front Polisario Saga' (2020) 2 *European Journal of Legal Studies* 117; C Macchi, 'With Trade Comes Responsibility: The External Reach of the EU's Fundamental Rights Obligations' (2020) 11 *Transnational Legal Theory* 409.

[125] Moreno-Lax and Costello (n 124); Kassoti (n 124).

[126] On the basis of Art 16 TFEU and Art 45 GDPR.

[127] C Ryngaert and M Taylor, 'Symposium on the GDPR and International Law: The GDPR as Global Data Protection Regulation?' (2019) *AJIL Unbound* 5, 6.

[128] C Kuner, *Transborder Data Flows and Data Privacy Law* (Oxford University Press, 2013) 129–33.

[129] *Schrems II* (n 108) paras 101, 104–05.

[130] Savirimuthu and Tzanou (n 96).

transborder data transfers and the main venue of the extraterritorial application of EU fundamental rights through potential legal challenges.[131] Regrettably, this leaves UK citizens (and EU citizens residing in the UK) in a 'zero-sum game':[132] since the UK's departure from the EU, there is no longer a fundamental right to data protection in the UK[133] and the potential extraterritorial application of the CFR will be primarily relevant in the fields of law enforcement and national security, but not in general, 'everyday' data processing situations.

C. Persisting Issues of the UK's National Security Regime

The IPA poses two main problems in the context of international data transfers: (i) the bulk metadata surveillance; and (ii) the bulk interception of communications.[134] Both issues have been identified as problematic in the CJEU's case law concerning international data transfers, making the fate of the Commission's adequacy decision on the UK uncertain.

A first problem concerns the 'bulk acquisition of metadata' under the IPA.[135] Such bulk acquisition covers data that is collected by telecommunication operators in the UK directly from the users of telecommunication services. There is no official definition of 'bulk powers' under UK law, but these are understood to include

> the collection and retention of large quantities of data acquired by the Government through various means (ie the powers of bulk interception, bulk acquisition, bulk equipment interference and bulk personal dataset acquisition and which can subsequently be accessed by the authorities.[136]

This could come within the CJEU's definition of 'generalised and indiscriminate' data retention, which the CJEU found to be incompatible with the CFR in *Privacy International* and, therefore, prohibited under EU law even if required by intelligence agencies for national security purposes.[137]

[131] This point was made in European Union Committee, *Beyond Brexit: Policing, Law Enforcement and Security* (HL 2019–21, 250) https://committees.parliament.uk/publications/5298/documents/52902/default/, which noted that 'now that the UK is a third country it will be held to higher standards by the EU in respect of data protection … it will no longer be able to benefit from the national security exemption in the EU Treaties' and 'there is abundant scope for legal challenge on data protection grounds'.

[132] Murray (n 118).

[133] CFR, Art 8. See M Tzanou, *The Fundamental Right to Data Protection: Normative Value in the Context of Counter-Terrorism Surveillance* (Hart Publishing, 2017).

[134] A further problem concerns the sharing of UK intelligence data with the other Five Eyes countries' agencies (USA, Canada, New Zealand, Australia). See European Parliament, 'The adequate protection of personal data by the United Kingdom', European Parliament resolution of 21 May 2021 on the adequate protection of personal data by the United Kingdom (2021/2594(RSP)) P9_TA(2021)0262, para 16(d).

[135] IPA, Part 6, ch 2.

[136] Commission adequacy decision on GDPR (n 1) para 216.

[137] *Privacy International* (n 110) para 81.

The Commission attempted in its adequacy decision to clarify that '"bulk power" does not equate to "mass surveillance"'.[138] More specifically, it drew a distinction between bulk powers which 'incorporate limitations and safeguards designed to ensure that access to data is not given on an indiscriminate or unjustified basis' and 'mass surveillance' undertaken without conditions or safeguards.[139] Pursuant to this, bulk powers in the UK: (i) can only be used 'if a link is established between the technical measure that a national intelligence agency intends to use and the operational objective for which such measure is requested';[140] (ii) are available to intelligence agencies only;[141] and (iii) are subject to a warrant issued by the Secretary of State and approved by a Judicial Commissioner.[142] Further, (iv) in choosing the means to collect intelligence, '[regard] must be given to whether the objective in question can be sought by "less intrusive means"', building on the principles of proportionality and necessity, and prioritising targeted over bulk collection.[143] Nevertheless, as was noted above, this Labour-suggested provision is generally regarded as toothless as its binding effect is dubious.

Yet, notwithstanding that the IPA provides for certain safeguards, including the 'double-lock procedure', the Commission seems to be walking on a tightrope here as the peremptory rule of the CJEU is that bulk data retention is prohibited in general – even when undertaken by intelligence authorities. The CJEU has only allowed, in *La Quadrature du Net*, a general, indiscriminate preventive data retention when Member States are confronted with a 'serious' threat to national security 'which is shown to be genuine and present or foreseeable'.[144] This is permitted for a limited period of time that is strictly necessary and cannot exceed a foreseeable period,[145] and is subject to limitations and strict safeguards that protect effectively the personal data of the persons concerned against the risk of abuse.[146] However, under the IPA, bulk surveillance is not exceptional as permitted in *La Quadrature du Net*; instead, it entails general bulk powers of intelligence agencies, which are not depended on a particular serious threat or time-limited. Furthermore, the limitations on the use of intelligence services' 'bulk powers' are not defined in the law itself – as required by the CJEU[147] – but are instead left to the discretion of the relevant Secretary of State subject to review by the Information Commissioner.[148] It seems, therefore, that the Commission

[138] Commission adequacy decision on GDPR (n 1) para 216.
[139] ibid.
[140] ibid para 217.
[141] ibid.
[142] ibid.
[143] ibid.
[144] *La Quadrature du Net* (n 111) para 136.
[145] ibid paras 137 and 138.
[146] ibid para 138.
[147] See *Schrems II* (n 108).
[148] See European Parliament resolution on the adequate protection of personal data by the UK, para 16(b); D Korff and I Brown, 'The Inadequacy of UK Data Protection Law: Executive Summary' (*Data protection and digital competition blog*, 30 November 2020) 6, www.ianbrown.tech/wp-content/uploads/2020/11/Korff-Brown-Submission-to-EU-re-UK-adequacy-ExecSumm-DK-IB201130.pdf.

has chosen to ignore the CJEU's data retention red lines in its adequacy decision concerning the UK.[149] Nevertheless, we argue that these are not going to magically disappear just because some procedures and limitations exist in the IPA. Legal challenges to the Commission's adequacy decisions on this basis might, therefore, be expected in the future, especially if there is a hardening of the UK's stance on these matters.

The second issue concerns the 'bulk interception' carried out by UK intelligence services.[150] This refers to 'the interception of communications in the course of their transmission sent or received by individuals who are outside the British Islands'.[151] For example, GCHQ's 'Tempora' programme, which was mentioned in the Snowden revelations, intercepts communications in real time through fibre-optic internet backbone cables, and allows for processing of the data at a later stage.[152]

Such bulk interception includes both the content of the communications as well as the metadata, and is capable of capturing EU-originating data, which are considered 'overseas-related communications'.[153] Access to the content of communications, however, constitutes a breach of the 'essence' of the right to privacy, according to established CJEU case law.[154] The CJEU first indicated this in *Digital Rights Ireland*,[155] and went on to hold in *Schrems I* – a case that concerned international data transfers to the USA – that the essence of the fundamental right to privacy was violated because the US mass online surveillance programmes granted access on a generalised basis not only to communications metadata but also to the actual content of electronic communications.[156] This pronouncement of the Court sets out another red line the Commission seemed to ignore in its UK adequacy decision, focusing instead on the different safeguards applicable to bulk interception.[157]

IV. Conclusion

As George Eliot stated, 'among all forms of mistake, prophecy is the most gratuitous'.[158] Nevertheless, two main conclusions arise from the study of the UK's

[149] Tzanou and Karyda (n 115). See also EDPB, 'Adequacy Referential', WP 254 rev. 01, https://ec.europa.eu/newsroom/Article29/item-detail.cfm?item_id=614108.
[150] IPA, s 136.
[151] Commission adequacy decision on GDPR (n 1) para 219.
[152] See European Parliament resolution on the adequate protection of personal data by the UK, para 12.
[153] ibid.
[154] Case C-362/14 *Maximillian Schrems v Data Protection Commissioner* [2015] ECLI:EU:C:2015:650 (*Schrems I*) para 94.
[155] *Digital Rights Ireland* (n 13).
[156] *Schrems I* (n 154) para 94.
[157] See Commission adequacy decision on GDPR (n 1) para 218ff.
[158] G Eliot, *Middlemarch* (1872) Part 1, ch 10.

political landscape in the context of national security, and law enforcement more broadly. First, bulk surveillance powers are here to stay. They are long rooted in the UK's socio-political environment, they reflect a basic consensus between the two main political parties and, thus, they appear irreversible.

Second, the issues related to these powers highlighted in the previous section are the UK's main vulnerabilities in the context of its data protection relations with the EU post-Brexit. Bulk powers and access to the content of intercepted communications constitute red lines for the CJEU and, thus, make the Commission's UK adequacy decision – which has not been yet scrutinised by the CJEU – a ticking time bomb.[159] They also demonstrate that the Commission opted for a proceduralised approach to UK bulk surveillance that fails to pay due attention to substantive requirements, including several CJEU's prohibitive rules.[160] Admittedly, the UK is no longer directly subject to the CJEU's jurisprudence, falling instead under the more permissive case law of the ECtHR, which has found bulk surveillance to comply with the ECHR if it is subject to specific conditions and safeguards.[161]

Nonetheless, it is safe to say that these problems are not going to disappear any time soon, making the EU–UK data privacy space even more uncertain – a characteristic of the EU–UK post-Brexit relations in general.

[159] See also Celeste (n 116) 214.
[160] See Tzanou and Karyda (n 115).
[161] See ECtHR (Grand Chamber) *Big Brother Watch et al* (n 101), para 323; Tzanou and Karyda (n 115) and discussion therein.

6

'Serious and Systemic'? Live Facial Recognition Technology in the UK and its Impact on Adequacy

ALLISON M HOLMES

I. Introduction

Following the UK's withdrawal from the EU, data protection and data sharing by and between law enforcement authorities has taken on a new importance. Continued information sharing between UK and EU authorities post-Brexit is contingent on maintaining a high level of personal data protection and the effective protection of fundamental rights. However, the powers of law enforcement can be at odds with these rights, notably the right to private life, particularly in the adoption of novel technologies that expand the scope of police powers of surveillance. This chapter examines one such technology – namely live facial recognition (LFR), utilised by law enforcement authorities in publicly accessible spaces – and how it impacts on these fundamental rights in a manner that puts these information-sharing arrangements at risk.

In assessing the impact of LFR on information-sharing arrangements post-Brexit, it is necessary to examine the adequacy decision that underpins law enforcement cooperation in this area.[1] In order to enable information sharing, the UK must ensure that it provides an adequate level of protection for personal data, in line with Article 36(3) of Directive (EU) 2016/680, the Law Enforcement Directive (LED).[2] This chapter argues that the use of LFR by the police in England

[1] Commission Implementing Decision of 26 June 2021 pursuant to Directive (EU) 2016/680 of the European Parliament and of the Council on the adequate protection of personal data be the United Kingdom (LED adequacy decision) C(2021) 4801 final.

[2] Directive (EU) 2016/680 of the European Parliament and of the Council of 27 April 2016 on the protection of natural persons with regard to the processing of personal data by competent authorities for the purposes of the prevention, investigation, detection or prosecution of criminal offences or the execution of criminal penalties, and on the free movement of such data, and repealing Council Framework Decision 2008/977/JHA (LED Directive) [2016] OJ L119/89.

and Wales represents a clear divergence from the EU standards governing the use of personal data.[3] This is indicative of a wider trend of divergence between EU and UK law that represents a threat to the overall adequacy arrangements governing data sharing between the EU and the UK. In order to analyse the divergences between the EU and the UK exposed by LFR, this chapter offers an assessment of the extant legal bases governing the use of this technology and current proposals to amend the powers of law enforcement in the UK in respect of LFR. In undertaking this analysis, the chapter examines the deficiencies in the legal framework governing LFR that negatively impact the protection provided to personal data and casts doubt on the finding that the UK's use of LFR provides protection that is 'essentially equivalent' to that of the EU.[4]

II. The Adequacy Decision

Following the referendum on the UK's EU membership on 23 June 2016 and during the subsequent negotiations surrounding the future of the EU–UK relationship, the British government emphasised the need to maintain stability and ensure 'unhindered' and 'uninterrupted' data flows between the UK and the EU post-Brexit.[5] During the Brexit negotiations, law enforcement agencies, government bodies and others repeatedly emphasised that the UK could face both economic and social isolation in circumstances where authorities could not share or receive law enforcement data on a cross-border basis. To that end, the final Trade and Cooperation Agreement governing the future relationship between the EU and UK specifically legislates for continued data sharing post-Brexit.

In particular, Part Three of the Agreement enables high-level data sharing and access to EU law enforcement systems and agencies.[6] A key facilitator of this information sharing is the LED, which stipulates transfer provisions for the

[3] The focus of this chapter will be on the use of LFR in England and Wales. The criminal justice systems of Scotland and Northern Ireland are devolved to the Scottish Parliament and Northern Ireland Assembly respectively. The technology has not been introduced in Scotland following a report of the Scottish Parliament, which noted that, given the potential discriminatory nature of this technology, 'there would be no justifiable basis for Police Scotland to invest in this technology'. See Justice Sub-Committee on Policing [Scotland], *Facial Recognition: How Policing in Scotland Makes Use of This Technology* (SP 2020-5, Paper 678). Similarly, as of the time of writing, there is no reported use of the technology in Northern Ireland.

[4] As confirmed and advanced in Case C-362/14 *Maximillian Schrems v Data Protection Commissioner* ECLI:EU:C:2015:650; Opinion 1/15 *Draft agreement between Canada and the European Union – Transfer of Passenger Name Record data from the European Union to Canada* ECLI:EU:C:2017:592; Case C-311/18 *Data Protection Commissioner v Facebook Ireland and Maximillian Schrems* ECLI:EU:C:2020:559.

[5] House of Lords Select Committee on the European Union; EU Home Affairs Sub Committee; Oral evidence: Data Protection Package; Matt Hancock, 1 February 2017.

[6] Trade and Cooperation Agreement between the European Union and the European Atomic Energy Community, of the one part, and the United Kingdom of Great Britain and Northern Ireland, of the other part (TCA) [2021] OJ L149/10, Part 3.

sharing of personal data between relevant law enforcement authorities.[7] The Directive provides data protection safeguards by explicitly tying data transfer provisions to fundamental rights considerations.[8] In the UK, these provisions are given domestic effect within Part 3 of the Data Protection Act 2018 (DPA).

For information sharing between the EU and the UK to be permitted under the LED, there are several distinct mechanisms that may be used, namely adequacy decisions, appropriate safeguards or derogations to specific situations.[9] While initially, following the UK's withdrawal, then Minister of State for Digital and Culture Matt Hancock would not be drawn on what mechanism would be used to ensure these transfers, subsequent agreements have provided a clear indication that adequacy decisions were the preferred mechanism for the continued sharing of data.[10] Adequacy decisions have a range of benefits. They represent the highest standard of protection for onward transfers of data guaranteed by any of the data sharing mechanisms provided for within the data protection instruments. This, in turn, means that fundamental rights are better protected. Further, they represent a positive development in terms of operational capabilities for law enforcement authorities because an adequacy decision removes the need for specific authorisation of transfers of personal data, resulting in an efficient mechanism for data sharing between relevant bodies.

In order for a third country to be considered as providing an adequate level of protection for personal data, there must be 'a level of protection of fundamental rights and freedoms … *essentially equivalent* to that guaranteed within the European Union'.[11] The criteria considered in assessing adequacy include consideration of the rule of law, respect for human rights and fundamental freedoms, the relevant legal framework, protection of the rights of data subjects, and mechanisms for ensuring effective remedies.[12] Similarly, independent supervisory authorities who ensure compliance with the data protection rules and possess adequate enforcement powers are required.[13] The final criteria for consideration are the international commitments of the third country and their participation in legally binding conventions or instruments, particularly those which relate to data protection.[14]

These elements were considered in the evaluation of the UK as a third country for the purposes of an adequacy decision under the LED. The close alignment between UK and EU data protection law was highlighted, with the structure and main components of the UK legal framework under Part 3 of the DPA governing

[7] LED Directive (n 2).
[8] ibid Art 35(3) and Recital 67.
[9] ibid Arts 36–38.
[10] Withdrawal Agreement 2019, Art 71.
[11] Case C-311/18 *Schrems* (n 4) [96].
[12] LED Directive (n 2) Art 36(2)(a).
[13] ibid Art 36(2)(b).
[14] ibid Art 36(2)(c).

law enforcement processing given considerable weight in the decision to award adequacy.[15] The adequacy decision also noted the extant oversight and redress mechanisms that provide remedies for data subjects whose rights might be impacted.[16] Notably, the Decision identifies the importance of the Information Commissioner and the Commissioner for the Retention and Use of Biometric Material as independent oversight mechanisms, with specific competencies in the area of law enforcement data processing.[17] Finally, the evaluation of the UK domestic regime considered the compliance with international instruments, and in particular the adherence to the European Convention on Human Rights (ECHR), the Council of Europe Data Protection Convention (Convention 108) and the subsequent amendments modernising this Convention (Convention 108+).[18] The compliance with the ECHR in particular is highly important to the finding of adequacy, and the need for continued adherence to this instrument was stressed by the European Commission (the Commission).[19]

Following this evaluation of the UK framework, two adequacy decisions were adopted on the 28 June 2021 – for the EU General Data Protection Regulation (GDPR) and LED respectively. Both decisions include additional safeguards to ensure continued compliance by the UK with the data protection obligations under the decisions. Under Article 3 LED, the Commission is obliged to monitor the legal framework underpinning the decision, 'including the conditions under which onward transfers are carried out and individual rights are exercised, with a view to assessing whether the United Kingdom continues to ensure an adequate level of protection within the meaning of Article 1'. This monitoring includes an obligation by Member States and the Commission to inform one another if there are indications that interferences with personal data by public authorities in the UK go beyond what is strictly necessary or lack effective legal protection.[20] If adequate protection is no longer ensured, the adequacy decision may be suspended, amended or repealed.[21] In particular, regard has to be had to the effectiveness of the exercise of individual rights in the areas covered by the adequacy decision, as well as the operation and oversight of relevant bodies. As such, while the current data protection framework within the UK meets the requirements for adequacy, developments in the data protection regime that alter these considerations concerning fundamental rights and oversight may impact on that finding.

[15] LED adequacy decision (n 1) Recitals 20–54.
[16] ibid Recital 158.
[17] ibid Recitals 93–108.
[18] ibid Recital 20; see also the European Convention on Human Rights and Convention for the protection of individuals with regard to the processing of personal data (Convention 108/108+).
[19] LED adequacy decision (n 1) Recitals 269, 277.
[20] ibid Art 3(2)–(3).
[21] ibid Art 3(4).

III. Case Study: Live Facial Recognition

It is within this context that the case study of live facial recognition technologies in public spaces offers a useful reference point to see how divergences in policies concerning the protection of personal data in the law enforcement sphere could impact on the finding of adequacy. In evaluating the impact of LFR, the legal framework that governs the use of these powers, the role of watchlists and the oversight arrangements must be considered against the potential impact on individuals' rights. Live facial recognition involves several distinct data processing operations. Members of the public are scanned as they pass fixed and mobile camera points. This can occur both on private property and within public spaces, the latter of which is the subject of analysis in this chapter. The images collected on the basis of this scan are then processed by a facial recognition algorithm, which creates a biometric template.[22] This template is compared to a database created from similarly processed images, which is known in the deployment as a 'watchlist'. If the algorithm detects a match, an alert is sent to the system and a decision is subsequently made on whether to intervene.

Live facial recognition necessarily engages data protection considerations. Fundamentally, it is concerned with the processing of biometric data. Biometric data is defined as 'personal data resulting from specific technical processing relating to the physical, psychological or behavioural characteristics of a natural person, *which allow or confirm the unique identification* of that natural person, such as facial images and dactyloscopic data' (emphasis added).[23] In creating biometric templates utilised for identifying individuals on the set 'watchlist', LFR necessarily satisfies these criteria. The classification of this information as biometric data is significant as the relevant data protection instruments identify biometric data as 'special category data', recognising that the processing of this category of data poses a particular risk to the rights and freedoms of natural persons.[24] Individuals' rights to both data protection and private life are implicated by the processing of this data.[25]

The potential impact on fundamental rights occasioned by the use of this data is even more significant when the use of LFR occurs in public spaces. Public spaces are broadly defined. The UK Information Commissioner's Office (ICO) has stated that in this context public spaces generally include spaces outside of a domestic setting, whether publicly or privately owned.[26] This encompasses areas open to

[22] P Fussey, B Davies and M Innes, '"Assisted" Facial Recognition and the Reinvention of Suspicion and Discretion in Digital Policing' (2020) 61(2) *British Journal of Criminology* 325, 326.

[23] See TCA (n 6) Art 523(d); LED Directive (n 2) Art 3(13).

[24] LED Directive (n 2) Recitals 51–52 and Art 10.

[25] Information Commissioner's Opinion, 'The Use of Live Facial Recognition Technology in Public Places' (ICO, 18 June 2021).

[26] ibid 12.

the public such as public squares, transport or buildings, but it can also extend to 'privately owned premises such as shops, offices, and leisure venues'.[27] Applying this technology to public spaces extends it beyond targeted use against individuals of interest to application to the wider public. Broad and indiscriminate use in public spaces has the potential to result in collateral intrusion of the rights of individuals whose biometric data is processed by the technology in a manner that is disproportionate to the aims sought.

Given the broad interference with individual rights that can result from the use of LFR in public spaces, it is necessary to evaluate whether it meets the criteria required for that interference to be justified. To that end, the use of the technology must be in accordance with law, strictly necessary and proportionate to the aims that are sought to be achieved.[28] Such an assessment is also important to determine the impact the use of this technology might have on the continued adequacy arrangement between the UK and the EU, as a failure to guarantee fundamental rights when data is processed in this manner is contrary to the requirements of the adequacy decision.

A. Legal Framework

For the use of LFR to amount to a justified interference, it must be in accordance with law. In England and Wales, there is no explicit statutory authority for the use of LFR. Rather, police powers in this area rely on common law, statute and delegated legislation to provide legal underpinnings for the use of the technology. In England and Wales, the powers of the police derive from common law and are not subject to exhaustive definition. They include 'all steps which appear to him necessary for keeping the peace, for preventing crime, or for protecting property from criminal damage … and they would further include the duty to detect crime and to bring an offender to justice'.[29] The common law power of the police can be extended to proactive powers provided that they enable the prevention and detection of crime. It has been further recognised that the common law powers of the police extend to obtaining and storing information for policing purposes.[30] However, relying on common law powers as the legal basis for LFR requires a broad interpretation that fails to account for the sensitive nature of the data involved and the potential intrusive nature of the technology. To ensure that the use of this technology meets the necessary quality of law, an explicit statutory provision would provide for a stronger basis.

[27] G Gonzalez Fuster and MA Nadolna Peeters, 'Person Identification, Human Rights and Ethical Principles: Rethinking Biometrics in the Era of Artificial Intelligence' (European Parliament, 2021) 10; UNESCO similarly defines a public space as 'an area or place that is open and accessible to all peoples'. L Montag et al, 'The Rise and Rise of Biometric Mass Surveillance in the EU' (EDRi, 7 July 2021) 8.

[28] ECHR, Art 8(2).

[29] *Rice v Connolly* [1966] 2 QB 414 [419].

[30] *Catt v Commissioner of Police of the Metropolis* [2015] UKSC 9 [7].

However, there remains no direct statutory authority for the use of LFR. Rather, existing instruments contain provisions that are interpreted in a manner that is then applied to the technology. Thus, the use of LFR is governed by provisions within the DPA, the Protection of Freedoms Act 2012 and the related Code of Practice provided for by that statute.[31]

Part three of the DPA provides authority for the processing of personal data for law enforcement purposes.[32] Any authority that processes sensitive data under this Act is required to ensure that the data is processed in a lawful and fair manner.[33] Such processing will only be lawful where either consent has been obtained for the processing or the processing is strictly necessary for law enforcement purposes.[34] Both of these requirements for processing further call for the controller to have an appropriate policy document in place at the time of processing.[35]

It is unlikely that the consent of the data subject will be an acceptable lawful basis for the processing of data because of the manner in which LFR is deployed in public spaces. Individuals may not be on advance notice of the areas in which LFR will be in operation at a particular time so will not be able to effectively exercise their freedom to choose whether to engage with such monitoring. Therefore, law enforcement authorities must meet the requirement that the processing is 'strictly necessary' for a set purpose as defined within the DPA.[36]

Strict necessity requires that the processing is 'necessary for the exercise of a function conferred on a person by an enactment or rule of law, and is necessary for reasons of substantial public interest'.[37] In the context of LFR, this further requires that alternatives to LFR are considered prior to the deployment of this technology.[38] It is important to note that in evaluating the strict necessity of the measure, the assessment should not be generalised, but one of direct personal evaluation.[39] Such a threshold is unlikely to be met when utilising LFR in public spaces.

In addition to provisions within the DPA that can apply to the area of LFR, the Protection of Freedoms Act 2012 provides for the regulation of the use of surveillance cameras. While not falling within the traditional definition of a surveillance camera, section 29(6)(d) of that Act can be interpreted to encompass

[31] Protection of Freedoms Act 2012, s 31(3); Surveillance Camera Code of Practice (3 March 2022).

[32] Law enforcement purposes are defined under the Data Protection Act 2018 (DPA), s 31 as: 'The purposes of the prevention, investigation, detection or prosecution of criminal offences or the execution of criminal penalties, including the safeguarding against and the prevention of threats to public security.'

[33] ibid s 35.

[34] ibid ss 35(4)(a) and 35(5)(a).

[35] ibid ss 35(4)(b), 35(5)(c) and 42.

[36] ibid Sch 8. Relevant set purposes within the DPA are defined as statutory purposes, the administration of justice and legal claims.

[37] ibid.

[38] ICO, 'The Use of Live Facial Recognition Technology by Law Enforcement in Public Places' (ICO, 31 October 2019) 14.

[39] *R (El Gizouli) v Secretary of State for the Home Department* [2020] 2 UKSC 10 [44].

LFR technology,[40] making it subject to the Surveillance Camera Code of Practice. Relevant authorities, including the chief officer of a police force in England and Wales,[41] must have regard to the Code and to any functions to which it relates. Also provided for within this instrument is the appointment of a Surveillance Camera Commissioner by the Secretary of State to ensure public confidence in surveillance systems by encouraging compliance with the Code, reviewing its operation, and proposing changes and advice concerning the Code where needed.[42] The role of the Surveillance Camera Commissioner has now been incorporated into the wider role of the Biometrics and Surveillance Camera Commissioner effective as of February 2022.

The Surveillance Camera Code of Practice is the only instrument within the legal framework of England and Wales that explicitly addresses the use of LFR, albeit in a manner that carries little legal effect. Entering into effect in February 2022, the Code sets out guidance for the use of these systems by public authorities. Any use of facial recognition systems under the Code needs to be justified and proportionate to the purpose sought to be achieved.[43] Notably, the Code offers no prescriptive requirements for how to satisfy the requirements, nor any specific operational, technical or competency measures that must be followed. The Code requires that authorities 'have regard' to this statutory guidance, meaning that it should be taken into account, and departures from the Code must be justified.[44] However, failures to act in accordance with the code do not merit liability in either criminal or civil proceedings. Therefore, as a legal instrument, it lacks the necessary rigour to ensure that the standards it sets are complied with by the relevant authorities.

In addition to the statutory guidance, LFR is also governed by the internal policies of individual police forces. These documents set out the legal authority for the use of LFR within that select police force. The police force similarly provides procedural guidance for the deployment of the LFR technology. For example, guidance may set the rank of the authorising officer for each deployment, how they should address the legality, necessity and proportionality of the deployment, and ultimately how this is balanced with individual rights considerations.[45] However, this guidance is advisory and bears no sanctions for failure to adhere to these set policies. Allowing the individual forces to set their own practices in

[40] The act defines 'surveillance camera systems as: (a) closed circuit television or automatic number plate recognition systems; (b) any other systems for recording or viewing visual images for surveillance purposes; (c) any system for storing, receiving, transmitting, processing or checking images or information obtained by systems falling within para (a) or (b); or (d) any other system associated with, or otherwise connected with, systems falling within para (a) (b) or (c).

[41] Protection of Freedoms Act 2012, s 33(5)(j).

[42] ibid s 34.

[43] Surveillance Camera Code of Practice, para 2.4.

[44] ibid para 8.

[45] Metropolitan Police Service, 'MPS LFR Policy Document', www.met.police.uk/SysSiteAssets/media/downloads/force-content/met/advice/lfr/policy-documents/lfr-policy-document.pdf.

this area can lead to inconsistent approaches being adopted by the various police constabularies, with some taking a more constrained approach and others using the technology more broadly.

The piecemeal governing framework for LFR was challenged in the case of *Bridges v Chief Constable of South Wales Police*, wherein whether the provisions were 'in accordance with law' was tested.[46] In holding that the legal framework was insufficient, the Court of Appeal emphasised the level of discretion left to individual police officers to determine both where the technology was deployed and who was on the relevant watchlists.[47] The Court held that 'the current policies do not sufficiently set out the terms on which discretionary powers can be exercised by the police and for that reason do not have the necessary quality of law'.[48] However, the Court's decision did not require such policies to be set out in statute. Rather, the Court accepted that internal policy documents within the police could satisfy the requirements for the use to be 'in accordance with law' so long as it sufficiently limited the discretion of individual officers.

This interpretation was welcomed by the government, which noted that a legal framework of existing legislation and published local police policies 'allows the police to exploit new technologies, including biometric identification and overt surveillance, for a policing purpose and where necessary and proportionate'.[49] However, the interpretation misrepresents the decision of the court and fails to recognise that the existence of the powers does not in itself render the exercise of those powers lawful. Nor does the government's interpretation offer an adequate explanation for what those internal policies should entail. In an attempt to proscribe unified guidance for internal force policy following the case of *Bridges*, the College of Police issued an Authorised Professional Practice (APP) for the use of LFR.[50] This guidance sets out the general approach to be taken by each police force. However, it is left to the discretion of the individual police forces to implement this in practice.[51] Notably, this guidance is only advisory and offers no clear lines of accountability where the guidance is not followed for satisfactory recourse mechanisms for individuals who may be impacted by the use of this technology.

This soft law fails to provide an adequate legal basis in domestic law to ensure the necessary requirements of the European Court of Human Rights (ECtHR) that the measure be 'in accordance with law'. While states are generally subject to a wide margin of appreciation when the question concerns interferences with

[46] *R (Bridges) v Chief Constable of South Wales Police* [2020] EWCA Civ 1058.
[47] ibid [91]–[92].
[48] ibid [94].
[49] HL Deb 4 November 2021, cols 1391–408.
[50] College of Policing, 'APP: Live Facial Recognition' (17 March 2022) www.app.college.police.uk/app-content/live-facial-recognition/.
[51] ibid.

qualified rights that are a result of the investigation, detection and prevention of crime, they must still ensure that the interferences with fundamental rights occasioned by the use of the technology can be justified. This requires that the measure be compatible with the rule of law, as evidenced by the accessibility and foreseeability of the provisions.[52] The provisions should not be so broad as to confer a wide discretion dependent upon the will of the individuals who apply it;[53] the open and discretionary nature of the APP guidelines do not confer the general quality of law that ECtHR precedent requires. Similarly to the Court of Appeal in *Bridges*, the ECtHR takes a relativist approach, noting the need to treat the surveillance differently depending on the impact on individuals.[54] In so doing, the ECtHR has held that due regard should be had to 'the possibility of rapid technological advances in this domain in particularly concerning technology for facial recognition and facial mapping'.[55] Particular attention must be paid to the interference with rights 'where the powers vested in the state are obscure, creating a risk of arbitrariness where the technology available is continually becoming more sophisticated'.[56]

In order to evaluate whether the UK is diverging from the EU standards in its data protection policies, it is useful to contrast the use of LFR in the UK with the proposed provisions of the EU Regulation of the European Parliament and of the Council Laying Down Harmonised Rules on Artificial Intelligence (the AI Act).[57] The proposed Act will be *lex specialis* to the GDPR and the LED, ensuring the provisions of the LED governing the processing of biometric data remain relevant in this area. However, the AI Act goes beyond the LED and provides specifically for the use of live facial recognition technologies within public spaces. The Act more precisely defines the areas in which the use of LFR in publicly accessible spaces is permitted than the internal policy documents and general guidance utilised in England and Wales. The approach of the UK government, relying on existing policy that does not adequately consider the technology, is in contrast to the EU's proposed AI Act. Notably, at EU level, policy requires that Member States implement national legislation concerning the use of real-time biometric technologies by law enforcement in publicly accessible spaces prior to its use.[58] The differing policy concerning legislation surrounding the police use of novel technologies is an element of wider diverging approaches to individuals' personal data between the EU and the UK.

[52] *Sunday Times v United Kingdom* App no 6538/74 (ECtHR, 26 April 1979) [48]–[50]; *Malone v United Kingdom* App no 8691/79 (ECtHR, 2 August 1984) [67].

[53] *Re Gallagher* [2019] UKSC 3 [17].

[54] *RE v United Kingdom* App no 62498/11 (ECtHR, 27 October 2015) [17].

[55] *Gaughran v United Kingdom* App no 45245/15 (ECtHR, 13 June 2020) [80].

[56] ibid [86].

[57] Proposal for a Regulation of the European Parliament and of the Council Laying down harmonised rules on artificial intelligence (Artificial Intelligence Act) (21 April 2021) COM (2021) 206 final.

[58] ibid Art 5(4).

B. Use of Watchlists

Further divergences are evident in the policies concerning the watchlists utilised in LFR deployments. Watchlists consist of biometric templates of individuals of interest, identified with reference to a particular deployment of LFR. Images of the public are compared against these watchlists to alert the police when a match is made. As these images and their processing are 'sensitive', it must only be done where 'strictly necessary'.[59] However, there remains little legal certainty around the creation of these watchlists, with the choice for the images for each deployment left to the discretion of the individual police forces.

This concern becomes particularly salient when the guidance from the College of Policing on the use of LFR is examined. While this guidance notes that individual force policy documents should detail their criteria for developing a watchlist, the APP sets out overarching advice regarding the creation of watchlists. Notably, this guidance provides a list of individuals who may be included in the LFR watchlist. The criteria for inclusion are: (i) those wanted by the courts; (ii) those suspected of having committed an offence, or where there are reasonable grounds to suspect an individual might commit an offence; (iii) those subject to bail conditions or other legal restrictions; (iv) missing persons deemed at risk of harm; (v) those presenting a risk of harm to themselves or others; and (vi) a victim or witness to an offence, or a close associate of an individual within any of the set criteria.[60]

The criteria within the guidance are broadly construed, and each criterion presents a unique set of issues that mean they are likely to fall foul of the requirements of necessity and proportionality in assessing their impact on fundamental rights. Several of the criteria pertain to those individuals who have committed or are suspected of committing a criminal offence. However, there is no threshold set for the seriousness of the offence for which the individual is suspected; both those who have committed minor summary offences and those who have committed serious crimes can be caught by the same provision. An appropriate evaluation of the proportionality of including an individual on a watchlist should have regard to the need to balance the individual's rights against the need of the police to prevent, investigate and detect crime. The use of these powers against individuals who are suspected of only low-level offences is likely to be disproportionate to the objective sought to be achieved.

The development of the watchlists further calls into question the necessity and proportionality when the wider criteria for inclusion are considered. Notably, the guidance covers individuals who are not suspected of any criminal offence. Given the impact on individuals' rights to private life and data protection occasioned by the use of the technology, there needs to be a strong justification case made for including these individuals on the watchlist. However, the guidance fails to provide

[59] DPA, s 35(5).

[60] College of Policing, 'APP: Live Facial Recognition' (n 50) para 2.5.

this justification or clarity on the approach that should be taken to ensure the interference is permissible. For instance, individuals who are classed as presenting a risk of harm to themselves or others are also eligible for inclusion. This criterion is vague and open to wide interpretation. Here, harm is broadly defined, including a risk of harm in relation to a person's welfare or financial harm. The level of harm required is assessed as medium risk, meaning that the harm is likely, but not serious.[61] The guidance on applying this criterion lacks clarity, setting the threshold as 'likely', but then subsequently noting that finding their location is 'critical to ensure their safety'.[62] Such contradictory language adds to the ambiguity of these provisions.

These issues are similarly evident in the criterion that permits the inclusion of victims, witnesses and/or those who are close associates on the watchlists. The application of the technology to these individuals is likely to be a disproportionate interference with the rights of those individuals. While the guidance offers suggestions as to how the proportionality of the inclusion of these individuals could be demonstrated, this set of suggestions fails to offer an adequate safeguard for the rights of those individuals. As these individuals are not the subject of investigations, any interference with their rights will only be proportionate in exceptional circumstances. The guidance does not offer a clear framework for how this threshold would be met. Nor does the guidance as a whole reflect the data protection requirements governing the 'sensitive' data that is used in LFR. Any inclusion on the watchlist, due to the sensitive nature of the data involved, requires that the processing be 'strictly necessary'; however, this requirement is not mentioned within the guidance.

Within the approach to the watchlists, there is a clear divergence from EU policy. At EU level, three specific uses are permitted in the creation of watchlists: targeted searches for specific potential victims of crime; prevention of specific, substantial and imminent threat to life or physical safety of natural persons or a terrorist attack; and detection, localisation, identification or prosecution of a perpetrator or suspect of a crime with a maximum sentence of at least three years.[63] This final criterion sets out 32 categories of offences that would qualify.[64]

[61] College of Policing, 'APP: Missing Persons' (24 March 2022) www.college.police.uk/app/major-investigation-and-public-protection/missing-persons/missing-persons.

[62] College of Policing, 'Watchlists' (21 March 2022) www.college.police.uk/app/live-facial-recognition/watchlist.

[63] AI Act (n 57) Art 5(1)(d).

[64] ibid Art 5(1)(d)(iii). These offences are set out in the Council Framework Decision 2002/584/JHA of 13 June 2002 on the European Arrest warrant and the surrender procedures between Member States [2002] OJ L190/1, Art 2(2). These categories of offences include: participation in a criminal organisation; terrorism; human trafficking; child sexual exploitation; illicit trafficking in narcotics; illicit trafficking in weapons; corruption; fraud; laundering of the proceeds of crime; counterfeiting currency; computer-related crime; environmental crime; facilitation of unauthorised entry and residence; murder or GBH; illicit trade in human organs; kidnapping and hostage-taking; racism and

Setting out distinct circumstances in which the powers can be used follows the reasoning in extant European case law that the protection of the fundamental right to respect for private life and the protection of personal data should only be interfered with insofar as is strictly necessary.[65] Such a qualification enables the principle of proportionality to be given due regard.

The categories of crime set out in the AI Act relate solely to 'serious crime'. This follows the approach of the ECtHR and CJEU, wherein a relevant factor in assessing the justification for the surveillance is the seriousness of the crime involved. A more serious crime will permit a more serious interference with the right to private life guaranteed under Article 8 ECHR.[66] As such, the watchlist used for deployments under the AI Act represents a more proportionate measure. This offers an important safeguard for fundamental rights. In contrast, the guidance set out by the College of Policing imposes no qualification that the offence must be a serious offence, nor is it limited to suspects and perpetrators. With the lack of relevant safeguards and the blanket and indiscriminate processing that results following the use of the technology, it is unlikely that such a broad approach would meet the requirements of strict necessity and proportionality under EU law, demonstrating an interference with fundamental rights in the processing of this personal data.

C. Oversight Arrangements

Within the finding of adequacy, a key determinant was the oversight and redress mechanisms for infringements of data subjects' rights. In finding the UK to be essentially equivalent to the EU in this regard, the adequacy decision emphasised the operational and functional independence of both the Information Commissioner and the Biometrics Commissioner.[67] The ICO is the primary oversight body concerning biometric data and therefore regulates the compliance with the DPA, which is engaged in the use of LFR.[68] The powers of the ICO encompass both the issuing of advice and enforcement notices for breaches of data protection

xenophobia; swindling; racketeering and extortion; counterfeiting and piracy of products; forgery; illicit trafficking in hormonal substances; illicit trafficking in nuclear materials; trafficking in stolen vehicles; rape; arson; crimes under the jurisdiction of the ICC; unlawful seizure of vessels; sabotage.

[65] Joined Cases C-203/15 and C-698/15 *Tele 2 v Post-och telestyrelsen* [2016] ECLI 970 para 96; see also judgments of 16 December 2008, C-73/07 *Tietosuojavaltuutettu vSatakunnan Markkinapörssi and Satamedia* [2008] ECLI 727 [56]; C-92/09 and 93/09 *Volker und Markus Schecke and Eifert* [2010] ECLI 662 [77]; C-362/14 *Maximilian Schrems v Data Protection Commissioner* [2015] ECLI 650 [92]–[96]; C-293/13 and C-594-12 *Digital Rights Ireland v Minister for Communication & Ors* [2014] ECLI 238 [52].

[66] See C-207/16 *Ministerio Fiscal* ECLI:EU:C:2018:788.

[67] LED adequacy decision (n 1) Recitals 93–99 and 50.

[68] DPA, s 116 and Sch 13 provides that the Information Commissioner must monitor and enforce these provisions.

provisions. In the context of LFR, the ICO has largely confined itself to an advisory capacity. In line with its statutory powers, the ICO has issued an opinion concerning the protection of personal data in the context of the use of LFR by law enforcement.[69] The purpose of this opinion is to provide guidance for law enforcement through all stages of the data processing involved in the use of LFR, but it is not a binding legal framework for the use of these powers. The ICO is empowered to issue enforcement notices for data protection breaches occasioned by the use of the technology.[70] However, such powers have yet to be exercised in this law enforcement context and it remains unclear whether these powers could extend to wider fundamental rights breaches beyond data protection occasioned by the used of the technology.

In addition to the data protection oversight offered by the ICO, the use of LFR also engages the role of the Biometrics and Surveillance Camera Commissioner. The Commissioner is independent of the government and issues reports on their functions – namely, for the purposes herein, on compliance with the Surveillance Camera Code of Practice and how the code is working.[71] However, the Commissioner has no enforcement or inspection powers regarding surveillance camera systems. As the updated Code of Practice classes LFR as a surveillance camera system, this means that the Commissioner has no enforceable oversight role with regard to this technology. The Commissioner is only able to provide advice and guidance, but no redress, for individuals impacted by the deployment of this technology.[72] This creates a lacuna in the oversight mechanisms for individuals whose rights may be impacted in a manner that effectively places them outside both the ICO and the Biometric Commissioner's remit.

For these individuals, oversight is left to the individual police forces who utilise the technology. The College of Policing guidance notes that

> Chief officers must establish their own internal governance arrangements for LFR. This should involve chief officer and PCC (or equivalent) oversight, with separation from operational decisions and decision makers where possible, to ensure sufficient independence and rigour when reviewing a force's use of LFR.[73]

However, there is no requirement within this guidance for either ex ante or ex post review of the technology by a body independent of the police. Such a lack of independent oversight is counter to the principles within the adequacy decision.[74]

Independent oversight is crucial in determining whether the use of the technology goes beyond that which is 'strictly necessary'. The courts will take several factors into account, including the existence of effective safeguards and guarantees against abuse. Such an assessment will examine the existence of judicial and/or

[69] ICO (n 38); DPA, s 116(2) read in conjunction with Sch 13(2)(d).
[70] DPA, s 149(2)(c).
[71] Protection of Freedoms Act 2012, ss 34–35.
[72] ibid s 34.
[73] College of Policing, 'APP: Live Facial Recognition' (n 50) 3.2.4.
[74] LED adequacy decision (n 1) 2.5.

independent scrutiny, and the affected parties' rights to remedy and redress for alleged violations of their rights. It is this independent review that ensures that these powers are not abused and provides public trust in the system. In the absence of such a check on the powers of authorised bodies, questions will arise over the validity and proportionality of their actions.

A lack of independent oversight of surveillance measures would be at odds with the extant jurisprudence on surveillance technologies. Independent scrutiny is crucial to ensure that the exercise of these powers comports with the rule of law and guarantee that those in power can be held accountable for their actions. It is worth noting that the courts have held that the requirement for effective oversight can be met absent formal judicial control. The lack of judicial oversight is not, in itself, sufficient to satisfy a finding that an oversight regime is inadequate.[75] However, the mechanism must meet the standards of independent oversight. The court must be assured that the oversight body is independent of both the government and the interested parties.[76] The use of internal scrutiny mechanisms within the relevant police force is unlikely to satisfy these criteria.

With regard to oversight, the AI Act offers a stricter regime, more in line with relevant fundamental rights standards. The AI Act aims to introduce a requirement that any real-time use of the technology by law enforcement authorities in publicly accessible spaces receive prior authorisation 'by a judicial authority or by an independent administrative authority of the Member State'.[77] By requiring ex ante oversight, the EU instrument proposes stronger safeguards than those set out in the UK guidance and is more likely to meet the requirements of necessity and proportionality.

D. The Public–Private Divide

Whilst the current LFR regime offers an indication that the processing of data under these mechanisms does not comply with the fundamental rights and oversight requirements of the adequacy decision, these concerns are amplified when examining private–public collaboration in the use of LFR. Collaborative use of LFR technology can take several forms, including where the police provide private owners of LFR with a watchlist of persons of interest to be deployed in a publicly accessible but privately owned space; where a match is generated by a privately owned system requiring police intervention; where a privately owned company sells the technology to a police force; or where different aspects of the system may

[75] *Klass and Ors v Germany* App no 5029/71 (ECtHR, 6 September 1978) para 56; *Szabo & Vissy v Hungary* App no 37138/14 (ECtHR, 12 January 2016) para 77.

[76] *S & Marper v United Kingdom* App nos 30562/04 and 30566/04 (ECtHR, 4 December 2008) para 77.

[77] AI Act (n 57) Art 5(3).

be subcontracted to a private party.[78] For the purposes of this chapter, the focus is on the first use, that of the provision of images for watchlists to private parties. This collaboration necessarily involves the sharing of biometric data that was originally processed by law enforcement with private entities, and raises additional data protection concerns.

In order for these collaborations to comply with data protection law, the parameters of the relationship must be clearly defined.[79] There should be explicit contracts or agreements to detail the information-sharing arrangements, having due regard for the legal basis for the processing and the necessary data protection principles.[80] As such use involves a law enforcement authority sharing the data, it must be shared for a clear policing purpose.[81] Sharing of data constitutes processing under the relevant data protection instruments and therefore there must be an appropriate legal basis for the sharing of the information.[82] However, the powers of the police to share data are broadly defined and can be governed by statute, common law or royal prerogative.[83]

The sharing of information between the police and private collaborators is not currently subject to explicit statutory regulation. In fact, the sharing of information between the police and private actors is excluded from the remit of much of the existing guidance. For instance, while the College of Policing's APP on LFR explicitly recognises the potential for police sharing data with private companies and/or other public sector organisations operating LFR systems, it states that such activities are outside the scope of the guidance.[84] Furthermore, private organisations are not subject to the Surveillance Camera Code of Practice, so the provisions on LFR set out in this instrument may not apply to private organisations utilising police-generated data. Sharing in this regard is therefore governed with a piecemeal approach. Where not explicitly provided for in statute, the police may use common law powers as the basis of their information sharing, provided they are exercised consistently with the requirements of the DPA, the UK GDPR and the Human Rights Act 1998, as well as applicable policy documents.

The lack of a clear legal framework means that information-sharing arrangements between the police and private collaborators can rely on general agreements that lack legal effect. Key questions must be raised about the parameters of the

[78] Biometrics and Forensics Ethics Group, 'Briefing Note on the Ethical Issues Arising from Public–Private Collaboration on the Use of LFR' (21 January 2021) www.gov.uk/government/publications/public-private-use-of-live-facial-recognition-technology-ethical-issues/briefing-note-on-the-ethical-issues-arising-from-public-private-collaboration-in-the-use-of-live-facial-recognition-technology-accessible.

[79] UK GDPR, Arts 5(2) and 24–29.

[80] ICO (n 38) para 4.9.2.

[81] The MoPI Code of Practice definition of 'policing purpose' is: protecting life and property; preserving order; preventing the commission of offences; bringing offenders to justice; and any duty or responsibility of the police arising from common or statute law.

[82] LED Directive (n 2) Art 3.

[83] LED adequacy decision (n 1) Recitals 29–30.

[84] College of Policing, 'APP: Live Facial Recognition' (n 50).

information that law enforcement could share on the basis of these agreements. General guidance exists as to key factors to consider for information sharing agreements.[85] However, these do not set enforceable conditions on law enforcement. Notably from a fundamental rights perspective, there is a lack of clear guidance as to the oversight regime or access to redress mechanisms for individuals whose data might be shared in this manner. In the absence of a clear legal framework, there is a risk that this information will be shared in instances where it is neither necessary nor proportionate to do so. There are also concerns about the ability to audit the use of the information by the third parties and any subsequent onward sharing of the data. In the absence of any regulation, data subjects will struggle to exercise their rights should they be impacted by these public–private collaborations.

IV. Conclusion

The use of LFR raises key questions concerning both the effectiveness of the exercise of individual rights in the areas covered by the adequacy decision and the operation and oversight of relevant bodies. In the absence of a clear legal framework and an assessment that the use of the powers is only done where 'strictly necessary', the interference with the sensitive personal data of individuals is disproportionate.

The lack of effective oversight over the use of the technologies is similarly indicative of a regime that is failing to give sufficient protection and redress for individuals as required under the adequacy decision. The expansion of the data processing abilities of law enforcement evidenced by LFR and the risk they pose to fundamental rights raises questions about the overall adequacy of the UK data protection regime. As the powers of law enforcement to adopt and utilise new technologies that implicate individuals' fundamental rights expand, the policies of the UK begin to diverge further from those of the EU. The extent of this divergence may very well impact on any continued finding of adequacy and the future of the EU–UK data sharing arrangements.

[85] College of Policing, 'APP: Information Sharing' (5 February 2020) www.app.college.police.uk/app-content/information-management/sharing-police-information/.

PART III

Parallel Challenges: Regulating Artificial Intelligence and Beyond

7

Regulation versus Innovation? A Comparative Analysis of EU and UK Policy Responses on Artificial Intelligence

LILIAN MITROU

I. Introduction

Artificial intelligence (AI) is undoubtedly at the forefront of technological development, since it has moved from the research laboratory to become part of our daily lives. While we are witnessing an exponential growth in AI, several ethical and human rights concerns. In addition, the perceived social impacts of AI uses have stimulated an extensive debate on how societies can profit from its benefits, while addressing and mitigating its risks.[1] The so-called 'algorithmic society'[2] is based on highly complicated, agile and unchartered technological and social structures, challenging the capability of current legal frameworks to address efficiently all the implications deriving from emerging technologies and the fourth industrial revolution.

The transformative power of AI, the risks and disruptive effects it may pose at the individual level but also on social structures and the enhanced asymmetries of knowledge, and especially power,[3] have – slightly and progressively, but definitely – shifted attention from the promulgation of ethical principles and codes to the discussion of legal frameworks and instruments.[4] Regulating AI as a part

[1] BC Stahl, R Rodrigues, N Santiago and K Macnish, 'A European Agency for Artificial Intelligence: Protecting Fundamental Rights and Ethical Values' [2022] *Computer Law & Security Review* 45.

[2] See O Pollicino and G De Gregorio, 'Constitutional Law in the Algorithmic Society' in HW Micklitz et al (eds), *Constitutional Challenges in the Algorithmic Society* (Cambridge University Press, 2021); JM Balkin, 'Free Speech in the Algorithmic Society: Big Data, Private Governance, and New School Speech Regulation' (2018) 51 *University of California Davis Law Review* 1149.

[3] P Nemitz, 'Foreword, Power in Times of Artificial Intelligence' (2020) 2(4) *Delphi – Interdisciplinary Review of Emerging Technologies* 158.

[4] NA Smuha, 'From a "Race to AI" to a "Race to AI Regulation": Regulatory Competition for Artificial Intelligence' (2021) 13(1) *Law, Innovation and Technology* 57.

of the governance of emerging technologies is no easy exercise, due to the uncertainties of their future developments, the large number of stakeholders involved, their interdependencies and, perhaps most importantly, the economic and societal benefits and risks they present.[5]

Even if the desirability and/or necessity of intervention by the legislator seems to be becoming undeniable, or at least is gaining ground,[6] preliminary issues and questions remain open to different approaches and strategic choices: what do we understand by the expression 'regulating AI'? Does it mean that the law should provide whether and how a 'technology' works? The answer to the question 'how should we regulate AI?' includes not only the goal, the approach and the scope of the regulation, but also the kind of regulatory schemes, instruments, tools and implementation mechanisms that could help achieve the regulatory objectives. But what are these objectives? The legislators are, like in many other cases, requested to respond to the challenge of how to maintain a balance between fostering innovation, protecting individuals' rights and addressing any potential unintended consequences – and that is no 'walk in the park'.[7]

This chapter aims at exploring these questions based on a brief analysis of the regulatory policy responses of the EU and the UK. My examination is based on the Proposal for an AI Act submitted by the European Commission (the Commission) on 21 April 2021 (AI Act Proposal) and the Strategy and Policy Papers published to date (August 2022) by the UK government. A critical restriction of the research lies in the fact that no legislative texts have been adopted (yet). Although neither the EU's nor the UK's regulatory framework has taken effect, the differences in approach between the two jurisdictions are clear. This chapter addresses the need for regulating AI and discusses the transition from the ethics debate to the introduction of legally binding rules. It highlights the difficulty in defining the 'object' and 'scope' of regulation, eg AI (systems), and presents the main regulatory policy choices of the EU and UK. Finally, it reflects upon the right timing for adopting provisions to regulate AI and upon AI regulation as an element and tool for digital sovereignty.

II. Why (and How to) Regulate 'Artificial Intelligence'?

A critical review of regulatory approaches presupposes an answer to the core question of why we should regulate AI. Is this general-purpose technology, regularly

[5] I Ulnicane, W Knight, T Leach, BC Stahl and W-G Wanjiku, 'Framing Governance for a Contested Emerging Technology: Insights from AI Policy' (2021) 40(2) *Policy and Society* 158.

[6] P Gomes Rego de Almeida, C Dennerdos Santos and J Silva Farias, 'Artificial Intelligence Regulation: A Framework for Governance (2021) 23(3) *Ethics and Information Technology* 505.

[7] Smuha (n 4) 62.

compared to electricity,[8] 'as transformative as the industrial revolution'?[9] Does AI raise fundamentally new ethical and legal challenges so that specific rules are required?

Artificial Intelligence presents the same features as other (still emerging?) disruptive technologies,[10] namely radical novelty, relatively fast growth, prominent impact, and at the same time uncertainty and ambiguity.[11] Independently of the – assumed or confirmed – exceptional nature or features of AI, scholars have argued that the decisive criterion is less the 'newness' of the technology, but rather the ways it enables changes in societal practices, behaviour or relations.[12] Despite the similarities between AI and other technologies, the scale, speed and complexity of AI are unprecedented, disrupting every industry and sector across the globe,[13] and having major impacts on the political system, labour market and welfare state.[14] As Aizenberg and van den Hoven underline that

> even if it is difficult to assess the way society perceived the impact of electricity on social environment and on rights and interests of persons, it is clear that as AI systems are increasingly becoming embedded in several social contexts, they also become highly relevant for fundamental rights.[15]

Many AI systems and applications are characterised by opacity, limited or no explainability, biased choices and design – and consequently possibly discriminatory and unpredictable outcomes. Another feature of AI that presents difficulties for the (applicability of) legal principles is the capacity of AI systems to develop and operate independently of human control.[16]

A preliminary issue is the (extent of the) necessity to launch legislative initiatives to regulate such innovative and unclassified relationships.[17] The answer to this issue and the choice of which regulatory strategy for AI depend on several

[8] S Lynch, 'AndrewNG: Why AI Is the New Electricity' (Stanford Graduate School of Business, 2017) www.gsb.stanford.edu/insights/andrew-ng-why-ai-new-electricity.

[9] R Gruetzemacher and J Whittlestone, 'The Transformative Potential of Artificial Intelligence' [2022] *Futures* 135.

[10] R Girassa, *Artificial Intelligence as a Disruptive Technology – Economic Transformation and Government Regulation* (Palgrave-Macmilan, 2020).

[11] D Rotolo, D Hicks and B Martin, 'What Is an Emerging Technology?' (2015) 44(10) *Research Policy* 1827.

[12] MM Maas, 'Aligning AI Regulation to Sociotechnical Change' in J Bullock et al (eds), *Oxford Handbook on AI Governance* (Oxford University Press, 2022).

[13] Big Innovation Centre/All-Party Parliamentary Group on Artificial Intelligence, 'International Perspective and Exemplars' (BIC/APPGAI, 30 October 2017) 10.

[14] Ulnicane et al (n 5).

[15] E Aizenberg and J Van Den Hoven, 'Designing for Human Rights in AI' (2020) 7(2) *Big Data and Society*.

[16] Ada Lovelace Institute, 'Regulate to Innovate-Report' (2021) 38.

[17] A Vorras and L Mitrou, 'Unboxing the Black Box of Artificial Intelligence: Algorithmic Transparency and/or a Right to Functional Explainability' in T-E Synodinou, P Jougleux, C Markou and T Prastitou-Merdi (eds), *EU Internet Law in the Digital Single Market* (Springer, 2021) 247ff.

factors regarding the complicated and unexplored nature of AI and the potential consequences and 'risks' of both technology and regulation. A first approach consisted in avoiding pursuing heavy-handed regulations and exploring the capabilities of current frameworks, and/or enacting tailored rules to target specific harms in particular application areas through dedicated regulatory bodies that are already charged with oversight of that particular sector.[18]

A key result of the consultation process conducted by the EU High-Level Expert Group on AI in 2019–20 was that 'while a number of the requirements are already reflected in existing legal or regulatory regimes, those regarding transparency, traceability and human oversight are not specifically covered under current legislation in many economic sectors'.[19] Similarly, the UK government assesses that AI 'is partially regulated through a patchwork of legal and regulatory requirements built for other purposes which now capture uses of AI Technology', such as the (also under revision[20]) UK data protection law, but it also needs to consider the 'ambiguity of the UK's legal frameworks and application of regulatory bodies to AI given these have not been developed specifically with AI technologies and its applications in mind'.[21]

A key parameter of the AI policies adopted is strictly related to the role of the state in the algorithmic era and its interplay with non-state agents and actors. Especially in the context of AI, the traditional role of the state seems to be significantly challenged by private entities that enjoy considerable informational and resource advantages.[22]

Since the mid-2010s, there has been a tendancy to develop ethical frameworks for mitigating the negative effects of AI and making it an ethically safe 'environment'. Over recent years, governments, intergovernmental and international organisations,[23] companies and private actors,[24] professional bodies and

[18] J New and D Castro, 'How Policymakers Can Foster Algorithmic Accountability' (2018) www2.datainnovation.org/2018-algorithmic-accountability.pdf.

[19] Commission, 'White Paper on Artificial Intelligence – A European Approach to Excellence and Trust' (2020) 9–10.

[20] Data Protection and Digital Information Bill, https://bills.parliament.uk/bills/3322.

[21] As presented to HM Government by Department for Digital, Culture, Media and Sport, *Policy Paper: Establishing a Pro-innovation Approach to Regulating AI* (CP 728, 2022) www.gov.uk/government/publications/establishing-a-pro-innovation-approach-to-regulating-ai/establishing-a-pro-innovation-approach-to-regulating-ai-policy-statement.

[22] V Koniakou, 'From the "Rush to Ethics" to the "Race for Governance" in Artificial Intelligence' (2023) 25 *Information Systems Frontiers* 71.

[23] Such as the EU High Level Expert Group (2019), the Council of Europe's Task Force on AI within the Commission for the Efficiency of Justice (2018), the UN Ad Hoc Expert Group on the Ethics of AI or the OECD's Expert Group on AI in Society (2019). Each of these expert groups produced a distinct set of principles and ethical guidelines for the steering of AI and algorithms towards ethical and, by extension, societally beneficial ends.

[24] As underlined by Koniakou (n 22), the broader domain of AI design, development and deployment is largely dominated by a handful of American, Chinese and some EU companies, such as Google, Amazon, Facebook, Apple, IBM, ATOS, Microsoft, Baidu, Alibaba and Tencent, which have developed and adopted ethical guidelines, in most cases before government and intergovernmental organisations engaged with AI ethics.

associations, research entities and (policy) think tanks around the world have actively published and/or adopted ethical guidelines. It is noteworthy that many, if not most, of these initiatives originate from industry actors rather than from regulatory bodies or more traditional actors in civil society.[25]

'AI ethics' and 'good and trustworthy AI'[26] came into the spotlight as part of international and national strategies[27] that aimed to deal with the opportunities and impacts of AI on the public and private sectors, while several state and non-state actors issued 'AI declarations' to affirm their intention to commit themselves to ethical AI innovation. Despite its rather limited normative effect, proponents of a soft law approach[28] suggest that ethical principles and guidelines offer a better and more flexible solution for AI governance.

Ethics of/for AI initially dominated the public debate and policy, but has not been met with universal enthusiasm. The 'ethics approach' has also been met with increasing scepticism, the criticism raised focusing on the risk of 'ethics washing', ie of drawing attention away from strong enforcement mechanisms towards weaker mechanisms, such as self-assigned commitments,[29] and trying to avoid or delay binding regulation.[30] Many critics have also highlighted that the plethora of ethical principles were characterised by a lack of consistency,[31] vagueness and a narrow understanding of responsibilities of AI developers,[32] while others stressed the attention paid to the structural constraints of private actors, like competition, which may lead them to 'choose between ethics and profit'.[33]

The published ethical frameworks, stressing human-centric elements and focusing, however vaguely, on principles such as transparency, explainability, privacy, accountability and fairness, have identified the numerous challenges to fundamental rights and the rule of law that AI poses, and have raised awareness

[25] An initial evaluation of 160 sets of AI ethical principles and guideline documents conducted by AlgorithmWatch (2021) showed that the majority of binding agreements and voluntary commitments that exist are proposed by the private sector. www.privacydesign.ch/2021/04/23/algorithm-watch-ai-ethics-guidelines-global-inventory/.

[26] See HM Government, *National AI Strategy* (CP 525, 2021) www.gov.uk/government/publications/national-ai-strategy.

[27] According to the OECD, in early 2020 at least 50 countries had developed, or were in the process of developing, national AI strategies. See A Jobin, M Ienca and E Vayena, 'The Global Landscape of AI Ethics Guidelines' (2019) 1 *Nature Machine Intelligence* 389.

[28] See L Floridi, 'Soft Ethics and the Governance of the Digital' (2018) 31 *Philosophy and Technology* 1. See also L Floridi et al, 'AI4People – An Ethical Framework for a Good AI Society: Opportunities, Risks, Principles, and Recommendations' (2018) 28 *Minds & Machines* 689.

[29] E Erman and M Furendal, 'The Global Governance of Artificial Intelligence: Some Normative Concerns' (2022) 9 *Moral Philosophy and Politics* 267.

[30] T Hagendorff, 'The Ethics of AI Ethics: An Evaluation of Guidelines' (2020) 30(1) *Minds and Machines* 99. See also B Mittelstadt, 'Principles Alone Cannot Guarantee Ethical AI' (2019) 1(11) *Nature Machine Intelligence* 501.

[31] A Tsamados et al, 'The Ethics of Algorithms: Key Problems and Solutions' (2022) 37 *AI & Society* 215.

[32] R Radu, 'Steering the Governance of Artificial Intelligence: National Strategies in Perspective' (2021) 40(2) *Policy and Society* 178.

[33] T Ferretti, 'An Institutionalist Approach to AI Ethics: Justifying the Priority of Government Regulation over Self-Regulation' (2022) 9 *Moral Philosophy and Politics* 239.

among professionals,[34] decision-makers and the general public. From this perspective, ethical principles can be regarded as 'precursors of the law',[35] summarising the variety of complex ethical issues and providing direction to legal rules.

However, such codes and guidelines cannot substitute for the law as they are too broad,[36] generic, vague and subject to various and different interpretations and materialisation to be able to shape and affect AI-actors' actions. Moreover, self-regulation solutions lack both public accountability and democratic legitimacy,[37] as well as a binding nature that enables the enforcement of the law, as only governments are able to build the necessary coercive processes, mechanisms and infrastructures to adjudicate conflicts and strike a fair balance between competing aims and values, rights and interests. However, both scholars and policy-makers do not necessarily consider ethics and legislative intervention as contradictory; rather, they see them as complementary ways to deal with AI challenges.[38]

In various AI policy documents, we can find a range of roles of the state with regard to AI governance. The state is often framed as a 'facilitator', laying the foundation for innovation and providing stakeholders with means and resources;[39] as a 'promoter', acting as proponent and exponent of change; as a 'moderator' of different views and attitudes on AI benefits and risks; as an 'arbitrator' or 'negotiator' between different social and political positions among agents; and as a 'guarantor', expected to ensure safety, security and, last but not least, fundamental rights and democracy risks.[40] These different roles are closely intertwined with the different regulatory approaches and goals.

III. Regulatory (Un)certainty and the Definition of AI

As disruptive technologies also challenge traditional regulative paradigms, how, when and to what extent AI should be regulated – on the national, transnational or international level – remains an open question.[41] What actually *is* AI as a field/

[34] L Stark and AL Hofmann, 'Data Is the New What? Popular Metaphors & Professional Ethics in Emerging Data Culture' [2019] *Journal of Cultural Analytics* https://doi.org/10.22148/16.036.

[35] P Nemitz, 'Constitutional Democracy and Technology in the Age of Artificial Intelligence' (2018) 376 *Philosophical Transactions of the Royal Society A: Mathematical, Physical and Engineering Sciences* 20180089.

[36] J Whittlestone, R Nyrup, A Alexandrova and S Cave, 'The Role and Limits of Principles in AI Ethics: Towards a Focus on Tensions' in *Proceedings of the 2019 AAAI/ACM Conference on AI, Ethics, and Society* (AAAI and ACM, 2019) 195.

[37] L Taylor, 'Public Actors without Public Values: Legitimacy, Domination and the Regulation of the Technology Sector' (2021) 34 *Philosophy & Technology* 897.

[38] Stahl et al (n 1).

[39] C Villani et al, *For a Meaningful Artificial Intelligence: Towards a French and European Strategy* (Conseil national du numérique, 2018).

[40] S Borras and J Edler, 'The Roles of the State in the Governance of Socio-technical Systems' Transformation' (2020) 49(5) *Research Policy.*

[41] Maas (n 12).

technology to be regulated? Despite the broad use of 'artificial intelligence', there is 'currently little consensus on a general definition, either within the scientific community or across national or international organisations'.[42] Conceptualising and framing AI is not only a methodological requirement; the way AI is defined is crucial for formulating the regulatory responses, with significant impact on the discourse, but also mainly on the scope, of regulatory intervention.[43]

The difficulty in defining AI is not confined to policy-makers, as actually there is no single or stand-alone technology but, rather, 'a deeply technical family of cognitive technologies',[44] which includes various applications. Hall and Pesenti, in their report for the UK government, understood AI as 'a set of advanced general purpose digital technologies that enable machines to do highly complex tasks effectively'.[45] The absence of a unitary definition complicates the adoption of AI-specific rules and affects the assessment and comparison of AI policies.

The Commission found that the notion of AI should be clearly defined to ensure legal certainty, given that the determination of what is regarded as an 'AI system' is crucial for the allocation of legal responsibilities under the new AI framework and its actual application. Based on a definition already used by the OECD[46] and the 'key functional characteristics of the software' (Recital 6 of the AI Act Proposal), the Commission proposed in Article 3(1) of the AI Act Proposal a broad, but technical definition of AI as

> software that is developed with one or more of approaches and techniques listed in Annex I … and can, for a given set of human-defined objectives, generate outputs such as content, predictions, recommendations, or decisions influencing the environments they interact with.

Annex 1 of the initial proposal laid out a list of techniques and approaches that are used today to develop AI.[47] Accordingly, the notion of 'AI system' refers to

[42] Department for Digital, Culture, Media and Sport (n 21).

[43] C Collins, D Dennehy, K Conboy and P Mikalef, 'Artificial Intelligence in Information Systems Research: A Systematic Literature Review and Research Agenda' (2021) 60 *International Journal of Information Management* 102383.

[44] M Kuziemski and G Misuraca, 'AI Governance in the Public Sector: Three Tales from the Frontiers of Automated Decision-Making in Democratic Settings' (2020) 44(6) *Telecommunications Policy* 101976.

[45] W Hall and J Pesenti, *Growing the Artificial Intelligence Industry in the UK* (Department for Digital, Culture, Media & Sport and Department for Business, Energy & Industrial Strategy, 2017) 8.

[46] According to the definition adopted by OECD, 'an AI system is a machine-based system that can, for a given set of human-defined objectives, make predictions, recommendations, or decisions influencing real or virtual environments. AI systems are designed to operate with varying levels of autonomy'. OECD, *Recommendation of the Council on Artificial Intelligence* (OECD/LEGAL/0449) 7.7.

[47] The Czech presidency has deleted Annex I and the corresponding empowerment for the Commission to update it by means of delegated acts and proposed instead the competence of the Commission to adopt implementing acts to further specify and update techniques under machine learning approaches and logic- and knowledge-based approaches (Czech General Approach Text of 11 November 2022 – 14336/22).

a range of software-based technologies that encompass 'machine learning', 'logic and knowledge-based' systems and 'statistical approaches'.[48]

The proposed definition has been contested by many EU Member States that consider it is 'ambiguous and too broad,[49] and that it fails to provide sufficiently clear criteria for distinguishing AI from more classical software systems'. These concerns prompted the Czech presidency of the EU, in the 2nd semester of 2022, to propose 'a new version of the definition, which narrows it down to systems developed through machine learning techniques and knowledge-based approaches and includes additionally the 'concept of autonomy'.[50]

The UK AI Strategy has largely avoided the challenge of defining AI, as 'Artificial Intelligence as a term can mean a lot of things, and the government recognises that no single definition is going to be suitable for every scenario'.[51] The UK government alluded to a broad definition, regarding AI as 'Machines that perform tasks normally requiring human intelligence, especially when the machines learn from data how to do those tasks', a definition 'sufficient for [its] purposes'.[52] In the AI Regulation Policy Paper, the UK government has confirmed the approach to 'regulate the use of AI rather than the technology itself', refraining from the EU approach to set out a relatively tighter and universally applicable definition.[53]

Despite the advantage of having 'maximum flexibility', the UK government also rejects the approach of putting 'no boundaries on what constitutes AI, and leave regulators or relevant bodies to decide what technology and systems are in scope as they see fit', and seeks to take the middle ground.[54] The AI Regulation Policy Paper focuses on setting out the core capabilities and characteristics of AI, eg 'adaptability' and 'autonomy', allowing regulators to set out and evolve more detailed definitions of AI according to their specific domains or sectors. Defining AI in various ways on a sector-by-sector basis ignores the dynamic character of AI (uses) and could increase uncertainty. The UK government itself acknowledges the shortcomings of this approach, stating that the lack of granularity taken by this approach could hinder innovation.

[48] Lilian Edwards argues that the AI Proposal 'takes an unhelpfully oversimplified view of the way in which AI systems function' as 'AI is not a product nor a "one-off" service, but a system delivered dynamically through multiple hands ("the AI lifecycle") in different contexts with different impacts on various individuals and groups'. L Edwards, 'Regulating AI in Europe: Four Problems and Four Solutions – Expert Opinion' (Ada Lovelace Institute, 2022).

[49] See M Ebers, VRS Hoch, F Rosenkranz, H Ruschemeier and B Steinrötter, 'The European Commission's Proposal for an Artificial Intelligence Act – A Critical Assessment by Members of the Robotics and AI Law Society' (2021) 4(4) *J* 589.

[50] Czech presidency (n 47).

[51] HM Government, *National AI Strategy* (n 26) 16.

[52] ibid 16.

[53] Department for Digital, Culture, Media and Sport, *Establishing a Pro-innovation Approach to Regulating AI. An Overview of the UK's Emerging Approach* (CP 728, 2022) 8, https://assets.publishing.service.gov.uk/government/uploads/system/uploads/attachment_data/file/1092630/_CP_728__-_Establishing_a_pro-innovation_approach_to_regulating_AI.pdf.

[54] ibid 8.

We should consider the quite uncertain approach of both the EU and the UK in defining AI in the context of their aim to ensure that the regulatory framework will remain 'flexible and future-proof',[55] and adaptable to technological developments. The fear that a legal framework adopted sometimes after several years of discussions and negotiations will become obsolete a short time after, or even before, its entry into force reflects the inherent difficulty of regulation keeping pace with technology. As emphasised in the Commission's White Paper on AI, 'Given how fast AI is evolving, the regulatory framework must leave room to cater for further developments'.[56] The attempt to address 'future risks and opportunities' and '[keep] up with fast moving technology' seems to be a driving force also for the UK approach. The common assumption that 'neutral' rules are preferable to technology-specific ones as they can be applied broadly regardless of the technological stage ignores or underestimates the 'tradeoff between flexibility and clarity' as 'the more specific the rule, the less discretion is granted to the interpreter'.[57] The grade of specificity defines the allocation of regulation, interpretation and enforcement powers to different legal actors that will be invited to resolve future uncertainties and legislative and/or enforcement gaps.

IV. Priorities and Approaches

Dealing with 'uncertainty' or – positively expressed – creating (a level of provisory?) certainty constitutes a goal that both the EU and the UK share. By introducing the AI Act Proposal, the EU aims to build an 'ecosystem of trust', as already proclaimed in the White Paper of 2020 as 'a policy objective in itself'.[58] From the EU's perspective, the rule of law and legal clarity are essential for '[giving] people and the confidence to embrace AI-based solutions, companies and public organisations the legal certainty to innovate using AI applications and encouraging businesses to develop them'.[59] Trust is interrelated with legal certainty and safety. Improving legal certainty is another objective that is explicitly present in the EU legislative initiative, as the EU seeks to ensure it to facilitate investment and innovation in AI. It also aims to ensure that AI systems placed on the EU market are safe and respect EU law, and to enhance governance and effective enforcement of EU law on fundamental rights and safety requirements applicable to AI systems.

Without this 'trust', organisations could be reluctant to invest in AI, because of concerns over whether these systems will work as intended (ie whether they are

[55] Czech presidency (n 47).

[56] Commission, 'White Paper on Artificial Intelligence – A European Approach to Excellence and Trust' COM (2020) 65 final.

[57] R Crootof and BJ Ard, 'Structuring Techlaw' (2021) 34 *Harvard Journal of Law and Technology* 347, 406.

[58] Commission (n 56).

[59] ibid 3.

effective, accurate, reliable and safe). Alternatively, if organisations were to adopt AI systems without understanding whether they are in fact trustworthy, they would risk causing real-world harm.

'Full (public) confidence of all parts of society in the use of AI technologies, in the science and the technologies and in the governance and regulation that enable them' is, according to the UK AI Council's Roadmap, published in January 2021, 'a precondition for the UK to "feel the full benefits of AI"'.[60] The AI Regulation Policy Paper confirmed that the maximisation of 'the full opportunities which AI can bring to [the] UK' has to be achieved 'while ensuring that we can build consumer, citizen and investor confidence in our regulatory framework for the ethical and responsible use of AI in our society and economy'.[61] Despite the common feature of ensuring 'trust/confidence', the texts adopted or negotiated by the EU and the UK indicate more divergences than convergences.

The Explanatory Memorandum introducing the official text of the EU AI Act frames the Commission's aim for the new law:

> AI should be a tool for people and be a force for good in society with the ultimate aim of increasing human well-being. Rules for AI available in the Union market or otherwise affecting people in the Union should therefore be human centric, so that people can trust that the technology is used in a way that is safe and compliant with the law, including respect for fundamental rights.[62]

Elsewhere, the Memorandum notes that AI is 'not an end in itself, but a tool that has to serve people with the ultimate aim of increasing human well-being'.[63] The EU legislator seems to prioritise the respect for fundamental rights and Union values as the first objective of the proposed legal framework, putting the attainment of legal certainty as a means to facilitate innovation second.[64] As noted in the report of the Ada Lovelace Institute,[65] 'different underlying objectives will not necessarily be mutually exclusive, but prioritisation matters', as 'choices about which to explicitly include and which to emphasise will have a significant effect on downstream policy choices', especially regarding the potential introduction of new regulatory institutions, approaches and tools.

In 2017, the UK Parliament invited the government to 'set the boundaries for what AI can and cannot do' by adopting 'forward-looking policies, prioritising the good of the wider public', and underlined that 'Government must evolve with

[60] UK AI Council, *AI Roadmap* (2021).

[61] K Kwarteng, 'Ministerial Foreword to the AI Regulation Policy Paper'.

[62] Commission, Explanatory Memorandum of the AI Act Proposal (21 April 2021).

[63] ibid.

[64] The Title V of ch 5 of the AI Act is entitled 'Measures for Support of Innovation'. AI-driven innovation is closely linked to the Data Governance Act, the Open Data Directive and other initiatives announced in the European strategy for data COM (2020) 66 final. However, scholars point out 'the absence of a substantial boost to innovation', as this aim is restricted to three articles and two measures. See VL Raposo, 'Ex Machina: Preliminary Critical Assessment of the European Draft Act on Artificial Intelligence' (2022) 30 *International Journal of Law and Information Technology* 88.

[65] Ada Lovelace Institute (n 16) 23.

technology to harness the opportunities and protect society from the risks'.[66] Some years later, the emphasis on cultivating and utilising AI technology's potential to contribute to economic growth was already visible in all the documents that lay down the UK's AI strategy and approach to regulation. The key aim seems to be to create a '(stable?) regulatory environment for businesses', 'designed to minimize unnecessary burdens and 'with unduly inhibiting AI innovation'.[67] Therefore, the UK government declared its commitment to 'proportionate regulation and, where appropriate, deregulation',[68] while clarifying that the response to the risks of digital technologies 'will be proportionate and will not overshadow the huge benefits that digital technologies bring'.[69] The support of 'responsible innovation' and 'unleashing the full potential of new technologies' takes precedence in the AI policy as stated in the AI Regulation Policy Paper. The 'actively pro-innovation approach'[70] is the key driver of the UK policy, to be achieved through a 'proportionate and "light-touch" and coherent regulatory framework'.

In the EU, when adopted, the AI Act, a part of the Commission's overall AI Package, will be the 'first comprehensive legislative measure globally containing binding rules on AI'.[71] By using this instrument of regulation,[72] the EU seeks to ensure a consistent approach across all Member States, in a process that will pre-empt national rules and lead to EU-wide (and not only) binding legislation on AI.[73] The AI Act will be a framework for regulating AI across all sectors.[74] Moreover, the AI Act has been designed to be complementary to cross-sectoral EU legislation, notably the EU General Data Protection Regulation (GDPR), and sectoral safety legislation, which is currently harmonised under the 'New Legislative Framework'.[75] The regulation of AI is complemented by an updated Regulation for Machinery Products, a revision of the 2006 Machinery Directive.

In the UK, governance of AI currently sits uneasily with traditional legal solutions and tools. Regardless of Parliament's incitement to 'act quick[ly] in guiding

[66] Big Innovation Centre/APPG AI 2017.

[67] 2021 Digital Regulation Plan. In July 2021, the Department for Digital, Culture, Media, and Sport (DCMS) released a policy paper actively promoting innovation.

[68] HM Government, 'Policy Paper: Digital Regulation: Driving Growth and Unlocking Innovation' (9 March 2022).

[69] ibid.

[70] Lilian Edwards, by assessing the lack of innovative ideas in the AI Regulation Policy Paper, has underlined that 'every second word [of the text] seems to be 'pro-innovation'. See R Bateman, 'Will the UK's "Light Touch" AI Regulation Plans Increase AI Risks?' (*#Risk London*, 1 August 2022).

[71] T Burri and F von Bothmer, 'The New EU Legislation on Artificial Intelligence: A Primer' (2021) http://dx.doi.org/10.2139/ssrn.3831424.

[72] Based on Art 114 of the Treaty on the Functioning of the European Union (TFEU), the approximation of laws to improve the functioning of the internal market.

[73] Burri and von Bothmer (n 71).

[74] With the exception of AI systems developed or used exclusively for military purposes.

[75] As explained by the Commission, the New Legislative Framework (adopted in 2008) aims to improve the internal market for goods and strengthen the conditions for placing a wide range of products on the EU market. It is a package of measures, including EU regulations, that aim to improve market surveillance and boost the quality of conformity assessments. See New Legislative Framework (europa.eu).

the norms and standards for AI and set the appropriate regulation where need be', the UK AI Policy is characterised by a stalling attitude with regard to the adoption of rules. The AI Regulation Policy Paper was presented as an interim report that sketched the choices, but the issuing of a White Paper was postponed first to late 2022, then to early 2023. In its policy statement on how it will approach AI governance and regulation, the UK government clarifies that it will abstain from the adoption of mandatory rules for AI, as it does 'not see a need for regulation at this stage'.[76]

The UK government deviates from the horizontal European approach 'to adopt a sectoral one in combination with "adaptive", "hybrid" or "de-centred" governance schemes'.[77] The National AI Strategy opted for a sector-led approach, rather than a European-style overarching approach, taking into consideration mainly that empowering regulators and industries to respond and work with innovators in their sectors to advise on the interpretation of existing regulations will enable a much faster response to individual harms.

The sectoral approach is intertwined with the key choice of the UK government to entrust different regulators to take a tailored stance for sectors ranging from broadcasting to healthcare. Existing regulators[78] have to lead the process of identifying, assessing, prioritising and contextualising the specific risks addressed by the cross-sectoral principles. The government does not propose to have any new or single AI regulator, or any coordinating body similar to the European Artificial Intelligence Board.[79] This sector-specific approach is actually a context-specific one, aimed at creating 'proportionate and adaptable regulation', while regulators are intended and expected to consider lighter-touch options, such as voluntary agreements or guidance-based approaches, eliminating burdensome or excessive administrative compliance obligations.

This means that more and more vertical regulators have to understand where and how AI is being used and anticipate the various associated consequences and risks. This approach faces concerns and criticism. A recent study of the Alan

[76] Department for Digital, Culture, Media and Sport (n 21).

[77] A Taeihagh, 'Governance of Artificial Intelligence' (2021) 40(2) *Policy and Society* 137.

[78] Such as Ofcom (Broadcasting), the Competition and Markets Authority, the Information Commissioner's Office (ICO), the Financial Conduct Authority and the Office of Communications, the Bank of England.

[79] The AI Act Proposal provides for the establishment of the European Artificial Intelligence Board, which will be composed of representatives from the Member States and the Commission. 'The Board should be responsible for a number of advisory tasks, including issuing opinions, recommendations, advice or guidance on matters related to the implementation of [the] Regulation, including on technical specifications or existing standards regarding the requirements established in [the] Regulation and providing advice to and assisting the Commission on specific questions related to artificial intelligence' (Rec 76). The Board is expected to facilitate an effective and harmonised implementation of this regulation by contributing to the cooperation of the national supervisory authorities and the Commission and providing advice and expertise to the Commission. For an analysis of the Board, see Stahl et al (n 1).

Turing Institute disputed the regulatory 'readiness' of regulators as it identified significant gaps across their systems, organisation and staff. As noted, 'an unprecedented demand for technical know-how and horizontal problem-solving can pose significant difficulties for regulators, particularly those who have not traditionally engaged with new and rapidly evolving technologies'.[80] Due to the 'siloed nature of the regulatory landscape', there is an obvious risk of multiple sets of guidance, overlap between regulatory mandates, gaps and the potential for issues to fall between them, narrow framing of AI around existing legislation, inconsistencies and contradictions. The government seems to be conscious of the possible disparity in terminology, lack of coherence and the ability of regulators to set and enforce rules, thus confirming that it 'may need to review the powers and remits of some regulators and ensure that there is a level of regulatory coordination'.[81]

V. Values, Principles and Risks

The UK AI Strategy[82] entails (brief) references to values, including fairness, openness, liberty, security, democracy, the rule of law and respect for human rights. Despite the confirmation that the UK's principles are deliberately value-focused, the AI Regulation Policy Paper contains no reference to the 'UK's broader values' that AI-driven growth and innovation should align with.[83] To ensure a coherent response, the AI Regulation Policy Paper suggests the 'cross-sectoral principles' that regulators would be tasked with interpreting and implementing within their regulatory remits should be in line with their existing roles. The principles proposed comprise a mixture of safety and security components, fundamental values such as transparency, explainability and fairness, and elements that should ensure accountability and the right to redress. It is questionable whether these principles will adequately serve to adjudicate between competing interests and views on specific questions.[84] Following the AI Regulation Policy Paper, UK regulators will decide if, when and how their regulated entities will need to implement measures to demonstrate that these principles have been considered or complied with, depending on the relevant context. It is noteworthy that transparency, explainability[85] and fairness are introduced as cross-sectoral guiding principles, but it will be the regulators who are entitled to assess and define the appropriateness of

[80] M Aitken, D Leslie F Ostmann, J Pratt, H Margettsand and C Dorobantu, *Common Regulatory Capacity for AI*. The Alan Turing Institute (2022).

[81] See Department for Digital, Culture, Media and Sport (n 21) 20.

[82] HM Government, *National AI Strategy* (n 26).

[83] Department for Digital, Culture, Media and Sport (n 21).

[84] Ada Lovelace Institute (n 16).

[85] This approach is based on the assumption that the logic and decision making in AI systems cannot always be meaningfully explained in an intelligible way, although in most settings this poses no substantial risk.AI Regulation policy paper.

transparency and explainability in order to decide in which contexts and specific instances fairness is important and relevant and, consequently, to translate these principles into specific guidance to support their being upheld in the respective sectors and contexts.

The UK government's AI Regulation Policy Paper relates the embedding of these principles in sector-based AI policies and applications along with the assessment of risk posed by a specific AI use and the way to respond to it. According to the AI Regulation Policy Paper, regulators should address issues where there is clear evidence of a real risk of missed opportunities and focus on high-risk concerns rather than hypothetical or low risks associated with AI. Interestingly, the AI Regulation Policy Paper associates high-risk with the diptych of 'appropriate transparency and explainability', which the Paper seems to consider as an entity. From this perspective, the British government also considers banning some high-risk AI uses in cases where regulators deem that decisions which cannot be explained should be prohibited entirely.[86] The introduction of high-level guiding principles subject to further definition and differentiation by the regulators reflects and responds to the choice of a proportionate and flexible approach, though the protection of fundamental rights will be variable while raising concerns with regard to enforceability.

On the other side, the AI Act Proposal aims to develop a 'human-centric approach'[87] so that new technologies function according to EU values and principles. By proposing the AI Act, European policy-makers adopt the ethical guidelines proposed by the High Level Expert Group (HLEG):[88] AI systems should be developed, deployed and used in a way that adheres to the ethical principles of respect for human autonomy, prevention of harm, fairness and explicability. These principles must be translated into concrete requirements to be met by the different stakeholders (developers, deployers and end users) to achieve trustworthy AI, the key requirements of which are (i) human agency and oversight, (ii) technical robustness and safety, (iii) privacy and data governance, (iv) transparency, (v) diversity, non-discrimination and fairness, (vi) environmental and societal well-being and (vii) accountability. Beyond adherence to ethical principles, in order to be trustworthy, AI systems should also be lawful (ie they must comply with all applicable laws and regulations) and robust from both a technical (safety, security)

[86] The AI Strategy does not mention any specific practices, such as social scoring, to be outlawed. The AI Regulation Policy Paper cites as an example of an application that may be banned the case where 'for instance in a tribunal where you have a right to challenge the logic of an accusation'.

[87] That means that they rest on commitment to their use in the service of humanity and the common good, with the goal of improving human welfare and freedom.

[88] Commission, Explanatory Memorandum to the AI Act Proposal (n 62) 13. The 'Ethics Guidelines for Trustworthy AI' were presented in 2019 by the AI High Level Experts Group (HLEG), a group of experts appointed by the Commission with the tasks of advising the Commission and providing assistance in the preparation of ethical framework and legislative proposals, as well as policy initiatives. The HLEG has worked closely with the AI Alliance, an online forum with over 4000 members representing academia, business and industry, civil society, EU citizens and policymakers.

and social perspective. The AI Act Proposal follows a largely procedural approach to AI by also addressing bias through data governance and transparency, and by aiming to remedy opacity through interpretability.

The Commission proposed a risk-based framework to regulate AI systems. The AI Act Proposal distinguishes different risk levels regarding AI systems and practices: (i) unacceptable risks (Title II); (ii) high risks (Title III); (iii) limited risks (Title IV); and (iv) minimal risks (Title IX). This approach should tailor the type and content of binding rules for AI systems to the intensity and scope of the risks that AI systems can generate.[89] The levels of risk in the proposed AI Act are based not on the underlying technology used, but on the potential impact on 'fundamental rights'.[90] In the EU model, developers, providers and users must comply with specific, differentiated, 'proportionate' obligations, based on the respective risk level, ranging from ex ante self-conformity assessments and registration to a European-wide public register (high risk) up to information and transparency obligations (limited risk), while for systems that pose minimal or no risk providers are encouraged to adhere to voluntary codes of conduct. In November 2022, the Czech presidency added the category of 'General purpose AI systems' to 'account for situations where AI systems can be used for many different purposes'.[91]

Aimed at ensuring a 'proportionate approach', the European risk framework that underpins the AI Act Proposal is in principle welcomed, 'as it offers a good balance between innovation-friendliness and a high level of proactive protection of fundamental rights'.[92] However, concerns have been raised and criticism expressed about various aspects regarding the parameters and processes of the risk-classification system. In the AI Regulation Policy Paper, the UK government points out that a fixed central list of risks and mitigations would '[fail] to allow for different levels of risk presented by seemingly similar applications of AI in different contexts'.[93]

The doubts with regard to the classification of AI systems expressed by Member States as 'high risk' indicate the concern that such an approach may also capture

[89] AI Act Proposal, Recital 14.

[90] 'What matters is the potential for harm, regardless of whether we're discussing an algebraic formula or a deep neural network': K Lum and R Chowdhury, 'What Is an "Algorithm"? It Depends Whom You Ask' (2021) *MIT Technology Review* www.technologyreview.com/2021/02/26/1020007/what-is-an-algorithm.

[91] In the General Approach Text of the Czech presidency (n 47), a general purpose AI system is defined (Art 3 1b) as 'an AI system that – irrespective of how it is placed on the market or put into service, including as open source software – is intended by the provider to perform generally applicable functions such as image and speech recognition, audio and video generation, pattern detection, question answering, translation et al'. According to the definition, a general purpose AI system may be used in a plurality of contexts and may be integrated in a plurality of other AI systems, and the Czech presidency's text clarifies that there may be circumstances where general purpose AI technology is integrated into another system which may become high-risk.

[92] EDPB–EDPS, Joint Opinion 5/2021 on the proposal for a Regulation of the European Parliament and of the Council laying down harmonised rules on artificial intelligence (Artificial Intelligence Act) 18 June 2021, 6.

[93] See Department for Digital, Culture, Media and Sport (n 21).

AI systems that are not likely to cause serious fundamental rights violations or other significant risks, thus leading the Czech presidency of the EU to propose the introduction of a supplementary horizontal layer on top of the high-risk classification: the significance of the output of the AI system as well as the immediacy of the effects.[94] Critics point out that the vast majority of AI systems will be subject just to the duty to ensure (some) transparency without being regulated in depth. In their Joint Opinion, the European Data Protection Board (EDPB) and the European Data Protection Supervisor (EDPS) noted that some of the provisions in the Proposal leave out the risks for groups of individuals or society as a whole, though these should be equally assessed and mitigated.[95] Despite the good and understandable intentions of the Commission to provide legal certainty, scholars underline that the classification model fails to capture the more nuanced reality of the way AI systems are used – and have an impact on fundamental rights.[96]

The question of timing is of utmost significance, as such an assessment has to be carried out when threats and risks are identifiable, but, at the same time, certain requirements based on the level of risk assigned must be met prior to its release.[97] Both the EDPB and scholars have suggested that including an obligation for third-party conformity assessment would further strengthen legal certainty and confidence in all high-risk AI systems.[98] Beyond the difficulties of self-assessment,[99] a major shortcoming of the EU concept is that the AI systems are to be (self-)assessed at market entry and not throughout their lifecycle. This timing is related to the scope of assessment: what seems to be important is the reasonably predictable uses and their effects and impacts, not the intended uses.

As AI systems are dynamic technologies, their deployment for different purposes and/or different contexts may change the initial classification. In any case, the qualification of a technology or procedure as 'limited risk' or 'minimal risk' mitigates the obligations and requirements set for AI systems providers and users, but it does not diminish the legal protection of the rights involved or the application of respective rules. Furthermore, the AI Act provides for ex post controls conducted by the national supervisory authorities, although it remains unclear on what basis and on what scale these controls will be carried out.[100]

[94] In the General Approach Text (see n 47), the Czech presidency has removed deep fake detection by law enforcement authorities, crime analytics and verification of the authenticity of travel documents from the high-risk use cases listed in Annex III, and added critical digital infrastructure and life and health insurance.

[95] EDPB–EDPS (n 92).

[96] N Smuha et al, 'How the EU Can Achieve Legally Trustworthy AI: A Response to the European Commission's Proposal for an Artificial Intelligence Act' (5 August 2021) http://dx.doi.org/10.2139/ssrn.3899991.

[97] Ebers et al (n 49).

[98] EDPB–EDPS (n 92) 37. See also Smuha et al (n 96).

[99] Ebers et al call for a more detailed classification of risks to facilitate industry self-assessment and support. Ebers et al (n 49) 593.

[100] Smuha et al (n 96).

In this respect, it is essential to adopt efficient monitoring, enforcement and redress regimes. Otherwise, regulatory proposals run the risk 'of providing the façade of legal protection, while in practice offering little meaningful and effective protection and collapsing into little more than self-regulation'.[101]

VI. (Human) Oversight, Enforcement and Redress

In the European AI debate, guaranteeing human autonomy and mitigating adverse effects of AI applications are closely linked with the requirement for human oversight.[102] Together with the obligations for ex ante assessment and risk management, human oversight is intended to facilitate the respect of other fundamental rights by minimising the risk of erroneous or biased AI-assisted decisions in critical areas such as employment.[103] When it comes to high-risk systems, appropriate human oversight measures should be identified by the provider of the system before placing it on the market or putting it into service. Despite the good intentions to ensure that there is a human in the loop to prevent harm or infringements of individuals' rights, the complexity and opacity of AI systems represent intrinsic challenges for human cognition.[104]

Although the UK government seems to ignore the need for human oversight, it combines the principle of transparency with the requirement for 'accountability for the AI and any specific outcomes'.[105] In this context, it considers that 'accountability for the outcomes produced by AI and legal liability must always rest with an identified or identifiable legal person – whether corporate or natural', and consequently the AI Regulation Policy Paper includes a 'cross-sectoral principle' to responsibility[106] for AI governance, without, however, providing any further guidance on the scope and means to ensure compliance.

With reference to enforcement, the model of the AI Act relies on (self-) conformity assessments and the combination of enforcement competences and powers of national authorities and the European Artificial Intelligence Board.[107] Article 59(1) of the AI Act Proposal requires Member States to designate or establish national competent authorities 'for the purpose of ensuring the application and implementation of [the] regulation'. A lot of questions have been raised

[101] ibid.
[102] This requirement was set by the HLEG Guidelines to be fulfilled by diverse governance mechanisms such as a human-in-the-loop (HITL), human-on-the-loop (HOTL) or human-in-command (HIC) approach. See High Level Expert Group, *Ethics Guidelines for Trustworthy AI* (Brussels, 2019).
[103] Memorandum to the AI Act Proposal (n 62).
[104] Vorras and Mitrou (n 17).
[105] Department for Digital, Culture, Media and Sport (n 21).
[106] In the UK approach as laid down in the respective documents, there is a quite vague and confusing parallel use of the terms 'responsibility', 'accountability' and 'liability'.
[107] Stahl et al (n 1).

about how these authorities should and could coexist and cooperate with existing authorities and bodies in the various domains and sectors covered by the AI Act, such as the data protection authorities. Potential overlaps of rules and competences may undermine the legal certainty and enforceability, and put additional compliance burdens on AI providers and users. Concerns have been expressed regarding the enforcement structure for being too complex and heavy to be served by under-resourced national authorities,[108] while even EU Member States have questioned the 'excessively decentralized, national level enforcement' data governance scheme as it may have 'limitations, notably due to insufficient capacities and know-how at the level of national authorities to implement and enforce AI rules effectively'.[109] It is noteworthy that the national supervisory authorities will not only deploy an 'arsenal' of powers for monitoring compliance with the AI Act similar to those under the GDPR but, moreover, they will be able to impose sanctions even above the GDPR level. Aiming at the introduction of 'effective, proportionate and dissuasive penalties', the EU Commission proposed a quite 'draconian' penalty regime in case of non-compliance with the AI Act, with fines potentially reaching €30 million or 6 per cent of global revenues, whichever is higher, for the most serious violations of the new AI framework.[110]

In contrast to the EU, the UK policy papers are silent on the sanctions that may be imposed by regulators. This is consistent with the approach of the UK government, which focuses on 'clear steers to the regulators' that 'do no not necessarily translate into mandatory obligations'. Instead, emphasis is put on the contestability of AI outcomes. According to the AI Regulation Policy Paper, regulators are expected to 'ensure the contestability of the outcome of the use of AI in relevant regulated situations'.[111] Although the title of the sixth cross-sectoral principle refers to 'routes to redress', there are no concrete indications about the nature and conditions of redress rights and mechanisms. Similarly, the AI Act Proposal is characterised by a lack of individual rights and respective complaint and redress mechanisms. Although Recital 38 implies 'effective redress' and 'effective remedy', enforceable, legal and procedural rights or any reference to judicial redress are missing,[112] with the exception of the criteria for the risk classification process for

[108] Smuha et al (n 96).

[109] See the Proposal as redrafted by the Czech presidency, which responded to these concerns by proposing to strengthen the role of the European Artificial Intelligence Board to enable it to provide support to the authorities competent for enforcing the AI Act.

[110] According to Art 71 of the AI Act Proposal, this is the case of breach of the rules concerning prohibited AI practices (Art 5). The European Parliament proposed to align the fines to the level adopted by the GDPR.

[111] Department for Digital, Culture, Media and Sport (n 53) 15.

[112] Ebers et al stress that neither individuals affected by AI systems nor civil rights organisations have the right to complain to market surveillance authorities or to sue a provider or user for failure to comply with the requirements (n 49). See also M Veale and F Zuiderveen Borgesius, 'Demystifying the Draft EU Artificial Intelligence Act – Analysing the Good, the Bad, and the Unclear Elements of the Proposed Approach' (2021) 22(4) *Computer Law Review International* 97.

AI systems under Article 7(2)(h)(I), which include considering whether processes for remedies are necessary for a particular AI system. In its report, the European Parliament proposed Amendments (269–70) to guarantee that individuals can complain to national authorities and seek a remedy if their health, safety or fundamental rights have been breached.[113]

VII. Some Concluding Thoughts on Regulating Artificial Intelligence and (Digital) Sovereignty

The AI Act Proposal is undoubtedly the most important and influential regulatory step taken on the international level and, if not the first, is certainly the most comprehensive one. The AI Act is explicitly positioned to become a global model, especially through its extraterritorial scope and the implications thereof. Due to the choice that AI will also be applicable to providers in third countries who place services with AI systems in the EU single market, as well as to providers whose AI systems produce outputs which are used in the EU,[114] the EU extends the scope of the AI Act beyond the borders of the EU to become a de facto global standard. The European legislator aims to place the EU in a position of leadership by both the example of good governance of AI and the 'Brussels effect' by standardising these practices in other jurisdictions,[115] while enhancing the goal of its 'digital sovereignty'.[116]

As explained by Celeste, the concept of digital sovereignty articulates the notion of sovereignty in the context of the digital ecosystem, over digital assets, which can be material and immaterial entities, thus potentially 'located' in a space

[113] Draft report on the proposal for a regulation of the European Parliament and of the Council on harmonised rules on Artificial Intelligence (Artificial Intelligence Act) and amending certain Union Legislative Acts (COM2021/0206 – C9-0146/2021 – 2021/0106(COD). The Czech presidency's General Approach Text (n 47) seems to respond to these concerns by adding a new Art 63(11), which provides that a natural or legal person who has reasons to consider that there has been an infringement of the provisions of the AI Act may make a complaint to the relevant market surveillance authority and may expect that such a complaint will be handled in line with the dedicated procedures of that authority.

[114] What is important is whether an AI system or service – for example, a loan management program based on machine learning – has an impact on European citizens, not where the company that provides it or uses it is located, whether physically or legally.

[115] The so-called 'Brussels effect' leads, under some conditions, to unilateral regulatory globalisation where regulations originating from a single jurisdiction penetrate many aspects of economic life across the global marketplace. For more about the 'Brussels effect', see A Bradford, *The Brussels Effect: How the European Union Rules the World* (Oxford University Press, 2020). See also T Christakis, '"European Digital Sovereignty": Successfully Navigating between the "Brussels Effect" and Europe's Quest for Strategic Autonomy' (2020) http://dx.doi.org/10.2139/ssrn.3748098.

[116] Some commentators allege that the externalisation of the EU's single market reflects imperialistic motives, while Kuner suggests that when 'a legal system strives for its standards to be accepted as universal values, it is inevitably engaged in a hegemonic struggle in which it seeks to have its own interests identified with the general interest'. See C Kuner, 'The Internet and the Global Reach of EU Law' in M Cremona and J Scott (eds), *EU Law beyond EU Borders: The Extraterritorial Reach of EU Law* (Oxford University Press, 2019) 112.

that transcends physical boundaries.[117] Although digital sovereignty is not limited to regulatory power, the European Council explicitly combined in October 2020 the goal of 'digital sovereignty' with the 'ability to define its own rules' – in other words, the ability to decide and act autonomously on the essential digital aspects of the future in the EU's economy, society and democracy.[118] In this context digital sovereignty is also considered as 'an ordered, value-driven, regulated and therefore reasonable and secure digital sphere'.[119]

The vision of the UK is clearly articulated in the Policy Paper on Digital Regulation: 'having exited the EU, we have the opportunity to build on our world leading regulatory regime',[120] thus claiming that the UK will become a 'global AI superpower' and promising to develop 'the most trusted and pro-innovation system of [AI] governance in the world'.[121] Whereas the EU maintains that it intends to cultivate a regulatory environment that guarantees a level playing field, where EU companies can compete with their foreign counterparts on equal terms,[122] commentators and scholars assess that the UK could achieve the desired leadership, or at least a competitive position in AI regulation could be achieved in some aspects of regulatory procedure and approach.[123] In this context, many view regulation as the 'missing link in the UK's overall AI strategy',[124] a gap that is critical to address if it is to become an AI superpower. Commentators emphasise that the geopolitical reality set constraints on the ability of the UK 'to establish a unique post-Brexit governance regime for AI', as 'the EU's shadow continues to loom large over UK policymaking'.[125] At the same time, the intended 'world leading data regime that is based on an approach of common sense and not box-ticking' is criticised as being 'misguided for ensuring ethical outcomes and innovation'.[126]

The AI governance field constitutes a global arena, where multiple states and stakeholders – struggling to reserve for themselves the leading position – compete to influence AI policies and governance.[127] Radu suggests that this is the new terrain of contestation in international relations, and is marked by uncertainty about the loss of control and human oversight.[128] It is highly questionable if a global

[117] See E Celeste, 'Digital Sovereignty in the EU: Challenges and Future Perspectives' in F Fabbrini, E Celeste and J Quinn, *Data Protection beyond Borders: Transatlantic Perspectives on Extraterritoriality and Sovereignty* (Hart Publishing, 2021) 211, 217–18.

[118] Hence the approach of L Moerel and P Timmers, 'Reflections on Digital Sovereignty' (EU Cyber Direct, 2021).

[119] J Pohle and T Thiel, 'Digital Sovereignty' (2020) 9(4) *Internet Policy Review*.

[120] HM Government, 'Digital Regulation' (n 68).

[121] HM Government, *National AI Strategy* (n 26).

[122] Christakis (n 115).

[123] Ada Lovelace Institute (n 16).

[124] ibid 9, 12.

[125] H Roberts, A Babuta, J Morley, C Thomas, M Taddeo and L Floridi, 'Artificial Intelligence Regulation in the United Kingdom: A Path to Global Leadership?' (1 September 2022) http://dx.doi.org/10.2139/ssrn.4209504.

[126] ibid.

[127] Koniakou (n 22).

[128] Radu (n 32).

AI governance could be applicable across different geographical, economical, cultural and legal contexts, and also in line with existing standards of democracy and fundamental rights.[129] On the other hand, the globalised and interdependent world economy also requires convergence on regulatory level.

As already analysed, there are several approaches to addressing the governance challenges posed by the disruptive technology of AI, ranging from deregulation to bold regulatory direction. It is questioned whether expertise and investments are attracted by flexible and vague approaches or by concrete and stable frameworks. As demonstrated by the GDPR experience, it seems important to move early to be able to lead global AI policy considerations. The issue of 'regulatory timing' seems to be unresolved: can the AI challenges be identified and addressed by attempts to predict sociotechnical changes in detail or by reactive responses which prefer to 'wait out' technological change until its societal impact has become clear? Adaptive and anticipatory regulative approaches, including provisions such as sunset clauses and obligatory reassessment, may serve as antidotes to mitigate the lack of clarity even decades after a technology's deployment.[130] However, as Collingridge states by summarising the 'control dilemma' faced by legislators, 'When change is easy, the need for it cannot be foreseen; when the need for change is apparent, change has become expensive, difficult and time consuming'.[131] Adopting technology-neutral provisions, such as those in the GDPR, seems to be the way to deal with the innovative and unclassified relationships deriving from the technological developments, and consequently to ensure that the law is sustainable over a sufficiently long period. But even regulation that is technology-neutral may in the end prove ineffective and not future-proof, as actually technology-independent rules are also premised on a set of assumptions made at a particular technological moment,[132] and the way its challenges and risks are perceived by the public, the stakeholders and the legislator.

[129] Taeihagh (n 77).

[130] Maas (n 12).

[131] D Collingridge, *The Social Control of Technology* (St Martin's Press, 1980) 29. See also EA Parson, 'Social Control of Technological Risks: The Dilemma of Knowledge and Control in Practice, and Ways to Surmount It' (2016) 64 *UCLA Law Review Discourse* 464, 467.

[132] Crootof and Ard (n 57) 410.

8

Regulatory Divergence: The Effects of UK Technology Law Reforms on Data Protection and International Data Transfers

EDINA HARBINJA

I. Introduction

The post-Brexit UK is characterised by a turbulent and chaotic political, economic and social environment and a lively and often disintegrated policy and law reform landscape. To deliver on Brexit promises of 'independence from Brussels',[1] the government has introduced law reform in various areas, with digital regulation and law being particularly significant and controversial. Shortly after Brexit, the government announced reforms in data protection, online safety, human rights and AI regulation, inter alia. After a period of intense political turmoil and prime minister resignations, we seem to be left with fewer reform proposals. At the moment, it seems that the human rights reform has been scrapped,[2] and the data protection and online safety reform have been delayed, contrary to the government's initial promises.[3] The AI regulation reform is ongoing, but comprehensive primary legislation in this area will not be expected any time soon.[4]

[1] HM Government, Briefing Notes, www.gov.uk/government/uploads/system/uploads/attachment_data/file/524040/Queen_s_Speech_2016_background_notes_.pdf; P Johnston, 'Do You Want Your Sovereignty Back? Then Vote Leave the EU' *The Telegraph* (8 February 2016) www.telegraph.co.uk/news/news/newstopics/eureferendum/12146990/Do-you-want-sovereignty-back-Then-vote-to-leave-the-EU.html. For more, see P Hustinx, 'Towards a Successful Cross-Border Regulatory Cooperation', ch 11 in this volume.

[2] S Payne and J Croft, 'Liz Truss Scraps Proposed British Bill of Rights' *Financial Times* (7 September 2022) www.ft.com/content/9b0a32fc-980b-4f00-9cf5-6c3f29756800.

[3] R Manthorpe, 'Online Safety Bill: Culture Secretary Nadine Dorries Vows to Get Tough on Tech Firms – as Executives Could Face Jail for Breaches' (*Sky News*, 4 November 2021) https://news.sky.com/story/online-safety-bill-culture-secretary-nadine-dorries-vows-to-get-tough-on-tech-firms-as-executives-could-face-jail-for-breaches-12459767; J Woodhouse et al, 'The Data Protection and Digital Information Bill 2022–23' (UK Parliament Research briefing, 6 September 2022) https://commonslibrary.parliament.uk/research-briefings/cbp-9606/.

Notwithstanding the uncertainty of the regulatory environment, it is apparent that current reforms have not been considered holistically. Their effects have been assessed rather in isolation, and the piecemeal approach results in regulatory discrepancy, inconsistency and divergence. Consequently, regulatory and law reform goals may be undermined, particularly regarding their impact on fundamental rights and freedoms.

This chapter examines aspects of this 'digital law reform package', and analyses the effects of a specific technology law reform on another area of law reform in the digital sphere. In particular, and in line with the overall subject matter of this book, I question the effects of online safety law reform (the Online Safety Bill) and AI regulation on data protection in the UK and commercial data transfers between the UK and the EU. The focus will be on the most significant proposal in these reforms that may compromise or otherwise impact the UK data protection regime, its adequacy and its relationship with the EU data protection regime. I challenge these proposals on the basis of their divergence and inconsistency, and conclude that the technology (and other) law reform must be approached holistically, or we risk unintended and adverse consequences, not only on the enforceability of these proposals, but also on the UK's data protection adequacy and, notably, data protection and privacy rights of individuals in the UK.

As a framework, the chapter endorses the regulatory alignment/divergence model developed by Armstrong. He submits that regulatory alignment/divergence in any given policy area will be a 'function of the operation and interaction of different modes of governance: hierarchy, competition, co-ordination, networks and community'.[5] Briefly, hierarchy is a coercive form of governance based on rules and discipline. In the context of Brexit, UK regulatory alignment/divergence is 'a function of the external discipline' of agreements between the UK and the EU, other instruments they are parties to and 'the institutional apparatus through which such instruments would be implemented and enforced'.[6] Firstly, in the context of data protection, the UK adequacy decision represents a hierarchical mode of governance. Secondly, competition as a form of governance means the market forces the extension of EU governance beyond its territory. An example of this may be companies applying EU General Data Protection Regulation (GDPR) standards of data protection outside the EU to simplify compliance and governance.[7] Thirdly, coordination entails voluntary mutual agreements and negotiations. An example would be the UK Withdrawal Agreement. Finally, governance by 'network' or 'community' includes public or private actors and the mechanisms

[4] HM Government, *Establishing a Pro-innovation Approach to Regulating AI* (CP 728, 2022) www.gov.uk/government/publications/establishing-a-pro-innovation-approach-to-regulating-ai/establishing-a-pro-innovation-approach-to-regulating-ai-policy-statement.

[5] KA Armstrong, 'Regulatory Alignment and Divergence after Brexit' (2018) 25 *Journal of European Public Policy* 1099, 1115.

[6] ibid 1104–05.

[7] On this point, see RA Costello, 'The Brussels Effect: Regulatory Standard-Setting and Constitutional Conflicts in Post-Brexit Privacy Law', ch 9 in this volume.

of transfer and diffusion, which result in 'common socialisation activities and joint knowledge production'.[8] Examples could include regulatory or academic knowledge production that may result in a greater regulatory alignment between the EU and the UK in different areas of technology regulation in the future.

The chapter approaches these questions of relevant law reforms comparatively, looking at the proposals in context and action, assessing their consequences and effects on individuals and society. It cross-references many relevant chapters in this book, where aspects of these reforms have been considered, mostly independently, focusing on one or two reforms.[9]

In section II, I briefly consider UK data protection adequacy to set out the scene for the assessment of the effect other law reforms may have on UK data protection adequacy. In section III, I consider the online safety reforms and their potential effect on regulatory divergence and data protection adequacy. Section IV looks at the government's approach to the regulation of AI in the context of data protection and adequacy, before offering conclusions and ways forward. The chapter will not focus on the proposed human rights reform, as it has been withdrawn for now. I will, however, mention it briefly to provide another example of the regulatory divergence and the resulting discrepancy that I assess in this chapter.

II. UK Adequacy Challenged

The UK data protection adequacy decision and the events that preceded it have been introduced in detail in chapter two, as well as in McCullagh's earlier excellent work.[10] In chapter three, Pearce also ably explores aspects of adequacy, questioning the unambitious proposal for law reform in the UK and arguing that the UK government could have proposed an even more radical data protection model.[11] Additionally, Erdos offers one of the most detailed analyses of the law reform proposal in his two recent pieces.[12] To avoid the repetition of these analyses, I will only briefly explore the most significant aspects of the data protection reform relevant to this chapter.

After the UK left the EU on 31 January 2020, the early data protection and technology law scholarship mostly focused on challenges associated with the UK being granted an adequacy decision by the European Commission

[8] ibid 1105.

[9] See chs 2 (K Mc Kullagh, 'Post-Brexit UK Data Protection: Staying the Course or Charting a New Direction?'), 3 (H Pearce, 'Brexit and Data Protection Law: A Missed Opportunity for Innovative Reform?'), 7 (L Mitrou, 'Regulation versus Innovation? A Comparative Analysis of EU and UK Policy Responses on Artificial Intelligence') and 9 in this volume.

[10] K McCullagh, 'Brexit: Potential Trade and Data Implications for Digital and "Fintech" Industries' (2017) 7(1) *International Data Privacy Law* 3; see also ch 2 in this volume.

[11] See ch 3 in this volume.

[12] D Erdos, 'A Bill for a Change? Analysing the UK Government's Statutory Proposals on the Content of Data Protection and Electronic Privacy' (7 September 2022). University of Cambridge Faculty of

(the Commission).[13] Following a period of uncertainty that saw the publication of the Commission's draft decisions,[14] the two final UK adequacy decisions were adopted on the 28 June 2021, allowing transborder personal data flows to continue between the EU and the UK.[15]

When assessing the data protection adequacy, the Commission had to determine whether the UK provides an 'essentially equivalent' level of protection to that in the EU. UK law did not need to mirror the GDPR entirely,[16] as long as it contained the core requirements set out in Article 45 GDPR and further elaborated on in Court of Justice of the EU case law, the EDPB's Recommendations on Essential Guarantees for surveillance measures[17] and the EDPB's 'adequacy referential'.[18] Importantly for the purpose of this discussion, the de jure substantive protection of personal data in UK law was assessed by reference to the criteria set out in Article 45(2) GDPR. The article requires the Commission to take into consideration not just the domestic data protection law *sensu stricto*, but also the rule of law, respect for human rights and fundamental freedoms, relevant legislation and the international commitments the UK has entered into. This provision thus compels the Commission to consider other legislation, case law and the rule of law more broadly, all of which may impact data protection and privacy in the UK, including the legislative proposals (once adopted) analysed in this chapter. This is a clear example of Armstrong's hierarchy as a coercive form of governance, where regulatory alignment is achieved through a set of rules and an adequacy decision.

Law Research Paper No 13/2022, http://dx.doi.org/10.2139/ssrn.4212420; D Erdos, 'Towards Effective Supervisory Oversight? Analysing UK Regulatory Enforcement of Data Protection and Electronic Privacy Rights and the Government's Statutory Reform Plans' (28 November 2022). University of Cambridge Faculty of Law Research Paper No 16/2022.

[13] See, eg C Kuner et al, 'The Global Data Protection Implications of "Brexit"' (2016) 6(3) *International Data Privacy Law* 167; A Murray, 'Data Transfers between the EU and UK post Brexit?' (2017) 7(3) *International Data Privacy Law* 149; L Moerel and R Tigner, 'Data Protection Implications of Brexit' [2016] *European Data Protection Law Review* 381; O Butler, 'The Implications of a "No-Deal" Brexit for Data Protection in the United Kingdom' (2019) 3(1) *Journal of Data Protection & Privacy* 8; P de Hert and V Papakonstantinou, 'The Rich UK Contribution to the Field of EU Data Protection: Let's Not Go for "Third Country" Status after Brexit' (2017) 33(3) *Computer Law & Security Review* 254; A Vanberg and M Maunick, 'Data Protection in the UK post-Brexit: the Only Certainty Is Uncertainty' [2018] *International Review of Law, Computers & Technology* 190; McCullagh, 'Brexit: Potential Trade' (n 10).

[14] Commission, 'Data Protection: European Commission Launches Process on Personal Data Flows to UK' (19 February 2021) https://ec.europa.eu/commission/presscorner/detail/en/ip_21_661.

[15] Commission, 'Data Protection: Commission Adopts Adequacy Decisions for the UK' (28 June 2021) https://ec.europa.eu/commission/presscorner/detail/en/ip_21_3183.

[16] Case C-362/14 *Maximillian Schrems v Data Protection Commissioner* (*Schrems I*) ECLI:EU:C:2015:650, para 81.

[17] EDPB Recommendations 02/2020 on the European Essential Guarantees for surveillance measures, adopted on 10 November 2020, https://edpb.europa.eu/our-work-tools/our-documents/preporki/recommendations-022020-european-essential-guarantees_en.

[18] Article 29 Working Party, 'Adequacy Referential' adopted on 28 November 2017, as last revised and adopted on 6 February 2018, WP254 rev.01 (endorsed by the EDPB, the Art 29WP successor body) https://edpb.europa.eu/our-work-tools/general-guidance/endorsed-wp29-guidelines. For a more in-depth analysis, see ch 2 in this volume.

In terms of the data protection law specifically, the UK government's intention was for UK data protection law to continue to adhere to the EU GDPR post-Brexit.[19] Nevertheless, the potential for divergence was never ruled out. The first sign of divergence arose in September 2021, when the Department for Digital, Culture, Media and Sport (DCMS) launched a public consultation and the law reform paper, 'Data: A New Direction'.[20] The paper outlined various proposed changes to the UK's data protection regimes, with legislative aims to reduce barriers to innovation, reduce compliance burdens on businesses, boost trade and improve public services.[21] Responses to the consultation were mixed, with vocal academic and social society critics suggesting that the proposal would weaken many established data protection rules and jeopardise the UK adequacy decision.[22] On 18 July 2022, the Data Protection and Digital Information Bill (the DPDIB) was introduced in the House of Commons to amend a number of provisions of the UK GDPR and the Data Protection Act 2018 (DPA).[23]

Despite the proposed reforms set out in the DCMS's consultation paper aiming to be substantive and innovative, they are, in reality, quite unambitious and do not seem to diverge radically from the EU data protection regime at first impression. Only a few significant proposals diverge from the GDPR to any extent.[24] Their impact is yet to be evaluated, as the final text has not yet been passed and so the law cannot be assessed in action. Indeed, as anticipated, the programme parliamentary discussion of the Bill originally planned for September 2022 has been postponed.

In her analysis of the DPDIB in chapter two, McCullagh argues that the proposed changes, 'if implemented in their current form, are unlikely to jeopardise the UK adequacy decision'.[25] Erdos shares this view, finding the reform proposal 'wide-ranging but not radical'.[26] McCullagh analyses the plan to retain the UK GDPR's definition of personal data with only minor amendments. The 'Data: A New Direction' consultation proposed revising the definition, but the DPDIB proposes that data will be identifiable if another person is 'likely' to 'obtain the information as a result of the processing' and the data subject 'will be, or is likely

[19] *Out-Law News*, 'GDPR Will Come into Force in the UK in 2018, Minister Confirms' (Pinsent Masons, 9 November 2016) www.pinsentmasons.com/out-law/news/gdpr-will-come-into-force-in-the-uk-in-2018-minister-confirms. See also E Celeste, 'Data Protection' in F Fabbrini, *The Law & Politics of Brexit: Volume III* (Oxford University Press, 2021).

[20] Department for Digital, Culture, Media & Sport (DCMS), 'Data: A New Direction' (10 September 2021) https://assets.publishing.service.gov.uk/government/uploads/system/uploads/attachment_data/file/1022315/Data_Reform_Consultation_Document__Accessible_.pdf.

[21] ibid.

[22] See, eg W Damen et al, 'Data Protection in Post-Brexit Britain: A Response to the Government of the United Kingdom's Public Consultation on Reforms to the Data Protection Regime ("Data: A New Direction")' (Leadership, Enterprise & Diversity Laboratory, University of Birmingham, 2021).

[23] Data Protection and Digital Information Bill, https://publications.parliament.uk/pa/bills/cbill/58-03/0143/220143.pdf.

[24] For more detail, see Erdos, 'A Bill for a Change?' (n 12).

[25] See ch 2 in this volume.

[26] Erdos, 'A Bill for a Change?' (n 12) 2.

to be identifiable' by that person 'by reasonable means'.[27] This limits the assessment of identifiability to the controller or processor and persons who are likely to receive the information, rather than anyone in the world.[28] The proposed change of definition would thus narrow the scope of what is considered personal data under the UK GDPR.[29] This, arguably, will provide controllers with more certainty that they have anonymised the data effectively so that they can 'use it more innovatively within their organisations, or when shared with organisations that adhere to similar standards on anonymisation and re-identification'.[30] Erdos offers a similar analysis, arguing that this would represent 'a plausible gloss on the definition found in the EU GDPR'.[31] The proposal mirrors the principle adopted in *Breyer*, and in McCullagh's view, which I share, it is unlikely to prove problematic when the UK adequacy decision is reviewed.

The second significant change relates to one of the lawful bases for the processing of personal data, ie the processing that is necessary for the legitimate interest of a data controller (Article 6(1)(f) UK GDPR). Currently, this ground can be used by a data controller to the extent that the controller conducts the so-called 'balancing test' and establishes that their interests are not outweighed by the interests of the individual.[32] In the 'Data: A New Direction' consultation, the UK government stated that applying the balancing test is too complex and forces organisations to inappropriately rely on consent as a lawful basis for processing. The government then proposed to remove the balancing test for a limited list of legitimate interests specified in the DPDIB.[33] The list includes matters of 'public interest', such as national security, public security, defence, emergencies, preventing crime, democratic engagement and safeguarding children/vulnerable adults. McCullagh submits that the list of categories is unlikely to prove problematic when the UK adequacy decision is reviewed. However, she also notes that the DPDIB further stipulates that the DCMS Secretary of State may, in the future, amend this list so that more processing may be conducted on a legitimate interest basis without necessitating a balancing test.[34] The amendments would need to undergo an affirmative resolution procedure, and the Secretary of State would explicitly have to regard data subjects' rights and fundamental freedoms, inter alia.[35]

Thirdly, and more concerningly, there are proposals in the DPDIB that would reduce the independence of the Information Commissioner's Office (ICO), the UK national data protection authority, which may attract scrutiny by the European

[27] Data Protection and Digital Innovation Bill (n 23) cl 1(2).
[28] Consistent with the EU case law.
[29] This reflects the position in Case C-582/14 *Breyer v Bundesrepublik Deutschland* ECLI:EU:C:2016:779, Opinion of AG Campos Sánchez-Bordona, para 65.
[30] DCMS (n 20) 46.
[31] Erdos, 'A Bill for a Change?' (n 12) 5.
[32] GDPR, Art 6.1(f).
[33] Erdos, 'A Bill for a Change?' (n 12) 7–8.
[34] See ch 2 in this volume.
[35] Data Protection and Digital Innovation Bill (n 23) cl 5.

Commission when the UK's adequacy decision is reviewed. Under the proposal, the ICO would be reorganised into a corporate board with the primary objectives of securing an appropriate level of data protection and promoting trust and confidence in the data processing. However, the ICO would also be formally required to take into account other objectives, such as tackling crime and 'promoting innovation and competition'.[36] The ICO will need to have regard to the government's strategic priorities (which will be set out by the Secretary of State in an official 'statement of priorities' laid before Parliament) when exercising its regulatory functions.[37] There is also a provision for the Secretary of State to approve statutory ICO Codes of Practice. Erdos adds another concern to this list, noting that 'the proposed changes do not effectively address the extremely limited reality of ICO enforcement action and, relatedly, the lack of an accessible mechanism to ensure that data subject complaints are properly handled'.[38] In his detailed analysis, he points to various deficiencies in the ICO's action, complaint handling, ineffective accountability and lack of holistic scrutiny. To address this, Erdos advances a couple of solutions, including the proposition that the Equality and Human Rights Commission should be required to review the ICO's regulation biennially from a human rights perspective and lay the review before Parliament for democratic scrutiny.[39]

Therefore, the question of the ICO's independence remains particularly concerning in the context of adequacy. McCullagh rightly posits that if the UK government uses these proposals to limit the independence and regulatory freedom of the ICO, they are likely to affect the adequacy when the UK adequacy decision is reviewed. These issues might also warrant close scrutiny by the Commission, as the European Data Protection Supervisor has observed 'that any changes that make it less independent or require it to push through a political agenda will naturally force the Commission to raise concerns, ask questions, and seek assurances'.[40] Additionally, the UK adequacy decision contains a sunset clause that is valid for four years, expiring on 27 June 2025 if the Commission has not renewed it by then.[41] In McCullagh's opinion, this combination of continuous review and a sunset clause 'will exert pressure on the UK to identify deficiencies and ensure that it does not diverge to a significant extent from the EU GDPR standard if the

[36] ibid cl 27, s 120B; Erdos, 'Towards Effective Supervisory Oversight?' (n 12) 3.

[37] Data Protection and Digital Innovation Bill (n 23) cl 28.

[38] Erdos, 'Towards Effective Supervisory Oversight?' (n 12) 3.

[39] ibid.

[40] N Hodge, 'EDPS: UK GDPR Reforms Could Create Friction with EU' (*Compliance Week*, 13 July 2022) www.complianceweek.com/data-privacy/edps-uk-gdpr-reforms-could-create-friction-with-eu/31851.Article.

[41] GDPR, Art 45(3); European Commission, Implementing Decision of 28 June 2021 pursuant to Regulation (EU) 2016/679 of the European Parliament and of the Council on the adequate protection of personal data by the United Kingdom, C(2021) 4800 final, https://ec.europa.eu/info/sites/default/files/decision_on_the_adequate_protection_of_personal_data_by_the_united_kingdom_-_general_data_protection_regulation_en.pdf Art 4, recitals 289–90.

UK is to secure a renewed adequacy decision in the coming years'.[42] McCullagh also believes that, once Brexit was perceived to be 'done' and was no longer the focus of intense political scrutiny in the UK, the UK government might be more accepting of the need to address deficiencies in the UK legal framework to retain it because of the economic consequences that would flow from the disruption of EU–UK personal data transfers. Erdos, however, is not so optimistic and points to the dangers of granting the government powers to amend data protection and e-privacy laws under statutory instruments outside the full and open democratic discourse through primary legislation, which 'may indicate that the direct changes set out in this Bill may simply be the first stage in UK data protection reform'.[43] His pessimism perhaps stems from the finding that 'almost all of the changes proposed are weighted in favour of those who control rather than who are the subject of personal data'.[44]

Other changes proposed in the DPDIB relate to the purpose limitation principle and research, archiving and statistical purposes, the solely automated decision-making right, and some of the compliance and accountability mechanisms (the data protection office obligation, data breaches, data protection impact assessments). These proposals have been analysed in detail by Erdos, so any further detail should be sought there. Importantly for this analysis, their introduction would not create a radical shift from the current regime either.[45]

In conclusion, the analysis above suggests that the proposed changes to the UK data protection law are indeed mainly evolutionary and are therefore likely to be favourably received during any review of the adequacy decision by the Commission.[46] I do, however, submit that the proposals affecting the ICO's independence and the DCMS Secretary of State having the power to add to the list of legitimate interest categories and amend the law through secondary legislation will increase divergence from the GDPR and, in tandem with other technology law reforms, could compromise the UK adequacy decision in the foreseeable future.[47] Looking at this relationship from the perspective of Armstrong's regulatory model set out above, the EU may need to resort to hierarchy as a regulatory model to maintain regulatory alignment. However, due to the importance of trade between the UK and the EU, cooperation and market as regulatory models may interact with hierarchy and allow for a level of divergence in the area of data protection and e-privacy that may not be entirely compatible with the requirement of 'essentially equivalent' data protection regimes.

[42] ch 2 in this volume.
[43] Erdos, 'A Bill for a Change?' (n 12) 23.
[44] ibid.
[45] ibid 5–11.
[46] ch 2 in this volume.
[47] ibid.

III. The Online Safety Bill

The Online Safety Bill seems to be a never-ending bundle of uncertainty.[48] Following the initial Online Harms White Paper,[49] the Bill was introduced in the Parliament in May 2021, and the current version includes amendments by the Public Bill Committee and Sunak's government.[50] Leiser and I have criticised the reform since its inception, and it is not my intention to rehearse these points again here.[51] Inter alia, we focused on the premise of the risk-based regulation, duty of care and the human rights implications of the Bill, emphasising the inadequate provision aimed at protecting privacy and the freedom of expression.[52]

The Online Safety Bill is a gigantic document of 230 pages. In the whole Bill, however, data protection as a term is mentioned only five times in the context of the disclosure of information to Ofcom, the UK's communications regulator.[53] The term 'personal data' is mentioned 11 times.[54] This may seem superficial, but I deem this an indication of the importance the Bill places on data protection and the right to privacy.

In the December 2022 iteration of the Online Safety Bill, there has been some improvement compared to the initially very vaguely defined service providers' duty to have regard to the importance of the protection of privacy and the freedom of expression.[55] The revised clause 20 expands on the duty about privacy and free speech, requiring service providers, when designing their processes and policies, to

> have regard to the importance of protecting users from a breach of any statutory provision or the rule of law concerning privacy that is relevant to the use or operation of a user-to-user service (including but not limited to, any such provision or rule concerning the processing of personal data).[56]

This is quite an imprecise provision, where the Bill seems to conflate privacy and data protection as mechanisms and concepts.[57] Leaving that conceptual

[48] M Leiser, 'The Online Safety Bill Is a Mystery Wrapped in a Riddle inside an Enigma' (*The Drum*, 17 November 2022) www.thedrum.com/opinion/2022/11/17/the-online-safety-bill-mystery-wrapped-riddle-inside-enigma.

[49] HM Government, 'Online Harms White Paper: Full Government Response to the Consultation', www.gov.uk/government/consultations/online-harms-white-paper/outcome/online-harms-white-paper-full-government-response.

[50] Online Safety Bill, as amended on report, 6 December 2022, https://bills.parliament.uk/bills/3137/publications.

[51] M Leiser and E Harbinja, 'Content not Available: Why the United Kingdom's Proposal for a "Package of Platform Safety Measures" Will Harm Free Speech' [2020] *Technology and Regulation* 780; E Harbinja and MR Leiser, '[Redacted]: This Article Categorised [Harmful] by the Government' (2022) 19(1) *SCRIPTed* 88, https://script-ed.org/?p=4050.

[52] ibid.

[53] Online Safety Bill (n 50).

[54] Counted by the author.

[55] Harbinja and Leiser (n 51).

[56] Online Safety Bill (n 50) cl 20.

[57] O Lynskey, *The Foundations of EU Data Protection Law* (Oxford University Press, 2015) ch 4.

distinction aside, the clause still broadly refers to the data protection regime and relates safety measures to complying with the data protection law and privacy. The provision emphasises the importance of having a robust data protection law that service providers need to comply with in the context of online safety. That also may sound quite superfluous since data protection compliance has been established much more strongly in data protection law, not only requiring service providers to '[have] regard to its importance', but also requiring their strict compliance with data protection principles and other provisions under the threat of a hefty fine. Therefore, compliance with the data protection law in clause 20 of the Bill appears quite vague and almost optional. On the other hand, this provision potentially invites scrutiny of the online safety law (if passed in this form) in the UK data protection adequacy assessment context. The link between online safety and data protection established here, albeit vague and insufficient, invites the Commission to consider the law, if adopted, in the context of the adequacy assessment. As noted in the previous section, the Commission is required to assess not only data protection law *sensu stricto*, but also the rule of law, respect for human rights and fundamental freedoms, relevant legislation, etc. The online safety legislation most certainly falls within this 'relevant legislation' remit.

While clause 20 refers to data protection very explicitly, other proposals in the Bill may impact data protection safeguards more impliedly. One of the biggest concerns related to the Bill's impact on privacy and data protection is the likely requirement that service providers proactively monitor personal data to comply with the duty of care.[58] This requirement is set out in clause 120, entitled 'Confirmation Decisions: Proactive Technology', which empowers Ofcom to require proactive monitoring by use of technology (eg algorithms, keyword matching, image matching, image classification or behaviour pattern detection). Ofcom can impose the use of such technology when ordering a service provider to comply with a duty pertaining to illegal content, children's online safety and fraudulent advertising. The clause also prohibits the use of this except when analysing 'user-generated content communicated publicly' and 'metadata relating to user-generated content communicated publicly'. However, the fact that the data is shared publicly does not mean that it is not personal or that the monitoring obligation does not extend to compromising user privacy and data protection rights. Under EU law, and in particular with regard to the e-Commerce Directive, a general monitoring obligation is prohibited and will remain so with the introduction of the Digital Services Act.[59] The UK has always had an unsettling stance towards this obligation, since Article 15 of the e-Commerce Directive appears nowhere in UK domestic legislation.[60] The Online Safety Bill confirms this.[61]

[58] G Smith, 'Mapping the Online Safety Bill' (CyberLeagle, 27 March 2022) www.cyberleagle.com/2022/03/mapping-online-safety-bill.html.

[59] Regulation (EU) 2022/2065 of the European Parliament and of the Council of 19 October 2022 on a Single Market for Digital Services and amending Directive 2000/31/EC (Digital Services Act) (Text with EEA relevance) [2022] OJ L277/1.

[60] G Smith, 'Time to Speak Up for Article 15' (CyberLeagle, 27 March 2022) www.cyberleagle.com/2017/05/time-to-speak-up-for-Article-15.html.

[61] Smith (n 58).

Another concern relates to end-to-end encryption (E2EE). Clause 106 of the Bill grants Ofcom a new power to issue notices to service providers requiring them to identify and take down terrorist content that is communicated 'publicly' by means of their services or child sex exploitation and abuse content being communicated 'publicly or privately'. The inclusion of 'private' communications raises concerns related to E2EE. In a recently published report,[62] Ryder and Wills take the view that the Bill, rather than forcing messaging platforms to abandon E2EE, will push them towards deploying a controversial technology called client-side scanning (CSS) to comply with notices issued by Ofcom. CSS refers to systems that scan message contents for matches or similarities to a database of problematic content before the message is sent to the intended recipient.[63] According to Ryder and Wills, CSS is 'likely to be the primary technology whose use is mandated'.[64] They thus conclude: 'The Bill notes that the accredited technology referred to c.104 is a form of "content moderation technology"', meaning 'technology, such as algorithms, keyword matching, image matching or image classification, which … analyses relevant content (c.187(2)(11)). This description corresponds with CSS.'[65]

Furthermore, a recent government amendment to the Bill provides that a provider given a technology notice has to make such changes to the design or operation of the service as are necessary for the technology to be used effectively. This is another argument in favour of concerns around requiring E2EE to be modified, 'which might, for instance, involve client-side scanning'.[66] The integrity of E2EE is crucial not only for the confidentiality and privacy of communications, but also for moral and essential cybersecurity reasons. Researchers have provided very solid evidence that compromising E2EE compromises the network security and safety of the same users we wish to protect.[67]

Provided that the Bill is passed, its actual impact is yet to be seen since a lot of its implications will depend on Ofcom's codes of practice and the relevant secretary of state's regulations. It will also depend on the relationship between data protection and online safety regimes, their overlaps and tensions. Ofcom and the ICO have issued a joint statement outlining their common objectives, shared competences and cooperation in implementing the online safety law.[68] Ofcom promises to engage with the ICO from an early stage in developing its proposals for the codes

[62] M Ryder KC and A Wills, 'Surveilled and Exposed: How the Online Safety Bill Creates Insecurity' (Index for Censorship, 31 October 2022) www.indexoncensorship.org/2022/11/new-legal-opinion-on-the-online-safety-bill/.

[63] ISOC, 'Fact Sheet: Client-Side Scanning', 24 March 2020, www.internetsociety.org/resources/doc/2020/fact-sheet-client-side-scanning/.

[64] Ryder and Wills (n 62) para 9.

[65] ibid 22.

[66] Smith (n 58).

[67] H Abelson et al, 'Bugs in Our Pockets: The Risks of Client-Side Scanning' (14 October 2021) arXiv:2110.07450 [cs.CR], https://doi.org/10.48550/arXiv.2110.07450; R Anderson, 'Chat Control or Child Protection?' (11 October 2022) arXiv:2210.08958v1 [cs.CY], https://doi.org/10.48550/arXiv.2210.08958.

[68] Ofcom and ICO, 'Online Safety and Data Protection: A Joint Statement by Ofcom and the Information Commissioner's Office' (25 November 2022) www.gov.uk/government/publications/

and guidance required by the Bill and, where appropriate, publish the ICO's formal responses to their consultations. The ICO commits to publishing its expectations on how safety technologies that use personal data should be developed in line with data protection law. They commit to collaborating within the Digital Regulation Cooperation Forum (DCRF).[69] Some of their planned actions include: building and maintaining a common understanding of the areas of overlap and tension between the data protection and online safety regimes; engaging with industry to understand the practical challenges of complying with both regimes; collaboration in developing policy and guidance; and 'establishing effective processes to maintain mutual awareness of our supervisory and enforcement actions'.[70] What is missing there is a much greater emphasis on the tensions within the general monitoring obligation and E2EE, as discussed above. These areas are mentioned in the statement as 'examples' rather than the major concerns that they are. Furthermore, the regulators promise to 'engage with industry to understand the practical challenges of complying with both regimes', seemingly and unfairly excluding civil society, academia and users. Finally, there does not seem to be a recognition of the regulatory capacities in this statement. Notwithstanding Erdos's findings about the ICO enforcement deficiencies, a question of these commitments' practical and effective viability arises.

In summary, what can be drawn from the face of the Bill and analysis of the likely consequences is that the Bill threatens to undermine privacy and data protection rights. The essence of this Bill, if adopted in this or similar form by Parliament, may affect the UK's data protection and privacy rights. The Bill is, therefore, likely to increase the level of regulatory divergence between the UK and the EU in the area of privacy and data protection, but also technology law and regulation more broadly. I submit that the European Commission should review the Bill in the context of the adequacy decision periodic review. In this exercise, the Commission would, again, exert hierarchy as a regulatory model to ensure that regulatory alignment is broadly maintained in the context of privacy and data protection rights.

The example of the proposed Human Rights Act reform would add to the divergence even further had the government decided to proceed with the reform. Fortunately, as it stands, the reform has been scrapped, but, given the political turmoil noted above, it is not difficult to imagine that a similar proposal could be tabled by a new government in the future.[71] To exemplify, the previous proposal

online-safety-and-data-protection-a-joint-statement-by-ofcom-and-the-information-commissioners-office.

[69] ibid 12.

[70] ibid.

[71] See the Bill of Rights Bill (2022) and the report of the 'Independent Human Rights Act Review', www.gov.uk/guidance/independent-human-rights-act-review#about-the-independent-human-rights-act-review; Ministry of Justice, 'Human Rights Act Reform: A Modern Bill of Rights – Consultation' (2022) ch 4.

barely mentioned data protection (only in Appendix 1: Examples of Relevant Domestic Legislation and Common Law Provisions, which cover articles within the Human Rights Act and in the context of Article 8 ECHR, where the DPA and the UK GDPR were mentioned). Privacy was mentioned a few times, but even that was insufficient, as it only appeared in the context of human rights balancing acts, ie the freedom of expression versus the rights to privacy balancing exercise by the courts.[72] The proposal placed a much greater emphasis on the freedom of expression, and the balance between this right and the right to privacy could arguably have been disrupted if the proposal had gone through.

IV. The Emerging UK AI Regulation

It is hard to offer solid answers as to what the UK AI regulation may look like. There are ongoing government consultations, so we can only draw some conclusions from the various consultation documents and strategies the government has introduced so far. Consequently, the impact of this reform on the data protection regime and adequacy is difficult to predict at the moment. However, we can derive some more general conclusions as to the nature and contours of this impact.

The National AI Strategy published in 2021 supported the proposals of the 'Data: A New Direction' consultation analysed above. The short-term goal is to 'determine the role of data protection in wider AI governance following the Data: A new direction consultation'.[73] This has changed due to the revisions introduced in the DPDIB, noted above. Amendments have been proposed to the GDPR Article 22 right related to automated decision-making and processing, but this is not a radical shift either.[74] In clause 11, the Bill provides additional statutory clarification of the thresholds, ie that automated decisions can include 'profiling and carrying out profiling', and that 'solely automated' means that 'there is no meaningful human involvement in the taking of the decision'. The Bill also narrows rights not to be subject to those decisions that are based entirely or partly on special categories of data. The Bill confirms and specifies that the safeguards that must apply when solely automated decision-making produces a legal or similarly significant effect include the provision of information and the enabling of them to make representations, to obtain human intervention and to contest a decision. Moreover, subject to parliamentary approval under the affirmative resolution procedure, the DCMS Secretary of State would be granted power under a statutory instrument to determine what is a 'similarly significant effect' and to amend the safeguards required of controllers in this area. Considering the substantive changes to this

[72] Ministry of Justice (n 71) ch 4, paras 206, 214, 215; see also ch 10 in this volume.

[73] HM Government, *National AI Strategy* (CP 525, 2021) 51, www.gov.uk/government/publications/national-ai-strategy.

[74] Erdos, 'A Bill for a Change?' (n 12) 16–18.

right, Erdos argues that these 'seriously narrow the circumstances when a data subject will be able to resist automated decision-making entirely'. Consequently, he argues, an emphasis is placed on the general safeguards that are subject to slightly expanded specification, which target the key risks that have been located in this area (transparency, fairness, etc).[75]

As analysed above, overall, the Bill includes few provisions that diverge from GDPR. However, the AI Strategy and the subsequent government consultation document both refer to innovation, trade and data flows as policy goals, noting that these would be championed 'while maintaining the UK's high standards for personal data protection'.[76] This is an extremely difficult balance to strike, and following the above analysis, it could be argued that the former goal may be championed to the detriment of the latter.

Turning to the proposed AI regulatory framework, it notably rejects primary legislation in most cases and relies on self-regulation, industry standards and regulation by the existing regulators and their forum – the DCRF.[77] Many commentators have expressed concerns around the proposal, ranging from concerns about the algorithmic governance and scrutiny to the actual power, capacity and legitimacy of the regulators and the DCRF. In chapter seven of this book, Mitrou compares the current attempts to regulate artificial intelligence in the UK and the EU. She notes that the EU AI Act proposal is 'the most important and influential regulatory step taken on the international level and, if not the first, is certainly the most comprehensive one'. Similar to the GDPR, the AI Act could become a global model, mostly due to its extraterritorial scope.[78] The UK, however, claims that 'having exited the EU, we have the opportunity to build on our world leading regulatory regime'[79] and become a 'global AI superpower', with 'the most trusted and pro-innovation system of governance in the world'.[80] Scholars find that the UK could achieve desirable leadership or a competitive position in AI regulation concerning some aspects of the regulatory approach.[81] However, they also view regulation as the 'missing link on the UK's overall AI strategy',[82] a gap that the UK needs to address to become an AI superpower. Researchers note that the reality sets constraints on the UK's ability 'to establish a unique post-Brexit governance regime for AI', as 'the EU's shadow continues to loom large over UK policymaking'.[83] At the same time,

[75] ibid 16–18.

[76] HM Government, *National AI Strategy* (n 73).

[77] HM Government, *Establishing a Pro-innovation Approach to Regulating AI* (n 4).

[78] See ch 7 in this volume.

[79] HM Government, 'Policy Paper: Digital Regulation: Driving Growth and Unlocking Innovation' (6 July 2021) www.gov.uk/government/publications/digital-regulation-driving-growth-and-unlocking-innovation.

[80] HM Government, *National AI Strategy* (n 73).

[81] Ada Lovelace Institute, 'Regulate to Innovate' (29 November 2021) www.adalovelaceinstitute.org/report/regulate-innovate/#:~:text=A%20report%20which%20sets%20out,beneficial%20for%20people%20and%20society.

[82] ibid 9, 12.

[83] H Roberts, A Babuta, J Morley, C Thomas, M Taddeo and L Floridi, 'Artificial Intelligence Regulation in the United Kingdom: A Path to Global Leadership?' (1 September 2022) http://dx.doi.org/10.2139/ssrn.4209504.

they criticise the UK's data protection reform as 'misguided for ensuring ethical outcomes and innovation'.[84]

Irrespective of the actual form and detail the UK AI regulation will adopt following the consultation, these concerns relate to the heart of the reform and its policy goals, which are unlikely to change. It is thus safe to assume that the reform may compromise data protection in favour of innovation and growth. This is, therefore, another area of divergence for the European Commission to consider when reviewing the UK's adequacy decision. This relationship, once more, cannot be viewed through the lens of regulatory cooperation, which would result in regulatory alignment. Instead, the effects of the UK AI regulation are currently predominantly viewed through the lens of hierarchy and the EU's threat of revoking data protection adequacy if the regulation impacts data protection adversely.

V. Conclusion

This chapter examined the potential effects of the UK's ongoing 'digital law reform package', including the new data protection, online safety and AI regulation Bills on data protection and international data transfers. I considered these effects through the lens of Armstrong's regulatory alignment/divergence model. I challenged the reform proposals on the basis of their divergence and inconsistency with EU law. I submitted that the technology (and other) law reform needs to be approached holistically, or we risk unintended and adverse consequences, not only on the implementation and enforceability of these proposals, but also on the UK's data protection adequacy and, notably, data protection and privacy rights of individuals in the UK. A piecemeal reform could lower data protection standards in practice and thus risk adequacy in international data transfers.

To address this, the UK government should consider the effects of hierarchy, cooperation,[85] market and network modes of regulation, and analyse their interactions in the area of technology law and policy. A comprehensive regulatory approach should be guided by the need to enable commercial data transfers with the EU and protect the digital rights of UK citizens. Currently, both policy goals seem to be undermined.

[84] ibid.

[85] For some useful suggestions, see ch 11 in this volume.

PART IV

Digital Sovereignty Tensions and Cross-Border Cooperation Mechanisms

9

The Brussels Effect: Regulatory Standard-Setting and Constitutional Conflicts in Post-Brexit Privacy Law

RÓISÍN Á COSTELLO

I. Introduction

Concerted legislative efforts from the EU – over the last decade in particular – have led to the recognition of the 'Brussels effect', a term used to refer to the increased global influence of the EU as an international standard setter for regulatory governance.[1] It has been claimed that the effect has been particularly marked in the area of data protection and privacy law, with the Union leading the way in setting standards for how data should be treated to best protect the privacy interests of individual citizens.

Although the first hints of the EU's global influence on privacy issues can be traced to the 1995 EU Data Protection Directive,[2] the diffusion of European privacy law has become more firmly established since the advent of the General Data Protection Regulation (GDPR).[3] Certainly, the impact of the Regulation has extended beyond even the traditional scope of influence enjoyed by other European initiatives. Graham Greenleaf estimates that there are now some 148 jurisdictions, globally, that have enacted data privacy laws, with 145 displaying the influence of the GDPR.[4]

[1] See the articulation offered by A Bradford, 'The Brussels Effect' (2012) 107 *North-Western University Law Review* 1; A Bradford, *The Brussels Effect: How the European Union Rules the World* (Oxford University Press, 2020).

[2] Directive 95/46/EC of the European Parliament and of the Council of 24 October 1995 on the protection of individuals with regard to the processing of personal data and on the free movement of such data [1995] OJ L281/31.

[3] Regulation (EU) 2016/679 of the European Parliament and of the Council of 27 April 2016 on the protection of natural persons with regard to the processing of personal data and on the free movement of such data, and repealing Directive 95/46/EC (General Data Protection Regulation) (Text with EEA relevance) [2016] OJ L119/1.

[4] G Greenleaf, 'Global Data Privacy Laws 2021: Despite COVID Delays, 145 Laws Show GDPR Dominance' (2021) 1 *Privacy Laws & Business International Report* 3; G Greenleaf, 'Global Tables of Data Privacy Laws and Bills' (2021) 169 *Privacy Law & Business International Report* 6.

Despite broad acknowledgement that the pattern of EU influence in the area of data protection is real, there has been little analysis of its central premise – that the Union is indeed exporting regulatory standards through this activity. This chapter interrogates the view that the Brussels effect is, indeed, a pattern of regulatory exportation and argues that, in fact, it should be understood as involving not only regulatory but also rights-based standards.

In this respect, it is important to remember that the GDPR is a document that identifies its purpose as protecting the fundamental right to data protection as enshrined in Article 8 of the Charter of Fundamental Rights of the European Union (the Charter) and Article 16 of the Treaty on the Functioning of the European Union (TFEU).[5] In addition, the Regulation itself is replete with references to fundamental rights,[6] and the objective of the document, articulated in Recitals 2 and 4 in particular, orients the Regulation towards 'the protection of natural persons with regard to the processing of their personal data'. While the recitals have interpretative value only, Article 1 GDPR encodes as a legally enforceable threshold the objective of the Regulation to protect the fundamental rights of natural persons, in particular the right to protection of personal data. This grounding objective, and the connection between the Regulation and fundamental rights, has been reinforced by the 2020 judgment from the Court of Justice of the European Union (CJEU) in *Schrems II*,[7] which emphasises that the GDPR should be read and interpreted in compliance with the Charter.[8] Indeed, it is increasingly difficult to maintain that the Regulation's standards can be shorn of the influence of the Charter or, through the requirements of Article 52 of the Charter, the European Court of Human Rights (ECtHR).

In this context, it is increasingly challenging to successfully disentangle the Regulation's status as a rights-based document from its function as a regulatory one – and thus to understand the extent to which its contents are, and should be, subject to regulatory exportation. In unpacking the facts and consequences of the Regulation's relationship to the Union's normative core, this chapter is particularly concerned with the implications of normative and regulatory integration within the GDPR for the UK's ability to offer an equivalent level of protection to personal data following Brexit. The chapter proceeds as follows. In section II, the Brussels effect itself is explained. In section III, the chapter examines the GDPR as a rights-based document, before moving, in section IV, to examine the consequences of the migration of European rights-inflected standards – like the GDPR – beyond the borders of the Union.

[5] Regulation (EU) 2016/679 (n 3).

[6] Charter of Fundamental Rights of the European Union [2012] OJ C326/391.

[7] Case C-311/18 *Data Protection Commissioner v Facebook Ireland Ltd, Maximillian Schrems* (*Schrems II*) ECLI:EU:C:2020:559.

[8] ibid [99]–[100].

II. Exporting Regulatory Standards

The migration of modern regulatory standards beyond the boundaries of the jurisdiction in which they were initially implemented is hardly new. The 'California effect' was first identified by David Vogel in 1999, and was a label ascribed to the shift in federal regulation in the USA that resulted from the spread of advanced regulatory standards based on California's law in the area of environmental policy[9] and, to a lesser extent, in regulatory standards governing information privacy.[10] California's data breach notification legislation is most frequently offered as exemplary of this trend – the standard enjoyed broad support at a state level in the USA and was adopted at a federal level as part of measures applicable to healthcare information data with the US HITECH Act in 2009.[11] The legislative standards introduced by the EU in the twenty-first century have led to a comparable pattern of regulatory exportation from the EU to other jurisdictions as the Union began to emphasise technology regulation and the rights to privacy and data protection as key concerns of the single market.[12]

While the 1995 Data Protection Directive perhaps hinted at this coming influence, the pattern became more firmly established with the GDPR, which entered into force in 2018, the influence of which has spread far beyond that traditionally enjoyed by European regulatory initiatives. The global creep of European data protection standards beyond the borders of the EU has led Tim Wu and Jack Goldsmith to posit that the Union has become 'the effective sovereign' in the area of data protection and privacy as a consequence of a combination of market power and concern for citizen privacy.[13]

Wu and Goldsmith were writing, however, some 12 years before this pattern would gain the momentum brought about by the GDPR. Indeed, it was only with the work of Anu Bradford, in 2018, that this international pattern of regulatory adoption of, and adherence to, EU standards was articulated as the 'Brussels effect'.[14] Bradford suggests that, unlike processes of political globalisation, in which

[9] D Vogel, *Environmental Regulation and Economic Integration* (Yale Centre for Environmental Law and Policy, 1999) www.iatp.org/files/Environmental_Regulation_and_Economic_Integrat.pdf.

[10] LM Elison and DN Simmons, 'Right of Privacy' (1987) 48 *Montana Law Review* 1; LM Elison and DN Simmons, 'Toward a Historic Understanding of Montana's Privacy Provision' (1998) 61 *Albany Law Review* 1681; C Hoofnagle, 'Comparative Study on Different Approaches to New Privacy Challenges, in Particular in the Light of Technological Developments' (European Commission, May 2010) http://ec.europa.eu/justice/data-protection/document/studies/files/new_privacy_challenges/final_report_country_report_b1_usa.pdf.

[11] The Health Information Technology for Economic and Clinical Health Act 2009.

[12] Directorate-General for Communications, Networks, Content, and Technology, 'Strategic Plan 2016–2020' (3 June 2016).

[13] T Wu and J Goldsmith, *Who Controls the Internet?: Illusions of a Borderless World* (Oxford University Press, 2006).

[14] Bradford, *The Brussels Effect* (n 1); D Michaels, 'Hot US Import: European Regulations' *Wall Street Journal* (7 May 2018); A Santariano, 'GDPR: A New Privacy Law Makes Europe World's Leading Tech Watchdog' *New York Times* (24 May 2018).

regulations are adopted after political agreement, or unilateral coercion as a result of threat or sanctions, the Union is presiding over unilateral regulatory globalisation that occurs through the operation of market mechanisms.[15]

In charting the rise of the EU's global regulatory influence, Bradford argues that the USA, in particular, has underappreciated the ability of the EU to leverage its market size to influence regulatory outcomes outside its borders. Bradford's argument is, fundamentally, one concerned with regulatory standards. She notes that the motivation for data protection is both internal (seeking to harmonise standards among Member States) and external (seeking to ensure European standards act as global standard setters), but the argument made is largely mechanical – focused on the patterns that permit regulatory exportation rather than what is being exported. This focus sidelines the rights-based character of the GDPR and does not engage with the idea that there may be an underlying or accompanying exportation of European rights standards alongside regulatory ones.

Other accounts are similarly limited. In an analysis that hints at the issue of rights-based rather than regulation-based standards, Schwartz notes that European regulatory dominance in the area of information privacy is not a function of markets, but a result of a more diffuse set of cultural processes that influence how the global community views privacy rights protection.[16] In this respect, Schwartz's starting point is a description of the GDPR as a privacy law rather than a regulatory standard, yet his account does not query whether the Regulation itself should be conceptualised as a normative rather than regulatory document or what the consequences of such a reconceptualisation would be.[17]

Schwartz's argument is that, rather than exercising unilateral power, the EU has engaged in a series of bilateral negotiations to ensure that third parties accommodate European thresholds of 'adequacy' into national law and that adequacy itself has been flexibly applied.[18] As such, the process of the Regulation's spreading regulatory influence is deeply and deliberately political. More broadly, Schwartz argues that within the EU there is broad political and policy buy-in on the normative importance of data protection, while the flexible and accessible design of the GDPR has made it a highly 'transplantable' legal model.[19] Although Schwartz takes an interest in the drivers of what Bradford refers to as the Brussels effect and locates the pattern at its heart in a broader array of soft power drivers in the form of cultural and policy influences, the account he gives specifically acknowledges (as Bradford's does) that the underlying buy-in to the importance of data

[15] Bradford, 'The Brussels Effect' (n 1).

[16] PM Schwartz, 'Global Data Privacy: The EU Way' (2019) 94 *NYU Law Review* 771.

[17] ibid 771, 773.

[18] An argument that would appear to now be effectively countered by the decision of the CJEU on the content and application of adequacy analysis in *Schrems II* (n 7).

[19] Schwartz (n 16) 771, 803.

protection and the Union's political power drives the creep of the Union's data protection model beyond its borders. However, he does not look to the content of what precisely is being exported as part of the effect – regulations or rights?

III. The GDPR – A Regulatory or Rights-Based Document?

It is worth extending the analysis of the Brussels effect beyond the generative patterns identified by Schwartz and Bradford in their accounts and identifying what (exactly) is being exported and adopted when the Brussels effect is engaged – not only to understand more precisely whether the effect is engaged, but also to identify the consequences of its presence. In this respect, it should be noted that while the efficacy of the GDPR, and the manner in which it allocates compliance burdens, has been disputed, there has been little controversy over the idea that the GDPR gives voice to the Union's constitutional values and was created to integrate and perpetuate the protection of Articles 7 and 8 of the Charter of Fundamental Rights in relationships between private individuals as well as between individuals and the state.

The EU specifically understands the GDPR as giving force to the right to data protection and the right to privacy, as those rights are contained in the EU's constitutional documents – in particular, through Articles 7 and 8 of the Charter of Fundamental Rights. Article 1 of the GDPR specifically provides that its purpose is the protection of the 'fundamental rights and freedoms of natural persons' – the right to protection of personal data. This is supported by the Recitals to the Regulation, which, although only of persuasive value, emphasise fundamental rights protection. Recitals 1 and 2 note the Regulation protects the rights included under Article 8 of the Charter, and the 'fundamental rights and freedoms' of individuals more broadly.

While the Regulation and these provisions are directed towards facilitating the single market and economic growth and trade,[20] the emphasis on rights is notable. Indeed, the Regulation specifically conceptualises the processing of personal data as 'designed to serve mankind' as part of ensuring that the right to protection of personal data is considered 'in relation to its function in society and be balanced against *other* fundamental rights' (emphasis added).[21]

To a significant extent, this reflects the Recitals of the Data Protection Directive,[22] which similarly emphasised that

> data-processing systems are designed to serve man; whereas they must, whatever the nationality or residence of natural persons, respect their fundamental rights and

[20] Recitals 5, 10.
[21] Recital 4, 51, 76 and 78.
[22] Directive 95/46/EC.

> freedoms, most notably the right to privacy, and contribute to economic and social progress, trade expansion and the well-being of individuals.[23]

Recognising these provisions, the Directive's objective is generally characterisable as the protection of fundamental rights and freedoms 'notably the right to privacy recognized in Article 8 of the ECHR [European Convention on Human Rights]'.[24]

The Recitals to the Data Protection Directive also note that the principles (notably the right to privacy) contained in it should be read as giving substance to those protections contained in the Council of Europe's Convention for the Protection of Individuals with regard to Automatic Processing of Personal Data.[25] The Recitals supported the objectives of the Directive contained in Article 1, which state that Member States 'shall protect the fundamental rights and freedoms of natural persons, and in particular their right to privacy with respect to the processing of personal data'. What is notable in the shift between the Directive and the Regulation is the emergence of a more clearly articulated emphasis on, and commitment to, fundamental rights. This is tied, in part, to the entry into force of the Charter of Fundamental Rights and the associated emphasis on fundamental rights mainstreaming within the Union.[26] However, it is arguable that it is also part of a more general emphasis on rights-oriented secondary laws and the constitutionalisation of EU law writ large following the Treaty of Lisbon.[27]

The result is that, although the GDPR is, both in name and in form, a regulatory law, inasmuch as it imposes notice and choice architectures based on conceptions of voluntariness, transparency and data limitation, it is also fundamentally oriented towards rights protection. In particular, the Regulation specifically seeks to ensure the promotion and protection of normative values as enshrined in the Charter that are extended to contexts that vertical constitutional protections cannot traditionally reach and which the horizontal application of constitutional guarantees would struggle to police effectively on a pro-active, ad hoc basis. The normative character of the Regulation has crystallised, most recently, in the decision of the CJEU in *Schrems II*.

A. The Decision in *Schrems II*

In its decision in *Schrems II*, the Court was asked to consider (as part of a broader range of issues referred from the Irish High Court) the validity of the Standard

[23] ibid Recital 2.

[24] ibid Recital 10.

[25] ibid Recital 11; Council of Europe, *Convention for the Protection of Individuals with Regard to the Automatic Processing of Individual Data* (ETS 108, 1981).

[26] O De Schutter, 'Mainstreaming Human Rights in the European Union' in P Alston and O De Schutter (eds), *Monitoring Fundamental Rights in the EU* (Hart Publishing, 2005).

[27] Treaty of Lisbon amending the Treaty on European Union and the Treaty establishing the European Community, signed at Lisbon, 13 December 2007 [2007] OJ C306/1.

Contractual Clauses Decision[28] and the Privacy Shield Decision[29] – the two mechanisms pursuant to which the data of European citizens were being transferred to the USA (and other third countries) under Part V of the GDPR.

In accordance with Article 45 of Chapter V, a country that is not a Member State (referred to as a third country) may benefit from an 'adequacy decision', which provides that data can be transferred to that jurisdiction on the basis that the third country has been certified by the European Commission (the Commission) as providing a roughly equivalent level of protection to that ensured under the GDPR.[30]

In the absence of an adequacy decision, a transfer of data can take place only if the exporter of personal data has ensured the application of appropriate safeguards for the transferred data in accordance with Article 46 GDPR.[31] Safeguards under Article 46 have generally taken the form of standard data protection clauses adopted by the Commission[32] that are included in contractual agreements concluded between the transferor (the data controller) and the transferee according to the Standard Contractual Clause (SCC) Decision Commission.[33]

In *Schrems II*, the European Court of Justice was asked to consider the level of protection applicable to data processed under the SCCs. The Court confirmed that the requirement for 'essential equivalence' with EU law under Article 45 GDPR applied equally to the SCCs under Article 46.[34] While the references to the Charter within the text of the GDPR would suggest it acted as a constitutional source, with the associated supremacy in interpretative and normative understandings of the Regulation, the CJEU confirmed in *Schrems II* that this was the case.

Still more significantly, the Court confirmed that the comparator within EU law to be used when assessing not only adequacy under Article 45 but also essential equivalence under Article 46 was the GDPR read in light of the Charter (and, as a result of the interpretative obligations of Article 52(3) of the Charter, the ECHR).[35] The Court confirmed that as Article 6 of the Treaty on European Union indicates, the fundamental rights enshrined in the ECHR constitute general principles of EU law (as well as the Charter corresponding to rights guaranteed by the ECHR).[36]

In those circumstances, the CJEU had, previous to the decision in *Schrems II*, held that the interpretation of EU law and examination of the legality of EU legislation must be undertaken in the light of the fundamental rights guaranteed by the Charter.[37] The Court has also consistently held that the validity of provisions of

[28] Commission Decision 2010/87 of 5 February 2010.

[29] Commission Implementing Decision (EU) 2016/1250 of 12 July 2016.

[30] GDPR, Art 45.

[31] ibid Art 46.

[32] ibid Art 46(2).

[33] Decision 2010/87 of 5 February 2010.

[34] *Schrems II* (n 7) [96].

[35] ibid [99]–[100], [97].

[36] ibid [98]; Case C-617/10 *Åkerberg Fransson* ECLI:EU:C:2013:105, [44]; Case C-524/15 *Menci* ECLI:EU:C:2018:197, [22].

[37] *Schrems II* (n 7) [99]. See also *Menci* (n 36) [24].

EU law, in the absence of an express reference to the national law of the Member States, cannot be construed in the light of national law.[38]

The Court specified that, in assessing whether the level of protection afforded by SCCs under Article 46 satisfied the requirement for 'essential equivalence', parties should afford particular consideration to both the clauses themselves and the relevant aspects of the legal system of the third country to which data was being transferred, as well as those matters set out in the non-exhaustive list included in Article 45(2) GDPR read in the light of the requirements of the Charter.[39]

The Court imposed the same analytical framework in assessing the Privacy Shield Decision – emphasising that the GDPR should be read in the light of the Charter and the rights contained therein – in particular Articles 7, 8 and 47.[40] In assessing the Privacy Shield Decision, the Court noted that it granted primacy to the requirements of US national security and law enforcement, which the CJEU interpreted as condoning interference with the fundamental rights of those persons whose data were transferred to the USA.

While the Court noted that interference with the rights protected in Articles 7 and 8 of the Charter were not prima facie impermissible, it found that, based on the evidence that had been furnished to the Court, access to, and use of, personal data by US authorities was not limited in a way that satisfied the requirement for essential equivalence.[41] In particular, the interferences were not limited to what was strictly necessary to achieve the legitimate objective[42] and were not necessary to genuinely meet objectives of general interest recognised by the Union (namely, to protect the rights and freedoms of others),[43] nor was the scope of the interference they permitted sufficiently or clearly defined.[44] The result, in the Court's assessment, was that access to and use of data under the Privacy Shield Decision were not circumscribed in a way that satisfied the requirements for essential equivalence.[45]

In particular, the Court noted that the provisions of both section 702 of the Foreign Intelligence Surveillance Act and Executive Order 12333 were disproportionate.[46] The former provision, in the Court's assessment, permitted

[38] Case C-11/70 *Internationale Handelsgesellschaft* ECLI:EU:C:1970:114, [3]; Case C-44/79 *Hauer* ECLI:EU:C:1979:290, [14]; Case C-135/15 *Nikiforidis* ECLI:EU:C:2016:774, [28]; *Schrems II* (n 7) [100].

[39] *Schrems II* (n 7) [105].

[40] ibid [122] et seq.

[41] ibid [171]–[173].

[42] ibid [167] and [176]. This is in line with Joined Cases C-92/09 and C-93/09 *Volker & Schecke* ECLI:EU:C:2010:662, [48]; Case C-291/12 *Schwartz* ECLI:EU:C:2013:670, [33]; Joined Cases C-465/00, C-138/01 and C-139/01 *Rundfunk & Others* ECLI:EU:C:2003:294, [74]–[75]; Joined Cases C-293/12 and C-594/12 *Digital Rights Ireland* ECLI:EU:C:2014:238, [33], [36]; Opinion 1/15 (*EU Canada PNR Agreement*) of 26 July 2017, ECLI:EU:C:2017:592, [124] and [126].

[43] *Schrems II* (n 7) [174] and [183].

[44] ibid [175] and [181].

[45] ibid [185].

[46] ibid [165]–[166], [180]–[181].

only a review of the objectives of acquiring foreign intelligence rather than an assessment of whether individuals were properly targeted as part of attaining such objectives and conferred no justiciable rights.[47] Similar issues were raised, in the Court's assessment, by the Executive Order.[48]

As a result, the Court found that the requirements of Article 45 GDPR and Article 47 of the Charter were not satisfied.[49] Most significantly, the Court noted that the Ombudsperson mechanism, introduced by the Privacy Shield Decision as a means of redress for the shortcomings identified in the Safe Harbour Decision, was insufficient to constitute an effective safeguard for the purposes of Article 47, which would necessarily require that data subjects had judicial recourse based on actionable rights – which the Ombudsperson mechanism did not and could not provide.[50]

In particular, the Court noted that the Ombudsperson was unable to issue binding decisions directed toward the intelligence services, rendering it ineffective as a safeguard of the rights protected by Articles 7 and 8 of the Charter.[51] Given these findings, the Court ultimately invalidated the Privacy Shield[52] on the basis that the primacy of US law enforcement requirements[53] resulted in an inevitable failure of the limitations and safeguards necessary to establish that interferences with the rights protected by Articles 7, 8, and 47 were justified and that as a consequence there could not be an essentially equivalent standard of protection for data subjects.[54]

B. *Schrems II* and the Brussels Effect

Following the decision in *Schrems II*, non-EU states must ensure that European constitutional (ie Charter) standards of privacy and data protection are vindicated with respect to European data transferred to their jurisdiction. Not only did the CJEU extend the substantive reach of EU constitutional rights in its judgment, but it also assessed US law in light of these European rights standards – under the rubric of the GDPR.

The decision in *Schrems II* thus exposed the true character of much of Europe's international influence in setting standards that, although ostensibly regulatory, are in fact fundamentally normative. Not only does the GDPR transmute the constitutional (Charter) values of Articles 7 and 8 into horizontal, uniformly

[47] ibid [179].
[48] ibid [184].
[49] ibid [186].
[50] ibid [191] et seq.
[51] ibid [196].
[52] ibid [201]–[202].
[53] ibid [164].
[54] ibid [168]–[185].

applicable standards, it does so through provisions that must explicitly be read in light of the rights contained in the Charter, and the constitutional framework to which they belong. In this respect, the GDPR is a fundamental and integrated component of the Union's constitutionalised system of rights protection centred on the Charter of Fundamental Rights.

Thus, while a 'true' Brussels effect exists in the context of consumer safety or climate-based regulatory standards, as Bradford argues, it subsists in those cases because such regulatory standards, though they may reinforce rights-related claims,[55] are not oriented specifically and primarily to securing discrete rights. In contrast, while the GDPR has certainly acted as an international standard setter in terms of the protection of personal data, and despite arguments about, and critiques of, the Regulation's efficacy, it is not seriously in doubt that the GDPR is a manifestation of the Union's constitutional values – created to integrate and perpetuate the protection of Articles 7 and 8 beyond a vertical constitutional setting.[56]

What emerges strongly from the decision in *Schrems II* is that while the GDPR is a regulatory document, it is also a normative one. The result is that the GDPR's international regulatory impact – borne of the factors that Bradford identifies and the political support that accompanies them – has generated an extraterritorial reach for European rights standards – an impact only reinforced following the decision in *Schrems II*. Following that decision, the extraterritorial reach of the GDPR and its normative standards is extended not only in circumstances in which the Regulation provides the model for laws adopted in other jurisdictions, but also where those jurisdictions receive and process EU citizen data in accordance with the principles of Part V of the GDPR, interpreted in light of the Charter.[57]

IV. Exporting Rights Standards

Regulatory, and legal, standards are not difficult to track when they migrate beyond the borders of their home jurisdiction. Though policy laundering may seek to obscure the origins of distinct provisions, the particular framework and thresholds of regulatory mechanisms are explicitly drawn and are thus explicitly mappable.[58]

[55] T Lock, 'Rights and Principles in the EU Charter of Fundamental Rights' (2019) 56 *CML Rev* 1201. For examples of the provisions of the Charter which take the form of principles rather than rights, see the protections of consumer protection under Art 38 of the Charter and environmental protection under Art 37 of the Charter.

[56] In this respect, the Regulation is applicable not only to those actors caught by 'vertical' legal relationships, as between a state and its citizens, but also applies in 'horizontal' legal relationships, ie between private parties.

[57] E Celeste, F Fabbrini and J Quinn (eds), *Data Protection beyond Borders: Perspectives on Extraterritoriality and Sovereignty* (Hart Publishing, 2021).

[58] On the phenomenon of policy laundering, see G Hosein, 'Policy Laundering and Other Policy Dynamics' in E Halpin, P Trevorrow, D Webb and S Wright (ed), *Cyberwar, Netwar and the Revolution in Military Affairs* (Palgrave Macmillan, 2006).

The underlying motivations of regulations are, similarly, discernible through policy and economic analysis when read in light of political concerns and can thus be interpreted, amended and supplemented to meet the requirements of importing jurisdictions. In contrast, the value presumptions and preferences that characterise rights protections and normative standards are both less easily discernible and less amenable to reduction to a form that can be predictably mapped as they travel to other jurisdictions and are often identifiable only in retrospect.

More fundamentally, rights-based standards are also culturally and socially specific – emerging in response to specific contexts and societal demands. In this respect, the right to privacy is exemplary. The right to privacy is variously guaranteed as a tort, a constitutional right and a human right in different jurisdictions, but in each case is framed in a manner conditioned by the nuance of the jurisdiction and time in which it emerged. Thus, continental civil law jurisdictions predominantly view privacy as a dignitarian right linked to concepts of self-ownership,[59] while common law jurisdictions often characterise privacy as a right related to rights in physical property.[60] Equally, while privacy is a right with a tortious structure in US law (in a model building on that initially proposed by Warren and Brandeis in their 1890 article[61]), it has equally been recognised as a constitutional right based on a range of US constitutional amendments (perhaps most notably the Fourth Amendment).[62] These latter constitutional conceptions of privacy in particular are specifically conditioned by colonial and post-colonial experiences of the suppression of political opposition,[63] while the tortious conceptions are specifically oriented by reference to the high thresholds imposed by North American conceptions of free speech.[64] In contrast, within EU Member States, privacy is generally characterised as a fundamental, constitutional right linked to dignity and is specifically understood as necessary in the context of limiting the state's collection of information following the use of databases of citizen information for discriminatory purposes during the twentieth century.[65] The focus of European privacy, while it embraces the classical, property-oriented ideas

[59] M Richardson, *The Right to Privacy: Origins and Influence of a Nineteenth Century Idea* (Cambridge Intellectual Property and Information Law, Cambridge University Press, 2017).

[60] ibid; SM Suter, 'Disentangling Privacy from Property: Toward a Deeper Understanding of Genetic Privacy' (2004) 72 *George Washington Law Review* 737; PM Schwartz, 'Property, Privacy and Personal Data' [2003] *Harvard Law Review* 117.

[61] SD Warren and LD Brandeis, 'The Right to Privacy' (1890) 4 *Harvard Law Review*.

[62] See H Gross, 'The Concept of Privacy' (1967) 42 *New York University Law Review* 34; DJ Solove, 'Conceptualising Privacy' (2002) 90 *California Law Review* 1087; FS Chilapowski, 'The Constitutional Protection of Informational Privacy' (1991) 71 *Boston University Law Review* 133; NM Richards, *Intellectual Privacy* (Oxford University Press, 2017); WL Prosser, 'Privacy' (1960) 48 *California Law Review* 383; C Fried, 'Privacy' (1968) 77 *Yale Law Journal* 475.

[63] WJ Cuddihy, *The Fourth Amendment: Origins and Original Meaning 602–1791* (Oxford University Press, 2009); NB Lasson, *The History and Development of the Fourth Amendment to the United States Constitution* (De Capo Press, 1970).

[64] See Warren and Brandeis (n 61).

[65] L Floridi, 'On Human Dignity as a Foundation for the Right to Privacy' (2016) 29 *Philosophy and Technology* 307.

of privacy based on state exclusion from the home, and those areas in which there is a reasonable expectation of privacy favoured by American courts, extends well beyond this to include a broader conception of a private life that is socially situated and premised on self-ownership and an understanding of press freedom that is far more circumscribed.[66]

This divergence between the socio-historical origins of privacy rights, together with the ambiguity as to the content of the right to privacy itself, make tracking the relative influence of one jurisdiction's jurisprudence on that of another particularly challenging.[67] What is of greater concern is the ambiguity, which[68] means that precisely what values are or should be imported when the Brussels effect takes hold is not clear.[69] The result is that there is a fundamental ambiguity as to the content of the standards and the precise borders of any mirroring of the Union's privacy jurisprudence in a manner that would satisfy the adequacy assessment outlined in *Schrems II* – assessed against the unwieldy and complex bulk of EU privacy law.

Exporting laws like the GDPR allows this amorphous body of constitutional privacy values – contested and poorly defined[70] – to stow away within the Union's regulatory standards as they migrate and assume a role in the national law of other jurisdictions. This fugitive rights aspect of the Brussels effect should be both acknowledged and questioned not only on the basis of principle (in order to accurately determine what we are speaking about when we refer to the Brussels effect), but also because rights, and particularly the right to privacy, have a cultural specificity that makes their export particularly problematic, resulting in the importation privacy solutions into jurisdictions whose privacy problems do not align with the remedial solutions provided by the GDPR and the Charter. For the UK, following Brexit, this has particular implications in terms of how privacy laws must be conceptualised in order to justify the existing adequacy decision.

V. Conceptualising Privacy in a Post-Brexit UK

In order to maintain the existing adequacy decision, the UK is required to critically examine the congruence of its own, domestic privacy laws not only with the

[66] See E Psychogiopoulou, 'The European Court of Human Rights, Privacy and Data Protection in the Digital Era' in M Brkan and E Psychogiopoulou (eds), *Courts, Privacy and Data Protection in the Digital Environment* (Edward Elgar, 2017); M O'Boyle, D Harris, E Bates and C Buckley, *Law of the European Convention on Human Rights*, 4th edn (Oxford University Press, 2018) ch 11; M Klamert, M Kellerbauer and J Tomkin (eds), *The EU Treaties and the Charter of Fundamental Rights: A Commentary* (Oxford University Press, 2019) 2115–27.

[67] *Ettore v Philco Television Broadcasting Co* 229 F 2d 481 (3rd Cir 1956) (Bigs CJ).

[68] *Wright v Secretary of State for Health* [2006] EWHC 2886 (Admin) [66] (Burton LJ).

[69] T Hervey, S Peers, J Kenner and A Ward (eds), *The EU Charter of Fundamental Rights: A Commentary*, 2nd edn (Bloomsbury, 2021) 184.

[70] ECHR, Art 8 has, for example, been described as 'the least defined and most unruly of the rights enshrined in the Convention': *Wright* (n 68) [66]. There also continues to be a significant degree of ambiguity as to the scope of Arts 7 and 8 of the Charter: see O Lynskey, 'Deconstructing Data Protection:

requirements of the GDPR, but also with the rich, often broad and sometimes ambiguous, interwoven network of European privacy values, including the content and jurisprudence of the Charter and of the ECtHR as a result of its influence on the Charter through Article 52. This may be particularly problematic given that the UK law does not recognise a discrete privacy interest in common law but, rather, an ECtHR-inflected cause of action in the form of the tort of misuse of private information (MOPI), which has developed from the equitable cause of breach of confidence when read in light of sections 6 and 7(a) of the Human Rights Act 1998 (HRA).[71]

Although the terminology of privacy was used in English law as early as the decision in *Prince Albert v Strange*,[72] no specific privacy action developed in English law until late in the twentieth century, with privacy interests generally being vindicated through property torts such as trespass and nuisance.[73] Although this failure of the common law was described as a 'glaring inadequacy',[74] there was nevertheless a reluctance among the judiciary to innovate and provide an alternative. In response to this reluctance, and following the introduction of the HRA in 1998, litigants began to rely on the existing, equitable action of breach of confidence, and sought to treat the court itself as a public authority under section 6 HRA. Following this approach, the courts (as public authorities[75]) were obliged to act in a manner compatible with the ECHR, thus giving rise to an indirect horizontal effect for the right to privacy under Article 8 ECHR,[76] which required the courts to interpret and apply common law doctrines in a manner that gave force to Convention rights. Over time, this had the effect of transforming the equitable action of breach of confidence into a tortious action of misuse of private information by reference to Article 8 ECHR.[77]

Despite this development of the MOPI action, there has been a marked reluctance on the part of the English courts to develop a general privacy action, or indeed to extend MOPI to a range of contexts that would mirror the broad swathe of activities caught by the ECtHR under Article 8.[78] The justification offered for

The "Added Value" of a Right to Data Protection in the EU Legal Order' (2014) 63 *International and Comparative Law Quarterly* 569.

[71] See J Rowbottom, *Media Law* (Hart Publishing, 2018) 59 et seq.

[72] See also in this respect *Clowser v Chaplin* (1981) 72 Cr App 342.

[73] Such as defamation (*Charleston v News Group Newspapers* [1991] FSR 62; *Tolley v JS Fry* [1931] AC 333); trespass (*Bernstein of Leigh v Skyviews & General Ltd* [1978] QB 479); nuisance (*Victoria Park Racing and Recreation Grounds Co Ltd v Taylor* [1937] HCA 45); and intellectual property (*Irvine v Talksport* [2002] EWHC 367).

[74] Law Commission, *Report No 110: Breach of Confidence* (Cmnd 8388, 1981) para 5.5.

[75] Pursuant to s 6(a) HRA.

[76] This requires the parties to rely on an existing cause of action which the Court must then enforce in a manner that complies with the HRA and Convention once the parties are before it. See *Douglas (No 3)* [2005] EWCA 595.

[77] *HRH Prince of Wales v Associated Newspapers Ltd* [2006] EWCA Civ 1776 (Lord Phillips); *Wainwright v Home Office* [2004] 2 AC 406, [34]; *Douglas and Others v Hello! Ltd* [2001] 2 WLR 992.

[78] Thus, the court noted in *Wainwright* that there is no general, all-encompassing tort of invasion of privacy which reaches beyond the protection of private information: *Wainwright* (n 77) [28]–[35].

the refusal to engage in such a development has been articulated by Lord Woolf CJ, who suggested in *A v B & C plc*[79] that the need for a stand-alone privacy right was minimal in circumstances where the existing action for breach of confidence served to cover the majority, if not all, of the interests infringed in privacy cases.[80] This view was echoed in *Wainwright v Home Office*, where there was a marked reluctance displayed by a majority of the bench – in particular on the part of Lord Hoffmann – to recognise a stand-alone privacy action.[81]

While the incorporation into domestic UK law of Article 8 ECHR through the HRA has had a profound impact on breach of confidence actions and the availability of privacy actions, the UK's jurisprudence continues to adopt an interpretation of privacy that is arguably more restrictive than the expansive capacity of Article 8 ECHR.[82] More fundamentally, there has been sustained criticism as to whether the test to be applied to determine whether a breach of privacy has occurred in UK law is sufficiently certain, in particular in the absence of a legislative basis. Alpin thus notes that the 'reasonable expectation of privacy' test developed by the English courts does not, particularly, lend itself to predictability and requires courts to draw guidance from existing legislation and jurisprudence.[83]

The viability of this drawing on sources beyond the common law in order to supplement the vision of privacy recognised by the English courts was cast into doubt by proposals to reformulate the UK's human rights framework by repealing and replacing the HRA.[84] While the proposals were later shelved, during their consideration they proposed replicating the content of the current HRA (thus enabling individuals to pursue a MOPI cause of action), which would have changed the manner in which ECHR rights could be enforced under domestic law by creating a system that would 'shield' the UK from adverse judgments of the ECtHR.[85] This would have placed the UK in the unenviable position of needing

This has been repeated in subsequent cases, notably in the recent decision of *Pryor v Liverpool Womens' NHS Foundation Trust* [2021] EWHC 2911 (QB).

[79] *A v B & C plc* [2003] QB 195, 205–06.

[80] Though, as Alpin notes, the decision does represent the first tentative hints of a reading of breach of confidence inclusive of a broader understanding of privacy rights and which later emerged with greater force in *Campbell v MGN Ltd* [2003] QB 633 (CA). See T Alpin, 'The Development of the Action for Breach of Confidence in a Post-HRA Era' (2007) 1 *Intellectual Property Quarterly* 19.

[81] See also *Wainwright v Home Office* [2002] QB 1334 (CA) [2004] 2 AC 406 (HL). On the decision in *Wainwright*, see M Lester, 'Wainwright v Home Office' (2004) 2 *European Human Rights Law Review* 193.

[82] The consultation paper published by the UK government following the completion of the Independent Human Rights Act Review would seem to support this position, with its advocating of common law sources and approaches to human rights following Brexit. See the discussion in M Elliott, 'The Common Law and the European Convention on Human Rights: Do We Need Both?' (Constitutional Law Matters, 2022) https://constitutionallawmatters.org/2022/02/the-common-law-and-the-european-convention-on-human-rights-do-we-need-both/.

[83] See Alpin (n 80); in this respect, see also the decision in *Green Corns Lrd v Claverly Group Ltd* [2005] EMLR 31.

[84] See the Bill of Rights Bill (2022) and the report of the 'Independent Human Rights Act Review' www.gov.uk/guidance/independent-human-rights-act-review#about-the-independent-human-rights-act-review.

[85] Ministry of Justice, 'Human Rights Act Reform: A Modern Bill of Rights – Consultation' (2022) ch 4.

to ensure that the legislative framework in place within the jurisdiction provides sufficient guidance to direct the decisions of domestic courts, and the activities of the government, in a manner reflective of the evolving privacy jurisprudence of the ECtHR and the CJEU, as well as the more specific provisions of the Union's secondary law, while simultaneously removing the obligation on the part of the state to comply with or consider itself bound by such decisions. While this particular proposal was subsequently not pursued, the underlying political desire for such a pivot, and a desire to minimise the impact of the ECtHR's influence, may remain, and may produce similar efforts in future.

Fundamentally, there is a perhaps more basic concern in looking to the development of privacy law in the UK following Brexit – namely, the distinct ideological framing of breach of confidence and privacy claims. Rights develop as a result of discrete socio-political contexts and in response to the historical experiences and contemporaneous concerns of their parent jurisdictions. Dignity and personality-based understandings of privacy, such as those adopted by the CJEU and the ECtHR, seek to recognise the relationship between privacy, dignity and personality within the European legal order as a 'first order' right.[86] This understanding is contextualised not only by the traditional dignitarian understandings that dominate civil law jurisdictions, but also by the experience of the Union's Member States in the Second World War – a period during which erosions of privacy were used to enable discrimination as well as political and religious targeting of communities.[87] In contrast, the development of breach of confidence actions in the UK and the historical contextualisation of privacy protections in the jurisdiction[88] show far more allegiance to proprietary and contractual relationships, as part of which confidence, and the associated protection from public scrutiny, is justified by reference to the relationship between the prospective applicant and the respondent initially, and subsequently by the 'private' nature of the material itself.[89]

The constitutionalisation of privacy in the EU is almost deliberately framed in a manner that rejects such a transactional lens. The result is that the GDPR and the jurisprudence of both the Charter and the Convention exist in a particularised constitutional context that cannot simply be mapped over the understandings of privacy in UK law but must, instead, be reconciled with them through judicial decisions guided by promulgated legislation and precedent. If, as it now appears, the UK chooses to diminish the influence of the ECtHR and defer to the content of the common law, the manner in which it can comply with or reflect the content of EU conceptions of privacy will be thrown into doubt. This is not only because the unquestioned importation of normative values may have fragmenting rather than

[86] Floridi (n 65).

[87] P-H Teitgen, *Establishment of a Collective Guarantee of Essential Freedoms and Fundamental Rights*, vol I (Council of Europe, 1949) 220, 272.

[88] See Richardson (n 59); more generally, see Cuddihy (n 63); Lasson (n 63).

[89] See *CTB v News Groups Newspapers Ltd* [2011] EWHC 1232 (QB); *PJS v News Group Newspapers* [2016] UKSC 26.

unifying impacts in the long term,[90] but also because a true 'Brussels effect' requires more than a mechanical translation of the values of the GDPR into national law.

Wu and Goldsmith have explicitly noted the counterintuitive and somewhat undesirable consequences that may develop from this importation of a fragment of European constitutionalism into a North American legal context, noting it generates the strange circumstance in which the 'United States, a country that did much to shed European rule centuries ago', faces the 'prospect of living under rules set by Europeans'.[91] No less so, the future of UK privacy law may be cast in doubt if the de facto and indeed the de jure adequacy of UK privacy protections are read in light of the requirements of the Charter.

VI. Conclusion

While a range of economic and political factors have led to the recognition of a 'Brussels effect' across a range of regulatory areas, it is worth looking beyond this immediately apparent pattern of regulatory influence attributed to the effect and to ask what, exactly, the EU is exporting when its legislative standards creep beyond its borders. This has only become more necessary in the aftermath of the decision in *Schrems II*, which has recast the GDPR's application beyond the borders of the EU in a strongly rights-based frame of reference. The decision has, in particular, forced attention to the normative character of the Regulation and the reality that, when speaking about and engaging with the Brussels effect, and assessing the integrity of any system that purports to be 'adequate' under the GDPR, states should do so with the understanding that it represents more than a regulatory trend. Not only does this mean that importing regulatory standards may now also result in an unintended importation of rights standards, but it may also mean that such a dual importation *must* take place to satisfy the requirements of the GDPR following *Schrems II*. For the UK, this raises particular challenges given the progressive attempts of the jurisdiction following Brexit to shed or minimise the influence of EU law and the jurisprudence of the ECtHR.

[90] As in Warren and Brandeis (n 61); Prosser (n 62); see also the subsequent fragmentation described by NM Richards and DJ Solove, 'Prosser's Privacy Law: A Mixed Legacy' (2010) 98 *California Law Review* 1887.

[91] Wu and Goldsmith (n 13) 177.

10

Brexit and the Risks of Digital Sovereignism

EDOARDO CELESTE

I. Introduction

Regaining sovereignty from the EU was a mantra of the Brexit campaign.[1] The Eurosceptic slogan 'Let's take back control' referred to an alleged erosion of sovereignty and supremacy of the powers of the UK Parliament by EU institutions.[2] Before the Brexit referendum, in a last attempt to reconcile UK sovereignty claims and its status as an EU Member State, UK Prime Minister David Cameron even proposed the idea of a 'Parliamentary Sovereignty Act', a plan that was soon dismissed as only a definitive departure from the EU would have achieved its objectives.[3] The EU, its laws and institutions were perceived as hampering the socio-economic development of an independent and sovereign UK, which relied on a century-long democratic tradition. However, it was clear that to regain that coveted independence a polite handshaking between former partners would not have sufficed. Especially in light of the complexity of the issues to be solved, uncoupling from the EU family could not be an overnight change.[4] As expected, the Brexit process resulted to be more akin a suffered divorce.

The post-Brexit restructuring of UK law in the digital field did not attract the headlines with even more challenging legal issues to be faced. One can argue that,

[1] See K Ewing, 'Brexit and Parliamentary Sovereignty' (2017) 80 *MLR* 711; G Gee, 'Regaining Sovereignty? Brexit, the UK Parliament and the Common Law' [2016] *European Public Law* 131; M Gordon, 'The UK's Sovereignty Situation: Brexit, Bewilderment and Beyond …' (2016) 27 *King's Law Journal* 333.

[2] J Ringeisen-Biardeaud, '"Let's Take Back Control": Brexit and the Debate on Sovereignty' (2017) 22 *Revue française de civilisation britannique* http://journals.openedition.org/rfcb/1319.

[3] See Gordon (n 1); B Wellings and E Vines, 'Populism and Sovereignty: The EU Act and the In–Out Referendum 2010–2015' (2016) 69 *Parliamentary Affairs* 309.

[4] See F Fabbrini (ed), *The Law & Politics of Brexit* (Oxford University Press, 2017); F Fabbrini (ed), *The Law & Politics of Brexit: Volume II: The Withdrawal Agreement*, 1st edn (Oxford University Press, 2020); F Fabbrini (ed), *The Law and Politics of Brexit. Volume III: The Framework of New EU–UK Relations*, 1st edn (Oxford University Press, 2021).

in the first phase, the UK limited itself to an ordinary, or consequential, reordering of its digital law following the departure from the EU. (Ordinary in the sense that no extraordinary amendment to UK law was introduced in the digital field following the Brexit referendum.) All changes were deemed to be necessary consequences of the loss of legal force of EU law following Brexit and the exercising of national regulatory prerogatives delegated by EU law itself. For example, through the introduction of the European Union (Withdrawal) Act 2018, the General Data Protection Regulation (GDPR) was retained in UK law through a mere relabelling, now being known in domestic law as the UK GDPR.[5]

Despite a series of pre-existing structural issues in the British legal system, in particular in the context of mass surveillance, data retention and immigration law,[6] the substantial maintenance of the integrity of UK law in the data protection field led to the adoption by the EU Commission of a decision determining the adequacy status of the UK data protection regime.[7] Such a recognition has allowed for the continued flow of personal data across the English Channel after the UK's departure from the EU, and more precisely after the end of the transition period agreed by both parties in the Trade and Cooperation Agreement (TCA), which finished in June 2022.[8]

However, after the seminal *Schrems I* case, decided by the Court of Justice of the European Union (CJEU) in 2015, adequacy decisions are not determinations regarded to be set in stone, but are conversely subject to regular monitoring to verify the subsistence of the conditions allowing for a safe transfer of personal data to the third state concerned.[9] Consequently, it was not expected that the UK would have introduced significant changes in its data protection regime lest it lose its adequacy status, which is functional to a multi-billion pound industry in the UK.[10]

The month of September 2021, only a few months after the adoption of the UK adequacy decision, marked the beginning of what could be described as a second, distinct phase of the process of development of UK digital law post-Brexit.

[5] See E Celeste, 'Data Protection' in Fabbrini, *The Law & Politics of Brexit: Volume III* (n 4).

[6] ibid.

[7] European Commission, Implementing Decision of 28 June 2021 pursuant to Regulation (EU) 2016/679 of the European Parliament and of the Council on the adequate protection of personal data by the United Kingdom, C(2021) 4800 final, https://ec.europa.eu/info/sites/default/files/decision_on_the_adequate_protection_of_personal_data_by_the_united_kingdom_-_general_data_protection_regulation_en.pdf.

[8] For a more detailed explanation of the clauses of the TCA related to data protection, see Celeste, 'Data Protection' (n 5).

[9] Case C-362/14 *Maximillian Schrems v Data Protection Commissioner* ECLI:EU:C:2015:650 (*Schrems I*); see T Ojanen, 'Making the Essence of Fundamental Rights Real: The Court of Justice of the European Union Clarifies the Structure of Fundamental Rights under the Charter: ECJ 6 October 2015, Case C-362/14, Maximillian Schrems v Data Protection Commissioner' (2016) 12 *European Constitutional Law Review* 318.

[10] See O Patel, D McCann and J Ruiz, 'The Cost of Data Inadequacy: The Economic Impacts of the UK Failing to Secure an EU Data Adequacy Decision' (UCL European Institute Report with the New Economics Foundation, 2020) www.ucl.ac.uk/european-institute/sites/european-institute/files/ucl_nef_data-inadequacy.pdf.

After an initial, consequential, legal reordering, the UK government, to general surprise, especially from the EU partners, announced its intention to reform UK data protection law in order to purge it from the burdensome box-ticking obligations derived from the bureaucratic EU data protection law and make it more business and innovation friendly.[11] After collecting feedback through a public consultation, which ran for 10 weeks from September 2021, the UK government introduced the Data Protection and Digital Information (DPDI) Bill in July 2022.[12]

In the public consultation and the documents accompanying the Bill, the government explicitly states its objective of regaining UK sovereignty in the digital field by adopting innovative legislation that would help the UK become a digital champion.[13] However, as experienced in other fields, the actual emancipation from the legal rules developed over decades with the other EU Member States for an integrated EU economy is a complex process, generating a plurality of tensions, not least from a digital sovereignty perspective. Indeed, the UK's attempt to introduce a new autonomous data protection model faces conflict, in an integrated digital economy where data are freely transferred, with the EU's recent attempts to protect its digital sovereignty by preserving fundamental rights guarantees over its data, for example by strengthening the de jure and de facto application of its data protection law beyond its borders.[14]

This chapter reconstructs and interprets the UK's recent policy moves in the data protection field using a digital sovereignty lens. It will be argued that, while the UK data protection reform is in line with the promises of Brexit of regaining national parliamentary sovereignty, it represents the first example worldwide of a nation deviating from rather than approaching the EU data protection model (section II). From a digital sovereignty perspective, European nations have understood that to compete with foreign superpowers like the USA and China it is necessary to advance a group strategy. In contrast to this trend, the UK data reform presents itself as an isolationist attempt to regain national digital sovereignty. UK digital sovereignty policies, if recontextualised from a global perspective, particularly considering their relationship with the EU, might be frustrated by the relatively small economic and regulatory relevance of the UK on the international plane (section III). Introducing a data protection reform without fully assessing its potential legal and economic impact and longer-term consequences

[11] Department of Digital, Culture, Media and Sport (DCMS), 'Data: A New Direction' (2021) https://assets.publishing.service.gov.uk/government/uploads/system/uploads/attachment_data/file/1022315/Dat a_Reform_Consultation_Document__Accessible_.pdf.

[12] UK Parliament, 'Data Protection and Digital Information Bill' https://bills.parliament.uk/bills/3322.

[13] DCMS (n 11).

[14] See E Celeste, 'Digital Sovereignty in the EU: Challenges and Future Perspectives' in F Fabbrini, E Celeste and J Quinn (eds), *Data Protection Beyond Borders: Transatlantic Perspectives on Extraterritoriality and Sovereignty* (Hart Publishing, 2021); F Fabbrini and E Celeste, 'The Right to Be Forgotten in the Digital Age: The Challenges of Data Protection Beyond Borders' (2020) 21 *German Law Journal* 55.

at the societal level risks representing a short-sighted form of digital sovereignism (section IV). Imposing to remain legislatively inert and subject to the inherited EU law is certainly not a potential solution to this sovereignist deviation. There is room for change, but the UK should carefully assess the consequences of losing its EU adequacy status, question itself on the democratic support for this policy move and explore its potential role in fostering a transnational conversation to develop cross-border synergies in the development of data protection and, more broadly, digital law (section V).

II. Regaining Digital Sovereignty: The Promises of Brexit

The DPDI Bill, introduced in July 2022, carries forward most of the proposed reforms announced by the UK's Department for Digital, Culture, Media and Sport (DCMS) in the public consultation launched in September 2021. In a nutshell, the Bill reforms the GDPR's accountability framework by removing the requirement for Data Protection Impact Assessments (DPIAs), for records of processing, and for the Data Protection Officer (DPO), replacing the latter with a 'senior responsible individual'.[15] Organisations will be able to refuse 'vexatious', and not only 'manifestly unfounded', subject access requests, or alternatively they will be able to charge a 'reasonable fee'.[16] The Bill transforms the Information Commissioner's Office, the UK national data protection authority, into an Information Commission, composed of up to 14 commissioners.[17] The Commission will be subject to 'strategic priorities' defined at ministerial level, and in enforcing data protection law, the new institution will have to pay regard to new objectives, such as 'the desirability of promoting' competition and innovation, the importance of preventing crimes and the need to preserve the security of the state.[18] The scope of Article 22 of the UK GDPR, which currently includes, in line with the GDPR, a ban on decisions reached solely by automated means that have a legal effect on the individual, as well as a right to human intervention in those circumstances where such decisions are allowed, is reduced. The Bill removes the ban and grants a right to human intervention only in case of 'significant' automated decisions producing an 'adverse legal effect' on the individual.[19] The proposed legislation introduces new legal bases for data processing in the form of a list of circumstances where a business organisation can process personal data for a legitimate interest without performing the so-called 'balancing test' required by Article 6(1)(f) of the GDPR, which consists in assessing whether the rights and interests of the data subject

[15] Data Protection and Digital Information Bill, respectively ss 17 and 18.
[16] ibid s 32.
[17] ibid s 27.
[18] ibid s 28.
[19] ibid s 11.

do not override the legitimate interest of the data controller.[20] A list of purposes that are deemed to be compatible with the original purpose of the processing is proposed as a means to increase the possibility of reusing collected data by softening the purpose limitation principle.[21] Lastly, but not certainly least, the Bill reforms the UK's adequacy mechanism for data transfers by replacing the criterion of adequacy with the requirement that the foreign data protection regime does not offer a 'materially lower' standard of protection.[22]

As affirmed by the DCMS when publishing the open consultation, with the reform, the British government wants to affirm the UK as a 'science superpower' at the forefront of digital innovation, especially in the field of artificial intelligence (AI).[23] In short, boosting 'responsible innovation' and acquiring a leading position in the teaching sector globally are the key objectives of the executive. In the consultation outcome document published on 23 June 2022, the DCMS reiterates the aspiration of transforming the UK into the 'most attractive global data marketplace'.[24] According to the government, this might be achieved by exploiting the legislative sovereignty that the UK has reacquired following Brexit. Reading the foreword from the UK Digital Secretary to the public consultation launched in September 2021, the sense of frustration vis-à-vis EU law is tangible.[25] The set of EU law regulating data is perceived as potentially hampering the development of the UK economy because of its 'complexity' and 'vagueness'. The UK wants to remain a world-leading regulator, excel in the AI field and continue to attract technology companies. To do so, according to the UK government, new, different and more 'agile' legislation is needed – hence the proposal of launching a public consultation, significantly entitled 'Data: A New Direction'.

By departing from the GDPR's accountability framework, organisations will have more capability to benefit from the personal data in their possession and therefore innovate, while at the same time maintaining a 'responsible' use of the data in their possession. Bureaucratic obligations imposed by the GDPR, such as DPIAs, mandatory reporting and the duty to appoint an independent DPO, are eliminated in the name of increased innovation and global competitiveness. In order to acquire a competitive advantage over the EU and, more broadly, on a global scale, the UK government is attempting to eliminate all legal obligations considered to be burdensome or formal box-ticking exercises for organisations processing data. In this scenario, the role of the Information Commission necessarily changes, becoming a promoter of innovation, with more 'effective powers' to monitor and steer the development of the UK digital economy.

[20] ibid s 5.
[21] ibid s 6.
[22] ibid s 45B.
[23] DCMS (n 11) 2.
[24] HM Government, 'Data: A New Direction – Government Response to Consultation', Introduction, www.gov.uk/government/consultations/data-a-new-direction/outcome/data-a-new-direction-government-response-to-consultation.
[25] DCMS (n 11).

From a transnational perspective, one can regard this recent policy move by the UK government with surprise. Indeed, only a few months before launching the public consultation on the data protection reform, the UK secured an adequacy decision from the EU Commission. This occurred just a couple of days before the end of the transition period, after which data transfers from the EU to the UK would not have been possible in the absence of a specific legal mechanism. As mentioned in the introduction, the case law of the CJEU has clarified that adequacy determinations must rely on a holistic assessment of the law of the third country in question. In practice, this means that the EU Commission, when assessing the adequacy status of a third country, has to take into account not only the data protection legislation of the foreign jurisdiction *sensu stricto*, but more generally all the elements of that state's legal framework that might have an impact on the right to data protection. After Brexit, the UK has become a third country from a data protection point of view, thus requiring a positive analysis of its data protection framework from the EU Commission in order to secure a continued free flow of personal data from the EU. The adequacy decision obtained in June 2021 already relied on unstable bases, given the existence of regulatory provisions in the UK that have been deemed to be contrary to EU fundamental rights, such as extensive mass surveillance and data retention powers in the field of national security and the restriction of data subject rights in case of data processing for immigration purposes.[26] The proposed data protection reform adds a further layer of instability, potentially increasing, if approved, the degree of divergence between EU and UK law, and thus making a suspension of the adequacy decision from the EU even more likely.

Yet, if one analyses the decision of the UK government from a national perspective, looking in particular at its positioning within the Brexit process, the recent move of the British executive is far less surprising. The proposed reform fully subscribes to the political agenda of Brexit, its rhetoric and in particular the claim that Brexit would eventually allow the UK to reacquire its lost sovereignty. Indeed, first of all, it is born from the assumption that EU law imposes unnecessary requirements, is bureaucratic and does not support innovation[27] – hence the need to get rid of EU norms in order to reacquire full independence in the nation's sovereign choices and finally incentivise a flourishing economy.

Interestingly, one can notice that the recent data protection reform is fully in line with this chain of arguments, and is the last of many fields that have been instrumentalised to pursue the Brexit agenda, even in absence of clear

[26] See Celeste, 'Data Protection' (n 5). See also European Parliament Resolution of 12 February 2020 on the proposed mandate for negotiations for a new partnership with the United Kingdom of Great Britain and Northern Ireland (2020/2557(RSP)) https://oeil.secure.europarl.europa.eu/oeil/popups/ficheprocedure.do?lang=en&reference=2020/2557(RSP).

[27] See Department for Exiting the European Union, 'Benefits of Brexit: How the UK Is Taking Advantage of Leaving the EU' (2022) www.gov.uk/government/publications/the-future-relationship-between-the-united-kingdom-and-the-european-union.

socio-economic evidence that this policy move will be successful from a general perspective.[28] Indeed, as will be highlighted in section IV, this reform risks pushing the EU Commission towards the unavoidable choice of suspending the UK adequacy decision, which will have a series of significant economic and compliance costs in the short to medium term.[29] Conversely, the proposed reform does not rely on solid empirical research demonstrating the advantages of the change from a business and innovation perspective, but solely on the opinions shared in the public consultation. On the contrary, various answers to the public consultation highlight how some of the proposed changes – in particular the removal of Article 22 on automated decision making and the lightening of some accountability requirements – might lead to a lower level of public trust in public and private institutions processing data in the UK as well as an increased diffidence from international partners wishing to transfer data to the UK.[30]

III. Digital Sovereignty Clashes: The UK Reform in the EU Context

In the field of data protection, the recent UK policy move is unique. Over the past few years, multiple countries have adopted data protection legislation drawing significant inspiration from the EU model or have been forced to bring their laws in line with EU standards, in what the scholarship has called the 'Brussels effect'.[31] The UK's decision of emancipating itself from EU data protection law, creating a new model drawing inspiration from different data protection regimes,[32] establishing new objectives for the activities of its national data protection authority, such as promoting innovation and global competition, as well as identifying new criteria and partnerships to create a new UK data protection galaxy of international data transfers is unprecedented. To date, the EU has played a central role as a global standard setter in the digital field, partially because of its economic relevance and partially because of its focus on fundamental rights, values that, at least in principle, are regarded as reference points in modern democratic states.

[28] See O Lynskey, 'EU–UK Data Flows: Does the "New Direction" Lead to "Essentially Equivalent" Protection?' (22 September 2021) https://dcubrexitinstitute.eu/2021/09/eu-uk-data-new-direction/, who argues that the UK may use data protection to pursue its political agenda. *cf* also Patel et al (n 10), who illustrate the economic impact of the failure to obtain an adequacy status from the EU Commission. Indeed, the announced data protection reform could lead to the similar situation of losing the adequacy status.

[29] *cf* Patel et al (n 10).

[30] *cf* Competition & Marketing Authority, 'CMA Response to Consultation on Data: A New Direction' (2021) para 9; Faculty of Advocates, 'Response from the Faculty of Advocates to The Consultation on Data: A New Direction' (20 December 2021).

[31] See RA Costello, 'The Brussels Effect: Regulatory Standard-Setting and Constitutional Conflicts in Post-Brexit Privacy Law', ch 9 in this volume; see Fabbrini et al (n 14).

[32] See B Treacy, 'Expert Comment' (2021) 22 *Privacy & Data Protection* 2.

However, apart from the direction that this policy move is taking, the UK's very idea of definitely severing its ties from the EU, regaining its legislative sovereignty and creating a new, independent regulatory dimension might be seen as an illusion. Indeed, in the hyperconnected digital society in which we live, especially in a transnational trade context, such as the one linking the EU and the UK, which was previously a single common market, the concept of rigid regulatory boundaries linked to sovereign physical territories does not correspond to reality. In the infosphere – as Floridi calls it – nation states struggle to apply the Westphalian notion of sovereignty as it is not necessarily true that, for instance, data physically located in one jurisdiction are exclusively subject to the laws of that country.[33] EU data protection law offers one of the clearest examples of extraterritorial effect, the GDPR itself explicitly having an extraterritorial scope of application.[34]

This phenomenon can be explained by the contemporary need of nation states to protect their digital sovereignty. The notion of 'digital sovereignty' has not received a univocal definition, as it would be hard to find consensus on the concept of 'sovereignty' itself.[35] Indeed, sovereignty is a historical concept that has evolved over the centuries from denoting a relative pre-eminence in a specific subject matter – as the medieval bishops had in all religious issues, notwithstanding the temporal power governing the territory where they were located – to an absolute capability to regulate the legal ordering within the physical boundaries of the nation state – the modern, Westphalian concept of 'national sovereignty'.[36]

The notion of 'digital sovereignty' stems from the traditional need of the nation state to exercise power over a newly emerged set of assets: it is 'control of the digital', as Floridi puts it in denoting the state's struggle to govern the data, software, standards, protocols, processes, hardware, services and infrastructure that underpin the digital society.[37] However, this contemporary form of sovereignty at the same time shares some of the elements that characterised this notion centuries ago. Indeed, the digital can hardly be caged within national boundaries – data circulate across nations; hardware is made of components built in different jurisdictions; virtual infrastructures serve the needs of customers and public institutions located in various states; private multinational companies conceive, manage and sell digital products and services on a global basis without tailoring their standards to the rules of all the countries where they are commercially active.

[33] L Floridi, 'The Fight for Digital Sovereignty: What It Is, and Why It Matters, Especially for the EU' (2020) 33 *Philosophy & Technology* 369.

[34] See Fabbrini et al (n 14); Fabbrini and Celeste (n 14); DJB Svantesson, 'Extraterritoriality and Targeting in EU Data Privacy Law: The Weak Spot Undermining the Regulation' (2015) 5 *International Data Privacy Law* 226; C Kuner, 'Extraterritoriality and Regulation of International Data Transfers in EU Data Protection Law' (2015) 5 *International Data Privacy Law* 235.

[35] See Celeste, 'Digital Sovereignty' (n 14).

[36] See GW White, *Nation, State, and Territory: Origins, Evolutions, and Relationships* (Rowman & Littlefield, 2004); Celeste, 'Digital Sovereignty' (n 14).

[37] Floridi (n 33) 371; see also P Hummel et al, 'Data Sovereignty: A Review' (2021) 8 *Big Data & Society* http://journals.sagepub.com/doi/10.1177/2053951720982012.

For this reason, nation states attempt to protect their sovereignty in the digital field not only by regulating what occurs in their physical territories – as they should do according to the traditional notion of Westphalian sovereignty – but also by putting in place one of two strategies: either they apply their rules extraterritorially or they try to attract digital assets into their territories. We can therefore identify two simultaneous policy trends that characterise digital sovereignty claims: one that is centrifugal, ie consists in extending a state's regulatory reach beyond its boundaries, and another one that is centripetal, ie attempts to attract important digital assets into the physical boundaries of the state so that the latter can better regulate and control them.[38]

An example of the first tendency is the above-mentioned extraterritorial scope of application of EU data protection law. By applying its law externally, the EU ensures that personal data related to EU residents, even when they leave EU soil and so are technically subject to the law of another jurisdiction, are processed according to EU law and standards.[39] An example of a policy aiming to preserve digital sovereignty in a centripetal way is the adoption of data localisation laws, which are pieces of legislation requiring personal data related to a country's data subjects to be processed and stored within that jurisdiction.[40] In this case, nation states remain anchored to the traditional Westphalian notion of sovereignty and instead of attempting to regulate a digital asset located in another jurisdiction, they impose the repatriation of those assets within national boundaries.

The UK's willingness to exercise and protect its digital sovereignty is not per se surprising. France and Germany were among the first states in Europe to have championed the idea that more protection of their national digital assets was needed in order not to succumb to regulatory and economic diktats from powerful countries at the forefront of digital innovation, such as the USA and China, and their multinational companies.[41] However, these states soon understood that fighting alone would do little to preserve or reconstitute their digital assets vis-à-vis the advanced state of development of foreign digital superpowers. Hence, they came up with the idea of developing a common policy to achieve digital sovereignty at the European level, transitioning from a national to a supranational perspective.[42] It is therefore also in this context that the UK data reform seems out of step with the recent policy trends. Not only is the UK the first country to depart from the EU data protection model, but it is also going against the tide by proposing an alternative regime that it hopes will ultimately be successful on a global basis.

[38] I first illustrated this distinction in Celeste, 'Digital Sovereignty' (n 14).

[39] See O Lynskey, 'The Extraterritorial Impact of Data Protection Law through an EU Law Lens' in Fabbrini et al (n 14); Svantesson (n 26).

[40] See E Celeste and F Fabbrini, 'Competing Jurisdictions: Data Privacy across the Borders' in G Fox, T Lynn and L van der Werff (eds), *Data Privacy and Trust in Cloud Computing* (Palgrave, 2020).

[41] See G Glasze et al, 'Contested Spatialities of Digital Sovereignty' [2022] *Geopolitics* 1; J Pohle and T Thiel, 'Digital Sovereignty' (2020) 9 *Internet Policy Review*.

[42] See Floridi (n 33).

However, the announced UK data reform does not simply denote an unconventional and maverick attitude; its likelihood of success may be questioned due to the disparity between the economic powers of the UK and the EU. EU digital sovereignty claims have emerged to challenge the American and Chinese economic imperialism in the digital field and preserve the EU's fundamental rights.[43] As said, the trend has been to escalate policy objectives from the national level to the supranational EU level in order to maximise the Member States' forces and be able to compete on the global level. The project to create a cloud made in the EU, the so-called Gaia X, which is an example of a centripetal trend,[44] as well as the recent solemn adoption of a Declaration of European Digital Rights and Principles,[45] which, in a centrifugal way, would work as a global manifesto of European digital values, are two examples of this tendency. At the same time, what we are currently observing in the UK is a national sovereignty-propelled – normative, rather than economic – spin-off from its much bigger neighbour, the EU, in order to be able to develop a new regulatory model in the digital field that would eventually lead to the UK taking a prominent role in the digital economy. We are therefore witnessing an uneven clash between national (UK) and supranational (EU) digital sovereignty policies, which, simply from an economic point of view, does not seem to leave much hope for the UK's ability to resist the Brussels effect, let alone play a 'London effect' that would affirm the UK as a global leader and standard setter in the digital economy.

An example of this inability that is already possible to provide relates to the UK's intention to conclude an agreement regulating data transfers from the UK to the USA.[46] This was an opportunity for the UK to gain an economic advantage over the EU, as the CJEU had twice invalidated the legal mechanism allowing personal data to be transferred to the USA.[47] However, the economic significance of the EU has led the USA to agree a new data pact with the group of 27 Member

[43] See C Hobbs et al (eds), *Europe's Digital Sovereignty: From Rulemaker to Superpower in the Age of US–China Rivalry* (ECFR, 2020).

[44] Federal Ministry for Economic Affairs and Energy and Federal Ministry for Education and Research, *Project GAI Act-X – A Federated Data Infrastructure as the Cradle of a Vibrant European Ecosystem* (Federal Ministry for Economic Affairs and Energy (BMWi) Public Relations Division, 2019); see also Celeste (n 14); A Pannier, 'The Changing Landscape of European Cloud Computing Gaia-X, the French National Strategy, and EU Plans' (Institut français des relations internationales, 2021); A Braud et al, 'The Road to European Digital Sovereignty with Gaia-X and IDSA' (2021) 35 *IEEE Network* 4.

[45] 'European Declaration on Digital Rights and Principles' (2022) https://digital-strategy.ec.europa.eu/en/library/european-declaration-digital-rights-and-principles; European Commission, 'Digital Rights and Principles: Presidents of the Commission, the European Parliament and the Council Sign European Declaration' (2022) IP/22/7683, https://ec.europa.eu/commission/presscorner/detail/en/ip_22_7683.

[46] A Dickson, V Manancourt and S Stolton, 'Distractions Plague UK's Post-Brexit Tech Plan' *POLITICO* (18 April 2022) www.politico.eu/Article/distractions-plague-post-brexit-tech-plan/.

[47] Case C-311/18 *Facebook Ireland and Schrems* ECLI:EU:C:2020:559; see M Tzanou, 'Schrems I and Schrems II: Assessing the Case for the Extraterritoriality of EU Fundamental Rights' in Fabbrini et al (n 14).

States rather than with the UK, which might have been seen as a rebel, but still dependent, satellite of the EU data protection galaxy.[48] Yet, notwithstanding the different sizes of these two competing players, the UK might still gain a short-term economic advantage. Indeed, their current links with the UK, and the still de facto embeddedness of Britain within the EU data protection galaxy, may prompt US and Chinese companies to relocate in the UK to obtain easy access to EU data.[49] However, this condition might only be temporary due to the possibility of the UK adequacy decision being suspended or invalidated.

UK digital sovereignty policies, if recontextualised from a global perspective, might be frustrated by the relatively minor economic and regulatory relevance of the UK on the international plane. Digital sovereignty strategies risk being reduced to short-sighted sovereignist claims.

IV. The Risks of Digital Sovereignism

The notion of digital sovereignism denotes the advocacy or adoption of sovereignist policies in the digital field. The scholarship also uses the terms 'digital statism', 'data' and 'tech nationalism'.[50] Basile et al identify three components of sovereignism in general, which can help us schematise and better define how this concept can be applied in the digital field: political, cultural and economic dimensions.[51] Digital sovereignism would denote policies that:

- from a political point of view, claim to regain control of national digital assets against the influence of foreign actors;
- from a cultural point of view, rely on the assumption that national identity, including its normative values and economic approach, are under threat; and
- from an economic point of view, are associated with protectionist or isolationist strategies.

Populism would be the gluing element of these three components as digital sovereignism is usually characterised by claims purporting that local regulators and

[48] See European Commission, 'Joint Statement on Trans-Atlantic Data Privacy Framework' https://ec.europa.eu/commission/presscorner/detail/en/ip_22_2087. At the time of writing, the EU Commission has initiated the procedure to adopt an adequacy decision on the new EU-US Data Privacy Framework. On the point see European Commission, 'Data Protection: Commission Starts Process to Adopt Adequacy Decision for Safe Data Flows with the US' (2022) IP/22/7631, https://ec.europa.eu/commission/presscorner/detail/en/ip_22_7631.

[49] See C Grant, 'Ten Reflections on a Sovereignty-First Brexit' (Centre for European Reform, 28 September 2020) www.cer.eu/insights/ten-reflections-sovereignty-first-brexit.

[50] Respectively, Floridi (n 33) 374; A Chander and UP Lê, 'Data Nationalism' (2015) 64 *Emory Law Journal* 677; Hobbs et al (n 43) 24.

[51] L Basile, R Borri and L Verzichelli, '"For Whom the Sovereignist Bell Tolls?" Individual Determinants of Support for Sovereignism in Ten European Countries' (2020) 21 *European Politics and Society* 235.

industry have lost the power to determine the destiny of national digital assets and that regaining that control would be the panacea to all economic and social problems.[52]

The UK's recent policy moves seem to go in a similar direction and can be qualified as an expression of digital sovereignism. They are politically pushed by the will of emancipating the UK from the EU regulatory influence. It is perceived that the UK digital economy and its assets are subject to bureaucratic sets of legislation that frustrate the UK's traditional pro-business approach to innovation. Although protectionist trends are not detectable, an isolationist strategy is well apparent, the UK being the first country to depart from the well-established and much imitated model of EU data protection. The whole is accompanied by a populist rhetoric that depicts EU data protection law as a set of outdated and burdensome norms imposed by Brussel's bureaucrats – as if the UK had not been one if the key players leading the development of this field of EU law over the past few decades.[53] De Hert and Papakonstantinou defined the UK as an actor that, after an initial phase of scarce engagement in the data protection field, later turned into a 'data protection enthusiast' with a very active role in 'co-shaping' EU data protection law, particularly in the law enforcement sector.[54] Despite this, the Brexit rhetoric posits the need to 'take control back' and adopt new rules that would be more innovation and business friendly and that would allow the UK to become a leader in the digital economy.

The UK sovereignist policy moves in the digital field, if justified from a political perspective as an attempt to give support to the Brexit claims, may have significant consequences, from both a legal and an economic point of view. Despite its regained legislative sovereignty, the UK is dependent on the EU Commission's adequacy decision in order to be able to receive EU data. Paradoxically, now that the UK is no longer part of the EU, it is even more subject to the Commission's scrutiny, as, being a third state, it is no longer implied that its legislation is in line with EU data protection standards.[55] Therefore, the UK adequacy decision theoretically works as a bridle on UK law. If the UK wants to maintain its adequacy status, it should avoid radically departing from EU law and keep following EU standards, in a sort of forced Brussels effect. Indeed, the CJEU has clarified that for the purposes of international data transfers, 'adequate' does not mean 'identical'; rather, a 'substantial equivalence' is required.[56] Now, if the DPDI Bill or a similar piece of legislation with equivalent content is passed into law, the UK will introduce significant reforms that in the eyes of the Commission will very probably

[52] See ibid.
[53] See P Hustinx, 'Towards a Successful Cross-Border Regulatory Cooperation', ch 11 in this volume.
[54] See P De Hert and V Papakonstantinou, 'The Rich UK Contribution to the Field of EU Data Protection: Let's Not Go for "Third Country" Status after Brexit' (2017) 33 *Computer Law & Security Review* 354, 356.
[55] See Celeste, 'Data Protection' (n 5).
[56] *Schrems I* (n 9); see also Ojanen (n 9).

be regarded as not providing an adequate level of protection to EU fundamental rights. In particular, the reform of the ICO and the dismantling of the data controllers' accountability framework seem to be significantly different from the EU approach and will necessarily lead to the withdrawal of the adequacy status from the EU Commission or its invalidation by the CJEU following an ad hoc litigation. From the political perspective, this outcome might also make the EU–UK relationship even more tense and might reduce the likelihood of success for future negotiations about a data transfer agreement.[57]

If the legal price to pay to adopt the UK's data reform were the loss of the adequacy decision, from an economic point of view, this might have a significant impact, especially in the short term. Indeed, the UK economy is deeply integrated with the EU economy. The UK's DCMS, in its impact assessment of the proposed data reform, calculated a potential loss of £1.4 billion, of which £1 billion is in reduced trading revenue and £420 million in compliance costs, due to the need to identify and implement alternative data transfer mechanisms, such as standard contractual clauses and binding corporate rules.[58] Moreover, the data reform, by enhancing the risk of loss of adequacy status, increases legal uncertainty among economic partners and generates preventive legal compliance costs among those firms that desire to adopt alternative data transfers mechanisms in fear of a sudden invalidation or suspension of the adequacy decision. From a consumer perspective, as many parties have observed in their answers to the DMCS's public consultation, the proposed reform might lead to an increased distrust in UK data controllers.[59] Indeed, by introducing a more business- and innovation-friendly regime, the UK government has unavoidably reduced the bureaucratic aspects of the GDRP that, however, precisely aim to protect data subjects' fundamental rights.[60]

UK digital policies are certainly not the only ones that risk incurring forms of digital sovereignism. Looking at the plank in our own eye, it is also true that EU digital sovereignty claims have potential sovereignist deviations – in particular, insofar as they adopt protectionist attitudes by subsidising the EU tech industry. In this regard, two examples can be presented. First is the already mentioned project Gaia-X, which aims to create a cloud in the EU.[61] After failed attempts to set up national clouds, the EU has understood the need to join together national forces as a single entity to compete with foreign digital players.[62] An EU cloud would allow

[57] See K Wynn, '"Data: A New Direction" – but Is It the Right One?' (2022) 22 *Privacy & Data Protection* 13.

[58] Department for Digital, Culture, Media & Sport, *Data: A New Direction – Analysis of Expected Impact* (2021) 22.

[59] The Law Society of England and Wales, 'Law Society Response: Department for Digital, Culture, Media & Sport Consultation, "Data: A New Direction"' (2021) para 4.

[60] See Lynskey, 'EU–UK Data Flows' (n 28); *cf* E Harbinja et al, 'Written Evidence Submitted by: British and Irish Law, Education and Technology Association (BILETA) Data: A New Direction Inquiry (DCMS)' (BILETA, 2021), who observe that the proposed data reform leads to an erosion of rights without necessarily fostering innovation.

[61] See above (n 44).

[62] See Celeste, 'Digital Sovereignty' (n 14).

critical public and private European organisations to store their data in servers located in the EU with the guarantee that EU fundamental rights and processing standards are respected, and without having to resort to foreign cloud providers. In this way, the EU seeks to achieve a higher level of digital independence from the risks connected to foreign service providers, but at the same time supports an industrial sector as well as research that did not emerge spontaneously in Europe, given the advanced stage of development and lower costs of non-European technologies and services.

The second example relates to the imposition of norms leading to a de facto obligation to process data within the EU. In the seminal *Digital Rights Ireland* case, for example, the CJEU imposed the condition that telecommunication operators must retain data for the purposes of public and national security in EU servers.[63] The consequences of this obligation are substantially equivalent to those just highlighted in relation to the project Gaia-X: an economic distortion is introduced by a legal obligation, which in principle is theoretically justifiable as a corollary of the need to preserve EU fundamental rights.[64]

These policies, however, if cynically regarded in terms of their produced economic effects, might be accused of being 'economically anachronistic', being merely supported by the need to promote digital autarchy, boost the EU economy and become leaders in the digital sector.[65]

V. Legitimising Digital Sovereignty Policies in a Plural Environment

Digital sovereignism is not an effective or successful policy in the long term. From an economic point view, short-term gains generated by protectionist attitudes are overcome by the lack of longer-term sustainability and the increase in costs related to legal compliance. From a political point view, digital sovereignist policies exacerbate tensions and hinder cross-border collaboration practices, which are essential in a closely connected digital environment. At the same time, digital sovereignty claims may well be legitimate and justified. Therefore, the conundrum, both in the UK and in the EU, currently lies in the definition of the boundaries between legitimate digital sovereignty claims and digital sovereignism.

Of utmost importance is reflecting on what would be the legitimate objectives to pursue through digital sovereignty policies. As shown in Table 1, in the case of the EU, the US and Chinese digital superpowers are seen as threats to the EU's possibility of protecting its fundamental rights. Following this argument, the EU

[63] Joined Cases C-293/12 and C-594/12 *Digital Rights Ireland* ECLI:EU:C:2014:238; see Celeste and Fabbrini (n 40); Chander and Lê (n 50).
[64] See also Celeste, 'Digital Sovereignty' (n 14).
[65] Floridi (n 33) 374.

desires to emancipate itself from this foreign predominance in the digital field by regaining an ability to produce, shape and control its own digital assets.[66] The EU's willingness to protect its fundamental rights is certainly legitimate, but it degenerates into a form of sovereignism when it becomes a justification to subsidise the EU tech industry or when it does not take into account the effect that an extraterritorial application of EU law has on the diversity and plurality of values and principles on the global level. Protecting EU digital rights should therefore be seen as the first lighthouse guiding the navigation of EU digital sovereignty policies in order to prevent their degeneration into forms of sovereignism. Digital constitutionalism, intended as the ideology that is pushing towards a rearticulation of fundamental rights in the mutated context of the digital society, can thus be used as a conceptual barrier to digital sovereignism in the EU.[67] This approach would also be in line with the human-centric attitude that the EU has promoted over the past decades, and is in particular stressing at the moment in the context of the development of a normative framework for artificial intelligence.[68]

Table 1 Comparison of EU and UK digital sovereignty policies

Actor	Foreign powers to circumscribe	Stated objectives	Sovereignist attitudes	Negative effects	Potential solutions
EU	China; USA	Protection of fundamental rights	Pursuit of digital autarchy Protectionism (Unjustified) data localisation Extraterritorial effect of EU law	Increased economic costs due to being made in the EU Slow innovation Regulatory imperialism, colonialism and the Brussels effect	Recognition of diversity International collaboration Collaborative standard setting
UK	EU	Support to innovation Simplification/ Debureaucratisation Economic leadearship	Populist arguments about EU law Reform proposed with evidence of net economic gains Isolationism	Relinquishment of EU fundamental rights Loss of public trust Creation of tensions with the EU (adequacy)	Collaborative standard setting International collaboration

[66] See, eg European Council, Remarks by President Charles Michel after the Special European Council meeting on 2 October 2020, www.consilium.europa.eu/en/press/pressreleases/2020/10/03/remarks-by-president-charles-michel-after-the-special-europeancouncil-meeting-on-2-october-2020/.

[67] For a more detailed illustration of the scholarship on digital constitutionalism, see E Celeste, 'Digital Constitutionalism: A New Systematic Theorisation' (2019) 33 *International Review of Law, Computers & Technology* 76; see also E Celeste, *Digital Constitutionalism: The Role of Internet Bills of Rights* (Routledge, 2022).

[68] See E Celeste and G De Gregorio, 'Digital Humanism: The Constitutional Message of the GDPR' (2022) 3 *Global Privacy Law Review* 4.

But also, an increased awareness of diversity and plurality should be sought. Otherwise, a stubborn and blind protection of EU fundamental rights risks leading to contestable results akin to imperialist or colonialist phenomena, when EU law is required to apply or is de facto applied extraterritorially by virtue of the principle of the law of the strongest. An apparent example of this threat was represented by the implementation of the right to be forgotten, as articulated by the CJEU in the seminal case *Google Spain*.[69] In the aftermath of the case, Google wondered whether the effect of delisting obtained on the basis of the exercise of the right to be forgotten by an EU resident should have the effect of compelling the search engine to eliminate the results in question from all the versions of its website worldwide. In the subsequent *Google v CNIL* case, the CJEU clarified that the delisting was not required on the global level but only on the versions of the search engine accessible from Europe, thus showing increased attention and respect towards the existence of other legal systems that do not share the same European values.[70]

UK digital sovereignty claims conversely aim to pursue different policy objectives. The protection of fundamental rights is not one of the priorities of the proposed data reform.[71] The UK conversely seeks to boost innovation, reduce bureaucratic tick-boxing practices imposed by the inherited EU data protection law and affirm itself as a leader in the digital sector. In light of this, one can observe that there is no common solution applicable to all potential digital sovereignist deviations. Indeed, arguing that digital constitutionalism and the promotion of diversity and pluralism should be the guiding principles to be pursued to avoid digital sovereignism in the UK would risk sounding like an attempt to impose an EU approach on a state that has voluntarily decided to leave the Union. The solution is not merely to ask the UK to reform its data protection law within the parameters of EU standards in order to maintain at all costs the adequacy status. However, at the same time, the UK should carefully assess whether the results of the Brexit referendum should be interpreted as a sign that the 'new direction' that the UK should pursue is one increasingly diverging from the hitherto shared European values. The UK should also evaluate the pros, cons and timing of its proposed reform, basing any amendments to the current normative framework on economic and legal justifications based, in turn, on empirical evidence.

[69] Case C-131/12 *Google Spain v APED* ECLI:EU:C:2014:317; on the aspect of extraterritorial application of the right to be forgotten, see DJB Svantesson, 'The Google Spain Case: Part of a Harmful Trend of Jurisdictional Overreach' (2015) EUI Working Papers http://cadmus.eui.eu//handle/1814/36317; P De Hert and V Papkonstantinou, 'Google Spain: Addressing Critiques and Misunderstandings One Year Later (2015) 22 *Maastricht Journal of European and Comparative Law* 624; B Van Alsenoy and Marieke Koekkoek, 'Internet and Jurisdiction after Google Spain: The Extraterritorial Reach of the "Right to Be Delisted"' (2015) 5 *International Data Privacy Law* 105.

[70] Case C-507/17 *Google LLC v Commission nationale de l'informatique et des libertés (CNIL)* ECLI:EU:C:2019:772; see also J Quinn, 'Google vs CNIL: Circumscribing the Extraterritorial Effect of EU Data Protection Law' in Fabbrini et al (n 14).

[71] See Lynskey, 'EU–UK Data Flows' (n 21).

Populist rhetoric and international arm-wrestling in the name of the Brexit promise of regaining a lost parliamentary sovereignty might not lead to an optimal solution for the UK economy and society, especially when the economic gains of the proposed reform are not clear and there is the risk of loss of public trust.

In parallel, the UK might reconsider its role as a contributor to the EU's, if not the world's, discussion on digital law. So far, the UK has played a crucial role in developing and enforcing EU data protection law. Even if no longer a Member State, the UK might still help share EU digital policies, by participating, for example, with a new role, in the works of the European Data Protection Board or in another institutional setting created ad hoc to foster collaboration between the EU and the UK. This solution would indeed represent a gain both for the EU, which would be more open to recognising foreign values and priorities, avoiding imperialist or colonialist trends, and for the UK, which would not have to resort to a frustrating and draining arm-wrestling with its bigger neighbour.

VI. Conclusion

Despite its promises, Brexit did not lead to a 'separate but equal' relationship between the UK and the EU.[72] Regaining national sovereignty in the digital field cannot rely on the assumption that a surgical exercise between legal, political and socio-economic frameworks that were not so long ago strictly linked is possible. It is not only a question of 'filiation' or the previous relationship. The digital society is largely interconnected. Data and digital goods and services circulate, are traded and shared across the world. The UK is an integral part of this complex mosaic and, even if no longer sharing the EU piece of the puzzle, it should take into account the effects of its policies on a transnational and cross-border level. The Brexit rhetoric of regaining legislative sovereignty and the idea of introducing brand new data protection legislation significantly diverging from the current one inherited from the EU seem to be based on a Westphalian notion of sovereignty that no longer holds in the digital society. The adoption and implementation of new digital law and policies have transnational effects, as it is not veracious to think that by leaving the EU the UK can get rid of the GDPR, as in any case the extraterritorial features of the latter will continue to exercise effects in the UK, be it willing or not. The UK has to consider its size and economic relevance on the global plane as the battle for digital sovereignty is dominated by big players, namely the USA and China, with the EU currently struggling to emerge as a single entity.

Introducing a data protection reform without fully assessing its potential economic impact and longer-term consequences at the societal level for the sake of demonstrating that the UK has finally emancipated itself from EU law risks being

[72] See K Lillington, 'Britain Looks to Weaken Rules on Data Privacy' *The Irish Times* (16 September 2021) www.irishtimes.com/business/technology/britain-looks-to-weaken-rules-on-data-privacy-1.4675042.

a short-sighted form of digital sovereignism. Populist arguments about the need to reacquire a long stolen parliamentary sovereignty and to reintroduce the traditional British pro-business regulatory approach here replace economic evidence and an analysis of the legal and political impact of the recently proposed data protection reform. A potential solution to this sovereignist deviation is certainly not to remain legislatively inert and subject to the inherited EU law. There is room for change, but the UK should carefully assess the consequences of losing its EU adequacy status. Indeed, adequate does not mean identical, and eventually the UK could play a role in fostering a conversation about reform at the EU level too. However, it is also important for the UK to question itself about the democratic mandate of this reform. UK people voted to leave the EU, but this does not necessarily imply consent to a sudden departure from EU data protection values as well, which would instead mark a constitutional value U-turn, not to say a crisis.

Widening the perspective, the question of the worldwide emergence, development and complementarity of different data protection systems in order to preserve national or regional digital sovereignty promises to be the legal conundrum of the next decade. The EU digital law model, which poses the human being and their fundamental rights at the centre, is having great success, being imitated by many states across the globe in what has been called the 'Brussels effect'. However, the EU strategy is not exempt from potential sovereignist deviations, especially when it comes to subsidising the emergence of a tech industry and services made in the EU. As occurred after the horrors of WWII, the exercise of sovereignty needs to be guided and circumscribed by the objective of preserving fundamental rights, and not by economic considerations. Digital constitutionalism thus emerges as a potential lighthouse to guide the navigation of EU digital strategies in this complex sea. Promoting a rearticulation and recognition of fundamental rights in the digital field might serve the twofold objectives of ensuring that digital sovereignty policies do not degenerate into forms of sovereignism and of promoting a constitutional recognition of digital rights.

At the same time, the EU needs to interrogate itself on the potential imperialist or colonialist consequences of its data protection framework. Alternative models based on different values and principles exist or are gradually emerging. This may well occur in jurisdictions that will become able to economically compete with the EU in the tech sector. Hence, to avoid an economic war eventually deciding which data protection model will prevail according to the law of the strongest, the solution is to foster international cooperation on data protection and digital regulation more broadly, and to understand its core objectives and how they can be achieved while supporting a plurality of values and technical innovation. To avoid a digital sovereignty arm-wrestle, this form of cross-border cooperation is necessary. Starting, of course, with our neighbours across the Channel.

11

Towards a Successful Cross-Border Regulatory Cooperation

PETER HUSTINX

I. Introduction

Data protection authorities from across Europe and beyond have been involved in efforts to develop the legal rules and standards that now exist in this field. That is certainly true for the Council of Europe Convention on Data Protection[1] and the Organisation for Economic Co-operation and Development (OECD) Privacy Guidelines[2] – two prominent founding documents on the subject – and the General Data Protection Regulation (GDPR),[3] as the present cornerstone of the EU legal framework.

The UK Information Commissioner's Office (ICO) and its predecessors have all actively contributed to these efforts, and their results continue to be relevant after Brexit. Moreover, in doing so, they also helped provide the basis for regulatory cooperation across borders in data protection. However, one question is now more relevant than ever before: how is this cooperation developing when it comes to the supervision and enforcement of current rules, especially where big global platforms are involved or other issues are at stake with a similar large impact?

As a part of its international strategy,[4] the ICO has invested in the development of a global framework for regulatory cooperation in data protection. These efforts have been quite successful and have started to bear tangible fruit in recent years.

[1] Convention for the Protection of Individuals with regard to Automatic Processing of Personal Data (ETS No 108) Strasbourg, 21 January 1981, as amended by Protocol (CETS No 223) Strasbourg, 10 October 2018 (also known as Convention 108+) https://rm.coe.int/16808ade9d.

[2] Guidelines governing the Protection of Privacy and Transborder Flows of Personal Data, 23 September 1980, as amended on 11 July 2013, www.oecd.org/sti/ieconomy/privacy.htm.

[3] Regulation (EU) 2016/679 of the European Parliament and of the Council of 27 April 2016 on the protection of natural persons with regard to the processing of personal data and on the free movement of such data, and repealing Directive 95/46/EC (General Data Protection Regulation, GDPR) [2016] OJ L119/1, https://eur-lex.europa.eu/legal-content/EN/TXT/?uri=CELEX:02016R0679-20160504.

[4] ICO International Strategy 2017–2021, https://ico.org.uk/media/about-the-ico/documents/2014356/international-strategy-03.pdf.

I will first briefly explain the main elements of this global framework and then consider what this might imply for the subject at hand – which essentially involves the scope for regulatory cooperation across borders at a more regional scale or in bilateral settings – with particular focus on the UK and the EU.

II. Global Framework

Data protection authorities (DPAs) from Europe and elsewhere have been meeting each other at annual conferences, both in Europe and other parts of the world, for many years. At the global level, this happened in the context of the International Conference of Data Protection and Privacy Commissioners, now known as the Global Privacy Assembly (GPA), with more than 130 members from all over the world.[5]

As chair of the GPA for a three-year period since 2018, the ICO, and Elizabeth Denham as the Information Commissioner, have played a leading role in modernising this body from a once-a-year conference to a year-round platform for collaboration and action.[6] The GPA has adopted a clear ambition and strategy, which also involves capacity building in regulatory and enforcement cooperation – that is, both regulatory cooperation and practical enforcement cooperation.[7]

One of its permanent working groups – the International Enforcement Cooperation Working Group, co-chaired by the Canadian, UK and US privacy enforcement authorities – is fully engaged in these subjects.[8] In the USA, the competent authority is the Federal Trade Commission – the regulator for privacy-related federal laws.[9] Other agencies are established at state level, inter alia in California.[10]

Among the Working Group's activities are the promotion of 'safe space' or 'closed enforcement sessions' to examine a variety of emerging digital risks, and the development of useful tools such as an Enforcement Cooperation Handbook and a repository to document and share professional experience.[11]

[5] The first meeting of the conference was in Bonn in 1979, the 41st meeting was a virtual event in 2021. For more information about the history, see https://globalprivacyassembly.org/the-assembly-and-executive-committee/history-of-the-assembly.

[6] The ICO chaired the Executive Committee and provided its permanent secretariat from 2018 to 2021. In 2019, the Conference decided on its strategic direction, and in 2021 the Assembly reaffirmed its strategic objectives.

[7] Global Privacy Assembly, Strategic Plan 2021–2023, https://globalprivacyassembly.org/wp-content/uploads/2021/10/2021022-ADOPTED-Resolution-on-the-Assemblys-Strategic-Direction-2021-23.pdf.

[8] International Enforcement Cooperation Working Group Report (July 2021) https://globalprivacyassembly.org/wp-content/uploads/2021/10/1.3e-version-4.0-International-Enforcement-Cooperation-Working-Group-adopted.pdf.

[9] For general information, see www.ftc.gov/about-ftc; about its Division of Privacy and Identity Protection, see www.ftc.gov/about-ftc/bureaus-offices/bureau-consumer-protection/our-divisions/division-privacy-and-identity.

[10] California Privacy Protection Agency, https://cppa.ca.gov.

[11] See International Enforcement Cooperation Working Group Report (n 8), notably 7–10.

In this context, different levels of cooperation must be defined, ranging from the quite general – the sharing of knowledge and experience with new technologies, such as artificial intelligence (AI), or investigation know-how, good practice and techniques – to the more specific, such as sharing intelligence and background on data controllers, or case-specific information on certain investigations. Each of these different levels of cooperation has its own specific needs and requires its own conditions and safeguards.

A. Enforcement Cooperation

As the DPAs involved in these forms of enforcement cooperation are all bound by their own national laws and typically lack a common legally binding framework, different instruments have been developed to overcome these handicaps and to allow regulatory cooperation to go forward where needed.

Since 2014, the GPA has developed a non-binding framework, the Global Cross Border Enforcement Cooperation Arrangement – an agreement for which these authorities are competent – that provides a common language and a pragmatic approach with sufficient details to create trust and allow an effective cooperation.[12]

So far, 16 authorities have committed to the Arrangement, including authorities from Australia, Canada, Estonia, Germany, Ireland, the Netherlands and the UK.[13] The typical way forward on this basis is that memoranda of understanding (MOUs) are used to shape the bilateral relationships between the individual parties as they see fit.[14]

B. Clearview AI

A good example of this approach is the joint investigation opened in July 2020 by the Office of the Australian Information Commissioner (OAIC) and the ICO into the personal information-handling practices of Clearview AI – an American facial recognition company that is globally active and describes itself as the 'World's Largest Facial Network'.[15] Clearview's facial recognition app allows users to upload a photo of an individual's face and match it to photos collected from the internet.

[12] See Enforcement Arrangement FAQs, https://globalprivacyassembly.org/participation-in-the-assembly/enforcement-cooperation-arrangement-faqs.

[13] See list of participants, https://globalprivacyassembly.org/participation-in-the-assembly/global-cross-border-enforcement-cooperation-arrangement-list-of-participants.

[14] See, eg Memorandum of Understanding between the ICO and the FTC, https://ico.org.uk/media/about-the-ico/mou/2618737/mou-us-federal-trade-commission-202012.pdf; Memorandum of Understanding between the ICO and the Office of the Australian Information Commissioner, https://ico.org.uk/media/about-the-ico/mou/2617355/oaic-ico-mou.pdf.

[15] See ICO press statement of 9 July 2020, https://ico.org.uk/about-the-ico/news-and-events/news-and-blogs/2020/07/oaic-and-ico-open-joint-investigation-into-clearview-ai-inc.

It then links to where the photos appeared. The system is reported to include a database of more than 10 billion images that Clearview claims to have taken or 'scraped' from various social media platforms and other websites.

Clearview's practices have caused controversy in the USA and led to critical comments from members of Congress.[16] The Canadian Privacy Commissioner also condemned Clearview's use of scraped biometric data.[17]

But the Australian and UK DPAs started a joint investigation under the GPA's Global Cross Border Enforcement Cooperation Arrangement and the MOU between the ICO and the OAIC, entered into half a year before. The two DPAs worked together on the evidence-gathering stage of the investigation. As both DPAs operated under their own country's legislation, any outcomes were considered separately.

In October 2021, the Australian DPA issued a 'cease and desist' order against the company and ordered the destruction of all scraped images collected from Australians.[18]

In November 2021, the ICO announced its provisional intent to impose a potential fine of just over £17 million on Clearview AI.[19] In addition, the ICO issued a provisional notice to stop further processing of the personal data of people in the UK and to delete it following alleged serious breaches of the UK's data protection laws.

In May 2022, the ICO issued a final decision in which it imposed a fine of £7.5 million for using images of people in the UK and elsewhere that had been collected from the web and social media to create a global online database that could be used for facial recognition. The ICO also issued an enforcement notice, ordering the company to stop obtaining and using the personal data of UK residents that is publicly available on the internet and to delete the data of UK residents from its systems.[20]

This is a good example of cross-border enforcement cooperation being about real issues and making a real difference to protections for the public. The harmful impact of Clearview's practices is usually not visible for the persons affected, but is no less real and may be experienced on the global scale.

The joint action at the evidence-gathering stage allowed a certain degree of burden sharing, with a division of tasks and better analysis, from different national perspectives. It is also increasingly important that DPAs coordinate and speak with one voice when global principles are at stake.

[16] See, eg US Senator Markey (D-Mass) on 8 June 2020, www.markey.senate.gov/news/press-releases/senator-markey-presses-clearview-ai-on-facial-recognition-monitoring-during-nationwide-protests.

[17] See statement of 3 February 2021, www.priv.gc.ca/en/opc-news/speeches/2021/s-d_20210203/.

[18] See the Australian decision, www.oaic.gov.au/__data/assets/pdf_file/0016/11284/Commissioner-initiated-investigation-into-Clearview-AI,-Inc.-Privacy-2021-AICmr-54-14-October-2021.pdf.

[19] See ICO press statement of 29 November 2021, https://ico.org.uk/about-the-ico/news-and-events/news-and-blogs/2021/11/ico-issues-provisional-view-to-fine-clearview-ai-inc-over-17-million/.

[20] See ICO press statement of 23 May 2022, https://ico.org.uk/about-the-ico/media-centre/news-and-blogs/2022/05/ico-fines-facial-recognition-database-company-clearview-ai-inc/. Both decisions are now under appeal.

The power and reach of multinational technology platforms over personal data is now unprecedented. Common action will create clearer and more forceful direction towards respect for data protection and privacy.

III. Council of Europe and the OECD

The Council of Europe Convention on Data Protection – known as Convention 108+ in its modernised form – also provides for the cooperation of supervisory authorities, inter alia by coordinating their investigations or conducting joint actions, and expects them to form a network as well.[21]

These authorities have indeed met annually at a separate conference,[22] but as most of them are also members of the GPA, there is less need for a more permanent platform like the GPA.

The OECD Privacy Guidelines also touch on the need for cross-border cooperation of privacy enforcement authorities, and the development of international arrangements that promote interoperability among privacy frameworks.[23] In a recent OECD document, 'interoperability' was referred to as the ability of privacy regimes or legal frameworks to work together to facilitate transborder data flows while ensuring the consistent protection of these data.[24] It can also enable and support convergence of frameworks.

In line with this, the OECD encouraged the early development of a Global Privacy Enforcement Network (GPEN).[25] This effort since 2010 now largely coincides with the GPA. The operational approaches are similar – the GPA and GPEN bring DPAs together, and MOUs then shape the bilateral relationships. Their different origins play no role in practice.

IV. EU and Brexit

The data protection authorities of EU Member States do not have to rely on a global framework for their interactions, as they all share the same EU legal framework – the GDPR, with a well-developed set of rules for cooperation and consistency. The GDPR provides for compulsory cooperation between competent DPAs, with

[21] Convention 108+ (n 1) Art 17, paras 1.b and 3.

[22] This conference is also known as the Spring Conference, as it has been held since the early 1990s, mostly in the spring.

[23] Privacy Guidelines (n 2) paras 20–21.

[24] Interoperability of Privacy and Data Protection Frameworks, DSTI/CDEP/DGP (2020)15/REV2, paras 9–13.

[25] Report on the Implementation of the OECD Recommendation on Privacy Law Enforcement Cooperation (2011) OECD Privacy Framework, 137–54, www.oecd.org/sti/ieconomy/oecd_privacy_framework.pdf.

one-stop shops and lead authorities for cross-border issues, mutual assistance, joint operations, where needed, and a European Data Protection Board (EDPB) with representatives from all national authorities to ensure consistency.[26]

The ICO was an integral and active part of this network before Brexit, and as one of the largest DPAs, also played a leading role in the enforcement working group. After Brexit, that was obviously no longer the case. This leads to the question how the regulatory cooperation in data protection between the UK and EU Member States is organised after Brexit.

The answer lies partly in Article 50 of the GDPR, on international cooperation. In relation to third countries and international organisations – and the UK is now a 'third country' – this provision expects both the Commission and supervisory authorities to take 'appropriate steps' to accomplish several relevant tasks.

One of those tasks is 'to develop international cooperation mechanisms to facilitate the effective enforcement of legislation for the protection of personal data'. Another is 'to engage … stakeholders in discussion and activities aimed at furthering international cooperation' in this field.[27]

It is interesting that both the Commission and supervisory authorities have a task here. Some initiatives may well require action from the Commission, such as proposals for EU legislation or formal international agreements, but other initiatives may well be taken by DPAs. In fact, much of the work already accomplished in the context of the GPA can be considered in this category.

The word 'appropriate' also appears in the context of Brexit. In the political declaration about their future relationship, the EU and the UK agreed to make 'arrangements for appropriate cooperation' between their data protection regulators.[28]

In the Trade and Cooperation Agreement (TCA)[29] between the EU and the UK, concluded in December 2020, both parties undertook 'to cooperate at bilateral and multilateral levels … Such cooperation may include dialogue, exchanges of expertise, and cooperation on enforcement, as appropriate, with respect to personal data protection.'[30]

In June 2021, further to Article 45(3) of the GDPR, the Commission also adopted an 'adequacy decision' with respect to the UK.[31] This meant that the level of protection in the UK was found 'essentially equivalent' to that in the EU, as a

[26] General Data Protection Regulation (n 3) Ch VII, Arts 60–76.

[27] ibid Art 50, first sentence, sub (a) and (c).

[28] Political Declaration setting out the framework for the future relationship between the European Union and the United Kingdom, 19 October 2019, paras 8–10, www.gov.uk/government/publications/new-withdrawal-agreement-and-political-declaration.

[29] Trade and Cooperation Agreement between the European Union and the European Atomic Energy Community, of the one part, and the United Kingdom of Great Britain and Northern Ireland, of the other part [2021] OJ L149/10, https://eur-lex.europa.eu/legal-content/EN/TXT/?uri=uriserv%3AOJ.L_.2021.149.01.0010.01.ENG&toc=OJ%3AL%3A2021%3A149%3ATOC.

[30] TCA, Art COMPROV.10: Personal data protection, para 3.

[31] Commission Implementing Decision of 28 June 2021 pursuant to Regulation (EU) 2016/679 of the European Parliament and of the Council on the adequate protection of personal data by the

result of which personal data could continue to flow freely from the EU to the UK, without additional safeguards.

However, the decision contained a 'sunset clause': after four years, a new determination will be necessary. The present decision could also be withdrawn if developments in the UK no longer justify an adequacy finding.[32]

A. Models of Cooperation

Not much progress in regulatory cooperation between the EU and the UK can be reported since. This may well be due in part to ongoing discussions on other issues, including on the position of Northern Ireland.

However, the ICO can see the opportunity for an agile and flexible arrangement that enables data sharing and better coordination. There will be important benefits from focusing on the achievement of real outcomes and ensuring that structures and formalities are proportionate: in other words, thinking more in terms of 'joined-up' regulation with strong incentives for multinational companies to take action to achieve high standards of compliance to common principles. This action needs to be timely and effective.

There are probably two main models of UK–EU cooperation in data protection:

- a centralised or integrated model built around the EDPB and one-stop shops with lead authorities, as currently provided in the GDPR; and
- a decentralised or loose-knit model built on bilateral relations and MOUs between ICO and targeted DPA's.

One could possibly also imagine a hybrid of these two models, where some activities are centralised and other are not. All options have their own obvious benefits and drawbacks, which will likely require a more careful analysis and eventually a good balance between the need for flexibility and consistency, and one-off or larger scale solutions, with an open eye for efficiency and effectiveness.

B. UK and Ireland

At this stage, the ICO is cooperating with several DPAs in the EU on a bilateral basis where needed, and with full respect for each other's applicable law. One very clear example is Ireland.

United Kingdom, C(2021) 4800 final, https://ec.europa.eu/info/sites/default/files/decision_on_the_adequate_protection_of_personal_data_by_the_united_kingdom_-_general_data_protection_regulation_en.pdf.

[32] ibid Arts 3 and 4. The explicit language of these two provisions, as further developed in recitals 281–90, is fully consistent with Art 45, paras 4, 5 and 6 of the GDPR and the relevant case law (notably CJEU judgment of 6 October 2015, Case C-362/14 (*Schrems*), paras 76 and 78 on the need for a strict review and periodical checks on adequacy).

Data flows between Ireland and the UK are a key issue, in addition to the movement of goods. Services, including in health, are also offered across the border and data flows are vital to their support. The cooperation between the Irish Data Protection Commission (DPC) and the ICO has always been strong and constructive. The ICO continues to engage with the Irish DPC when in the public interest.[33]

In this respect, the leading role that the DPC plays in regulating some big global players – such as Google, Apple, Facebook, Amazon and Microsoft – with a European establishment in Ireland should be noted.

The two offices also recently shared experience on children's privacy. The ICO's 'Age-Appropriate Design Code'[34] – mandating online service providers to take the best interests of child users into account – went live in September 2021 after a 12-month transition period, and the Irish DPA has issued new guidance.[35]

C. The Role of Adequacy

All this goes with an important proviso – the UK's adequacy status under the GDPR. If the present adequacy decision is withdrawn or not continued after four years, the situation will become a lot more difficult, also for regulatory cooperation across borders.

To be very clear on this point: 'essential equivalence' is not cast in stone and does not require a carbon copy of the GDPR. There is clearly a margin for national variations.[36] What matters, however, is that a country's laws and practices provide an essentially equivalent level of protection. In other words, its laws and practices must be able to deliver essentially the same results as the EU legal framework. Convention 108+ of the Council of Europe has also been recognised as a benchmark for high standards in this respect.[37]

However, if essential elements of protection are missing, that would create a serious obstacle. This is relevant because a UK data reform consultation[38] has been ongoing, and the UK government – under different Cabinets – has been considering how to proceed. Any proposals for legislative change will subsequently be discussed in Parliament.

In its public response, the ICO has been open to the consultation. It is good practice to review laws to see how they are working. But in the ICO's view, the UK

[33] See also Memorandum of Understanding between the ICO and the Irish DPC, concluded on 14 July 2022, www.dataprotection.ie/sites/default/files/uploads/2022-07/Redacted%20-%20MoU%20-%20ICO%20and%20Irish%20DPC%20Signed%2014072022.pdf.

[34] https://ico.org.uk/for-organisations/guide-to-data-protection/ico-codes-of-practice/age-appropriate-design-a-code-of-practice-for-online-services/.

[35] 'The "Children's Fundamentals" – A Guide to Protecting Children's Personal Data' (18 March 2021) www.dataprotection.ie/en/dpc-guidance/blogs/the-children-fundamentals.

[36] CJEU in *Schrems* (n 32) para 73; CJEU judgment of 16 July 2020, Case C-311/18 *Schrems II*, para 94. See also GDPR (n 3) recital 104.

[37] See GDPR (n 3) recital 105.

[38] 'Data: A New Direction' (10 September 2021) www.gov.uk/government/consultations/data-a-new-direction.

must continue to have high standards, which are vital to trust and confidence in the data economy and to what the public expects.[39]

In her foreword to the ICO's response in October 2021, Elizabeth Denham, then still the Information Commissioner, emphasised the crucial value of an independent regulator and expressed concerns that certain elements of the proposals did not sufficiently safeguard this independence.[40] Elsewhere, she also mentioned the key role of the fairness principle, especially in relation to new technologies, such as AI. In the ICO's view, it would not be wise to limit the scope of this important principle.[41]

In June 2022, the UK government published its response to the consultation, and in July a Data Reform Bill – referred to as the Data Protection and Digital Information Bill – was introduced to Parliament.[42]

The new Information Commissioner, John Edwards, seemed fairly satisfied[43] with the state of play, and by early September the Bill was about to be debated in Parliament when the debate was postponed for further consideration.[44] Meanwhile, a new consultation by the government has been announced.[45]

Any further comments on the substance of the Bill would be inappropriate at this stage, and in any case exceed the scope of this chapter.

V. Final Remarks

It would be remiss to conclude these notes without mentioning another kind of regulatory cooperation, in which data protection regulators may be taking part.

[39] 'ICO Response to DCMS Consultation 'Data: A New Direction' (6 October 2021) https://ico.org.uk/about-the-ico/news-and-events/news-and-blogs/2021/10/response-to-dcms-consultation-foreword/.

[40] ibid 2–5.

[41] 'The Certainty of Change: Regulation in a Time of Political and Social Challenges', speech delivered to BCS, The Chartered Institute for IT, 26 November 2021, https://ico.org.uk/about-the-ico/news-and-events/news-and-blogs/2021/11/the-certainty-of-change-regulation-in-a-time-of-political-and-social-challenges/.

[42] For a brief statement of the Information Commissioner, see https://ico.org.uk/about-the-ico/media-centre/news-and-blogs/2022/06/statement-in-response-to-the-government-s-announcement-on-the-upcoming-data-reform-bill/. For the government's response, see www.gov.uk/government/consultations/data-a-new-direction/outcome/data-a-new-direction-government-response-to-consultation. For the Bill introduced to Parliament on 18 July 2022, see https://publications.parliament.uk/pa/bills/cbill/58-03/0143/220143lp.pdf.

[43] See his statement at n 42.

[44] S Waterfield, 'Could Liz Truss Change the UK's New Data Laws after Parliamentary Debate Is Postponed?' *Tech Monitor* (5 September 2022) https://techmonitor.ai/policy/privacy-and-data-protection/data-protection-and-digital-information-bill-liz-truss; M Gooding, 'Data Protection Bill "Paused" as Digital Secretary Hints at Changes to UK's GDPR Replacement' *Tech Monitor* (4 October 2022) https://techmonitor.ai/policy/geopolitics/data-protection-and-digital-information-bill-gdpr-brexit.

[45] R Morrison, 'New Consultation Could Delay UK's Post-Brexit Data Laws' *Tech Monitor* (1 November 2022) https://techmonitor.ai/policy/geopolitics/data-protection-bill-uk-gdpr-replacement-brexit, quoting a DCMS official saying that 'data adequacy with the EU is at the heart of the approach we are taking going forward'.

That is cooperation across relevant sectors – both national and international – to ensure better outcomes in a digital economy, and in our increasingly digitalised societies in general.

The ICO is fortunate to be member of such a joined-up approach to digital regulation in the Digital Regulation Cooperation Forum, established in July 2020 together with the Competition and Markets Authority and the Office of Communications, and now also including the Financial Conduct Authority.[46]

In March 2021, the Forum published its first annual plan of work.[47] Priorities include responding strategically to industrial and technological developments, developing joined-up approaches and building shared skills and capabilities: in other words, essential work to jointly address the challenges of a digital age.

All this is ultimately meant to underscore how regulatory cooperation across borders or relevant sectors can bring new perspectives and new energy, which is bound to benefit both the participants in that cooperation and their ultimate stakeholders, to which we all belong.

Regulatory cooperation across sectors is a relatively new phenomenon, where the UK is playing a leading role and other countries are following.[48] Regulatory cooperation across national borders – both in and outside the EU – is also developing on an increasing scale. Both are very welcome, as the power and reach of multinational technology platforms over personal data is unprecedented.

Regulatory cooperation between the EU and the UK could follow different models, as set out in this chapter. At this stage, most cooperation is taking place on a bilateral basis where needed, especially between the UK and Ireland. To what extent other models will be feasible will probably also depend on the outcome of discussions on other issues, including on the position of Northern Ireland.

However, the subject of adequacy – more specifically, whether the UK will be able to preserve its adequacy status under the GDPR – will no doubt continue to play a key role as well, not only as a precondition for a successful cross-border regulatory cooperation, but also in a much larger context.

[46] See https://ico.org.uk/about-the-ico/what-we-do/digital-regulation-cooperation-forum/.

[47] DRCF Workplan 2021/22 (10 March 2021) www.gov.uk/government/publications/digital-regulation-cooperation-forum-workplan-202122. For information on more recent developments, see https://ico.org.uk/about-the-ico/what-we-do/digital-regulation-cooperation-forum/.

[48] eg the Netherlands and Australia. See introduction to DRCF Workplan 2022/23 (28 April 2022) www.gov.uk/government/publications/digital-regulation-cooperation-forum-workplan-2022-to-2023.

INDEX

www.ingramcontent.com/pod-product-compliance
Ingram Content Group UK Ltd.
Pitfield, Milton Keynes, MK11 3LW, UK
UKHW020809290926
15470UKWH00003B/1057

9 781509 966486